SUPERPOWER
AT
SEA

*Written under the auspices of
the Center of International Studies,
Princeton University*

---

*A list of other Center publications
appears at the back of the book*

SUPERPOWER
AT
SEA

U.S.
Ocean
Policy

Finn Laursen

PRAEGER

PRAEGER SPECIAL STUDIES • PRAEGER SCIENTIFIC

New York • Philadelphia • Eastbourne, UK
Toronto • Hong Kong • Tokyo • Sydney

Library of Congress Cataloging in Publication Data

Laursen, Finn.
  Superpower at sea.

  Bibliography: p.
  Includes index.
  1. Maritime law—United States.   2. United States—
Foreign relations.   3. United States—Politics and
government.   I. Title.
JX4422.U5L35   1983   341.4′5′0973   83-21222
ISBN 0-03-069536-8

Published in 1983 by Praeger Publishers
CBS Educational and Professional Publishing
a Division of CBS Inc.
521 Fifth Avenue, New York, NY 10175 USA
© 1983 by Praeger Publishers

3456789 052 987654321

Printed in the United States of America
on acid-free paper

TO MY FAMILY

ACKNOWLEDGMENTS

My interest in ocean politics goes back to the early 1970s when the issue appeared on the international agenda. Professor John Logue of Villanova University was a special contributor to this interest. Later I decided to write my dissertation on the topic at the University of Pennsylvania. The encouragement I received at Penn, especially from Professors Norman Palmer, Alvin Rubinstein, Donald Smith, and Henry Teune, was much appreciated. While I continued my research at the European University Institute in Florence, Italy, I had very useful discussions with Professors Hans Daalder, Peter Ludlow, Pierre Salmon, and the late Sir Andrew Shonfield.

The present book was largely written while I spent the academic year 1980-81 as John Parker Compton Visiting Fellow at the Center of International Studies, Princeton University. I am grateful to the Center and especially its director, Professor Cyril E. Black, for this opportunity. The scholarly community at the Center was very stimulating indeed.

Because of President Reagan's decision to review U.S. ocean policy the book was only finished after I returned to Denmark. While in Denmark I had particularly useful discussions with my good friend Jesper Grolin. Needless to say, none of my intellectual mentors should be held responsible for errors of fact or interpretation in this book.

Research support from the Danish Social Science Council is also gratefully acknowledged.

Excerpts from some of the author's previously published works appear herein by permission of the publishers. Portions of Chapters 2 and 8 are drawn from material published in "Security versus Access to Resources: Explaining a Decade of U.S. Ocean Policy," World Politics, Volume 34, No. 2 (January 1982). Copyright (c) 1982 by Princeton University Press. Reprinted by permission of Princeton University Press. Portions of Chapter 3 are drawn from material published in "The Law of the Sea and International Security: Aspects of Superpower Policy," in Finn Laursen, editor, Toward a New International Marine Order, copyright (c) 1982 by Martinus Nijhoff Publishers.

Finally, I want to thank the secretaries at the Department of Public Finance and Policy, Odense University, for typing the final manuscript.

PREFACE

This study examines the development of U.S. ocean policy from the late 1960s to 1982, when President Ronald Reagan decided not to sign or ratify the new United Nations Convention on the Law of the Sea, which had been negotiated over more than a decade, first within the United Nations Seabed Committee, 1968-73, and then within the Third United Nations Conference on the Law of the Sea (UNCLOS III), 1973-82.

From the first U.S. proposals, worked out by the Nixon administration in 1970, to the final days of the Carter administration in 1980, the United States played a very active role in the international negotiations. Various compromise proposals were put forward in the hope of reaching a widely accepted international agreement that would bring law and order to about 70 percent of the earth's surface and underlying waters and seabeds. This study traces these U.S. proposals as well as unilateral steps taken by the United States during the period under study. Substantively, the aspects of security, offshore petroleum, fishing, and deep seabed mining are covered. These have been by far the most salient political issues.

In an effort to try to explain the policies described, the study applies four analytical models, namely, a modernized version of classical realism (statist goals), international interdependence, bureaucratic politics, and domestic politics. All four models can help to describe and explain some aspects of U.S. ocean policy in this period, but domestic politics is found to have the greatest explanatory power. It explained the passage of the Fishery Conservation and Management Act of 1976, and the Reagan shift away from multilateralism in 1981 and 1982.

Since domestic pressures have been in the direction of unilateral U.S. actions, the findings have raised serious questions about the possibility of strengthening international law. Thus this study, which is a case study of foreign policy making, has important implications for world order politics. However, it is largely left to the reader to determine what these implications are. Suffice it to suggest here that it will take more international education, different domestic power structures, and more trust between nations before the rule of law can progress significantly in international affairs. For the moment it seems that suboptimal solutions will remain common internationally.

Analytically the study suggests the importance of studying the domestic politics of foreign policy and of developing a more coherent model of domestic politics for this purpose. The findings that international interdependence played a minor role and that bureaucratic politics was epiphenomenal constitute a challenge to the views of many scholars who have emphasized those factors.

Finn Laursen

CONTENTS

Page

ACKNOWLEDGMENTS   vii

PREFACE   ix

Chapter

1   OVERVIEW OF PROBLEM   1

    From Grotius to UNCLOS III   1
    Trusteeship Zone or Exclusive Economic Zone   6
    Species Approach or Zonal Approach   7
    International Agreement or Unilateralism   8
    Notes   12

2   ANALYTICAL PERSPECTIVES AND HYPOTHESES   15

    Statist Goals   15
    International Interdependence   18
    Bureaucratic Politics   20
    Domestic Politics   22
    Summary and Extensions   25
    Notes   27

3   THE POLITICS OF SECURITY   31

    The Fear of Creeping Jurisdiction   31
    Naval Missions   34
    Seabed Arms Control   36
    The 1970 Nixon Proposal   38
    The 1971 U.S. Straits Proposal   39
    International Developments   40
    Notes   42

4   THE POLITICS OF OFFSHORE PETROLEUM RIGHTS   47

    The Oil Lobby   47
    Allies of the Industry   53
    Congressional Action   55

Chapter   Page

        International Developments   56
        Acceptance of Enclosure   60
        Notes   63

5   THE POLITICS OF FISHING   67

        The Species Approach   67
        Voices of U.S. Coastal Fishermen   72
        Congressional Action (1973-75)   73
        The Fishery Conservation and Management Act (1976)   77
        The President's Signature   83
        Notes   85

6   THE POLITICS OF DEEP SEABED MINING   91

        The Nixon Proposal and the Mining Industry   91
        Third World Maximalism   95
        The Parallel System   99
        Congressional Action (1971-76)   104
        The Informal Composite Negotiating Text (1977)   110
        Moving toward Unilateral Action   113
        The Deep Seabed Hard Mineral Resources Act (1980)   117
        Notes   122

7   THE DRAFT CONVENTION AND THE REAGAN REVIEW   131

        International Progress   131
        The Mining Industry Strikes Back   134
        The Reagan Review   136
        The Eleventh Session of UNCLOS III   143
        Reagan's 'No'   146
        Notes   149

8   EXPLANATORY ASSESSMENTS   155

        Statist Goals   155
        International Interdependence   159
        Bureaucratic Politics   162
        Domestic Politics   165
        Notes   171

9   CONCLUDING REMARKS   175

        Notes   182

	Page
SELECTED BIBLIOGRAPHY	185
INDEX	203
ABOUT THE AUTHOR	210

1

OVERVIEW OF PROBLEM

FROM GROTIUS TO UNCLOS III

The traditional ocean regime of the freedom of the seas has been breaking down in the twentieth century. This breakdown has been followed by efforts to establish a new regime, that is, rules and regulations to govern the various uses of the oceans. With the purpose of establishing such a new regime, the Third United Nations Conference on the Law of the Sea (UNCLOS III) was convened in December 1973. The conference eventually lasted nearly a decade. In the spring of 1982 it finally agreed to a new Convention of the Law of the Sea.

The work of UNCLOS III was preceded by the work of a United Nations General Assembly Seabed Committee (1968-73). It was in view of those preparatory negotiations that the Nixon administration made a major law of the sea proposal in 1970. Between then and the Reagan administration's decision in the summer of 1982 not to sign the new Draft Convention on the Law of the Sea, U.S. ocean policy went through a series of major changes. The purpose of this study is to trace those changes and try to offer explanations. Why did the Nixon, Ford, and Carter administrations actively work for an international law of the sea agreement? And why did the Reagan administration decide to vote against and not sign the proposed convention in 1982?

Before trying to answer these questions a short introduction to the classical law of the sea may be in order. The traditional ocean regime was known as "the freedom of the seas." That regime is associated with the Dutch legal theoretician Hugo Grotius, who had defended it in Mare Liberum (1609).[1] Beyond a narrow territorial sea, according to that regime, everybody could freely navigate and fish. Most nations claimed a territorial sea of three nautical miles, a few claimed four, six, or twelve miles. In this zone the coastal state exercised its sovereignty. However, foreign vessels were supposed to have a right of "innocent passage," that is, they could transit as long as they did not do any harm to the coastal nation. What this meant in practice was never very well defined, giving the coastal state some freedom of interpretation.

Grotius' concept of the freedom of the seas had prevailed over an alternative system—that of dividing the seas the way in which land territory had been divided, that is, in areas of national jurisdiction. Such a system was advocated by the British scholar John Selden in Mare Clausum (1635), and the Portuguese and Spanish governments had worked for it. However, the Netherlands was the dominant maritime power at the time, and freedom was perceived to be in Dutch commercial interest. Later on Great Britain became the dominant maritime power and the British defended the freedom of the seas just as much as the Dutch had originally done—with exceptions during wars.[2]

However a gradual erosion of the traditional ocean regime has taken place, especially since the Second World War. The Truman Proclamations in 1945 are important in this respect. In one of the Proclamations it was stated that

> the Government of the United States regards the natural
> resources of the subsoil and sea bed of the continental
> shelf beneath the high seas but contiguous to the coasts
> of the United States as appertaining to the United States,
> subject to its jurisdiction and control.[3]

The Proclamation talked about a "need for new sources of petroleum and other minerals," and a need for "conservation and prudent utilization." Extension of jurisdiction was said to be "reasonable and just," because the continental shelf is "an extension of the landmass of the coastal nation and thus naturally appurtenant to it." It was further suggested that "self-protection compels the coastal nation to keep close watch over activities off its shores."[4]

The second Proclamation claimed a right of the coastal state to create national fishing conservation zones. Such zones would be necessary in certain cases because "the progressive development of new methods and techniques contributes to intensified fishing over wide sea areas and in certain cases seriously threatens fisheries with depletion." However, the Proclamations in no way abridged "the right of free and unimpeded navigation of waters of the character of high seas," nor did they extend the limits of the territorial waters of the United States.[5]

Despite the explicit limitations of the Truman Proclamations it has been argued that they started what has become known as "creeping jurisdiction." Chile followed in 1947 by claiming a 200-mile maritime zone. In this case it was especially a claim to the living resources of the seas. The resource involved was mainly that of offshore whaling. Shortly after the Chilean extension Peru followed, also claiming a national zone of 200 nautical miles. In this case it was mainly tuna and anchoveta resources that were important. The measure was first of all directed against U.S. distant-water fishing. Ecuador became the third Latin American state to claim 200 miles in 1951. [6]

The Latin American extensions all claimed that the Truman Proclamations constituted a precedent. Since the west coast of Latin America has a narrow continental shelf, a distance principle was chosen instead of a geomorphological one. That it should be 200 miles was rather accidental.

The idea that there should be some international codification of the law of the sea led to the first two United Nations Conferences on the Law of the Sea in Geneva in 1958 and 1960. The first Geneva conference agreed to four conventions, including a Convention on the Continental Shelf, which codified the central idea of the Truman Proclamations by establishing that the coastal state has jurisdiction over the natural resources of the continental shelf out to the 200-meter isobath or beyond "to where the depth of the superjacent waters admits of the exploitation of the natural resources of the said areas." [7] This concept of exploitability was not a very fortunate one from the point of view of setting a limit to "creeping jurisdiction." Technological progress, it could be argued, would legalize national claims to deeper and deeper parts of the continental shelf. Nor was the 1958 conference able to establish an agreed outer limit to the territorial sea. In 1960, at the second conference, a U.S.-Canadian proposal of a six-mile territorial sea combined with an additional six-mile fisheries jurisdiction failed by a single vote to get the required two-thirds majority. [8] Under these circumstances the freedom of the seas could still be seen as threatened.

In 1967 the law of the sea was again put on the United Nations agenda. The topic was introduced by Malta's Ambassador Arvid Pardo. In a famous speech he talked about new pressures on ocean resources and dramatized the wealth of the manganese nodules on the deep ocean floor, which had so far not been exploited, but would become exploitable very soon. The manganese of these nodules would, at the 1960 world rate of consumption, last 400,000 years; the copper 6,000 years; the nickel 150,000 years; and so forth. [9] This was bound to spark the imagination of a world that was increasingly concerned about the physical limits of production. [10] Many new countries, which had recently become independent, now entered the game of ocean politics. They viewed the traditional international legal order as the product of and as serving the interests of the rich industrialized countries. They were determined to influence the new emerging ocean regime.

After Pardo's speech, the General Assembly set up an ad hoc committee, which in 1968 became a permanent committee, the Committee on the Peaceful Uses of the Sea-Bed and the Ocean Floor beyond the Limits of National Jurisdiction, commonly referred to as the Seabed Committee. This committee produced various reports and drafted various resolutions. One 1970 resolution claimed the oceans beyond the limits of national jurisdiction to be the "common heritage of mankind" and called for the establishment of a new international regime:

> The area shall not be subject to appropriation by any means by States or persons, natural or juridical, and no State shall claim or exercise sovereignty or sovereign rights over any part thereof.
>
> No State or person, natural or juridical, shall claim, exercise or acquire rights with respect to the area or its resources incompatible with the international régime to be established and the principles of this Declaration. [11]

The outer limit of national jurisdiction, however, was not defined at this time.

In the following years the Seabed Committee continued to produce reports and resolutions and eventually to prepare UNCLOS III, which met for eleven sessions between 1973 and 1982 (see Table 1).

It was on the final day of the spring 1982 eleventh session in New York that UNCLOS III adopted the new Convention on the Law of the Sea. There were 130 countries voting in favor, 4 against, and 17 abstaining. Apart from the United States, the three countries voting against the convention were Israel, Turkey, and Venezuela. Among the countries abstaining were the Soviet Union and her East European allies, and West European countries such as West Germany, Italy, the Benelux countries, and the United Kingdom. Most Third World countries voted in favor. So did Australia, New Zealand, Canada, France, Japan, and the Scandinavian countries. Then followed some final drafting changes that were adopted at a short session in New York in September, and in December 1982, the new convention was signed by 113 states and the United Nations Council for Namibia at a final session in Montego Bay, Jamaica. Never before had a new U.N. convention received so many signatures on the first day it was opened for signature. [12]

TABLE 1

UNCLOS III Sessions and Texts

Session	Place	Dates	Negotiating Texts and Final Convention
1	New York	December 3–December 15, 1973	
2	Caracas	June 20–August 29, 1974	
3	Geneva	March 17–May 9, 1975	Informal Single Negotiating Text (ISNT) Third UNCLOS, Official Records, vol. 4:137–81
4	New York	March 15–May 7, 1976	Revised Single Negotiating Text (RSNT) Third UNCLOS, Official Records, vol. 5:125–85
5	New York	August 3–September 17, 1976	
6	New York	May 23–July 15, 1977	Informal Composite Negotiating Text (ICNT) Third UNCLOS, Official Records, vol. 8:1–70
7, part 1	Geneva	March 28–May 19, 1978	
7, part 2	New York	August 21–September 15, 1978	
8, part 1	Geneva	March 19–April 27, 1979	ICNT, Revision 1 (A/Conf. 62/WP. 10/Rev. 1) 28 April 1979
8, part 2	New York	July 16–August 24, 1979	
9, part 1	New York	March 3–April 4, 1980	ICNT, Revision 2 (A/Conf. 62/WP. 10/Rev. 2) 11 April 1980
9, part 2	Geneva	July 28–August 29, 1980	Draft Convention (Informal Text) (A/Conf. 62/WP. 10/Rev. 3) 22 September 1980
10, part 1	New York	March 9–April 17, 1981	
10, part 2	Geneva	August 3–August 28, 1981	Draft Convention on the Law of the Sea (A/Conf. 62/L. 78) 28 August 1981
11, part 1	New York	March 3–April 30, 1982	
11, part 2	New York	September 22–September 24, 1982	U.N. Convention on the Law of the Sea (A/Conf. 62/122) 7 October 1982
Signing Session	Montego Bay Jamaica	December 6–December 10, 1982	

Source: Compiled by the author.

TRUSTEESHIP ZONE OR EXCLUSIVE
ECONOMIC ZONE

It was in 1970 that President Richard Nixon announced a major
new ocean policy of the United States. It is not the purpose here to
present a detailed study of how the 1970 policy was developed. [13]
But the 1970 policy, which was the United States' initial ocean
strategy, is a natural point of departure, and it is the purpose here
to study the major changes that have followed in U.S. policy since
then.

The major aim of the 1970 policy, according to President
Nixon, was to get nations to "renounce all national claims over the
natural resources of the seabed beyond the point where the high seas
reach a depth of 200 meters (218.8 yards)." Beyond this 200-meter
isobath, resources would be considered the common heritage of mankind and an international regime would be set up to regulate exploitation. However, the continental margin part of the international
area would be a trusteeship zone. [14] Here the coastal states would
"act as trustees for the international community." Beyond the continental margin "agreed international machinery would authorize
and regulate exploration and use of seabed resources." [15] In practice this meant that the coastal state would issue licenses for the
continental margin area and a new international authority, to be established, would do so for the area beyond. In both areas exploitation should give important revenues for international community
purposes. Another important part of the 1970 policy was the conditional acceptance of a 12-mile limit for the territorial sea, the condition being free transit of international straits. [16]

It can be argued that the 1970 policy tried to stop "creeping
jurisdiction," and that it especially tried to satisfy the interest of
free naval mobility. The policy also stressed the importance of find-
ing internationally negotiated rather than unilaterally legislated solutions.

Important changes took place in U.S. policy after 1970. The
first major change concerned the acceptance of wider coastal state
jurisdiction over coastal area resources. Although the Nixon proposal tried to arrest the process of "creeping jurisdiction," the
United States had dropped the idea of a trusteeship zone by the time
of the Caracas session of UNCLOS III in 1974. Instead the United
States now gave conditional support for the idea of a 200-mile economic zone. John R. Stevenson, U.S. representative to UNCLOS III,
said that

we are prepared to accept, and indeed we would welcome
. . . a 200-mile outer limit for the economic zone,

provided it is part of an acceptable comprehensive
package including a satisfactory regime within and
beyond the economic zone and provision for unimpeded
transit of straits used for international navigation. [17]

A satisfactory regime for the economic zone was one that would
separate resource uses and nonresource uses. Coastal state jurisdiction should apply to the former, but there should still be "freedom of navigation, overflight, and other nonresource uses."[18]

A first major question to be asked is: why did the United
States decide to support the idea of a 200-mile economic zone at
(or before) the Caracas conference? As late as 1972 John Stevenson
had expressed U.S. objections to the idea, stating mainly that there
would be a danger that economic jurisdiction would be expanded to
interfere with other uses. It was also suggested that such a zone
was not the best way to ensure optimum utilization of fisheries consistent with sound conservation practices. The migratory habits of
different species should be taken into account. Stevenson further
suggested that since most petroleum and gas resources are located
in the continental margin, such a 200-mile zone would largely include these resources and create problems of equitable sharing. [19]
And yet, despite these objections, the United States had decided to
support the idea conditionally by 1974.

SPECIES APPROACH OR ZONAL APPROACH

The 1970 Nixon proposal had not addressed the issue of fishing policy; but the issue was on the international agenda. As the
development of more efficient fishing technology, including distant-
water factory ships, increased the fishing effort to the point of overfishing a number of species, the traditional freedom of the seas was
becoming obsolete. A common resource, which had traditionally
been res nullius, but which had become private property by capture,
now needed to be managed to assure optimum yield. [20] Should such
management be national or international?

The initial U.S. response to this problem was a proposal introduced in the U.N. Seabed Committee in 1971, which called for
a "species approach." Three kinds of fish stocks would be treated
in three different ways. The proposal would maintain a regulatory
role for "appropriate international (including regional) fisheries organizations." These organizations would determine "the allowable
catch" for different species. For coastal stocks there would be a
coastal state preference. But for highly migratory species (mainly
tuna), international regulation was prescribed in such a way that

there would be no coastal state preference. Finally, concerning anadromous species (mainly salmon), a preference would be given to the state in whose fresh waters the stock in question spawns.[21]

The second major event in U.S. ocean policy in respect to the establishment of coastal zones was the U.S. decision to go unilateral in the fisheries area, namely, the passing and signing of the Fishery Conservation and Management Act of 1976 (FCMA). By this Act the United States unilaterally extended its jurisdiction over fishing out to 200 miles off its coasts from March 1, 1977. Why did Congress pass this bill and why did President Gerald Ford sign it? The event must especially be seen as rather puzzling because the administration kept advising Congress against unilateral measures until late in 1975. Under Secretary for Security Assistance Carlyle E. Maw stated before the House Committee on International Relations on September 24, 1975: "The President supports the establishment of a 200-mile fisheries zone by negotiation: he strongly opposes unilateral claims to jurisdiction over the high seas. . . ."[22]

Similarly, John Norton Moore, chairman of the National Security Council (NSC) Interagency Task Force on the Law of the Sea, said on the same occasion that "the Administration has recently concluded a thorough evaluation of our interim fisheries policy, and the President has determined strongly to oppose measures unilaterally extending our fisheries jurisdiction."[23] John Norton Moore gave a number of reasons why unilateral action might be counterproductive. There would be a risk of confrontation with other nations off U.S. coasts, and the step could seriously harm U.S. distant-water fishing interests as well as the development of universal fisheries conservation obligations. Also, it could harm UNCLOS negotiations and mean a serious setback to the development of international legal institutions. The step, it was further argued, would be inconsistent with existing international law.[24] And yet, Congress went ahead, and President Ford signed the bill early in 1976.

INTERNATIONAL AGREEMENT OR UNILATERALISM

The FCMA represented a policy of national enclosure. So did the international idea of a 200-mile exclusive economic zone in which the coastal state would have sovereign rights to the natural resources, be they fish or minerals. However, it was clear from the beginning of the international negotiations that national enclosure would not be an option for the deep ocean floor. A number of resolutions referred to an area "beyond the limits of national jurisdiction." Eventually, as an increasing number of states made claims to 200-mile zones and claims to continental margin resources beyond 200 miles in cases where the margin extends further out, the area "beyond national jurisdiction" was limited to the deep ocean floor. The main resource at stake on the deep ocean floor are so-called polymetallic or manganese nodules, containing nickel, copper, cobalt, manganese, and other minerals. To regulate the exploitation of manganese nodules on the deep seabed the United States originally proposed an International Seabed Resource Authority that would have licensing responsibilities, but would not itself directly conduct exploration and exploitation activities.[25] And this was still basic U.S. policy by the time of the Caracas conference.[26]

However, speaking to the American Bar Association in Montreal, Canada, on August 11, 1975, Secretary of State Henry Kissinger supported what has become known as a parallel or dual access system—a system that will allow both private companies and an International Seabed Authority (ISA) to mine the deep seabeds. Certain conditions were set. The new international organization should preserve the rights of all countries and their citizens to directly exploit deep seabed resources, and it should insure fair adjudication of conflicting interests as well as security of investment. Further, the decision-making procedures should reflect and balance the interests of the participating states. And the organization should not have the power to control prices or production rates. On these conditions the United States could agree to a system where the ISA would conduct mining operations on behalf of the international community. And the United States was also prepared to explore ways of sharing deep seabed technology with other countries.[27]

Secretary Kissinger restated the central aspect of this policy in New York in April 1976 during the fourth session of UNCLOS III: "The United States accepts that an 'enterprise' should be established as part of the International Seabed Resource Authority and given the right to exploit the deep seabeds under the same conditions as apply to all mining."[28]

It was suggested that this parallel system could work in a way by which each individual contractor would propose two mine sites for exploitation. Of these the ISA would select one for exploitation by its own "Enterprise," or it could be made available to developing countries. The remaining site would be available for the contractor to mine. Revenue sharing and transfer of technology was still part of U.S. policy. But Kissinger now added a new element. The United States was prepared to accept a temporary limitation on production of seabed minerals, tying such limitation to the growth in the world nickel market, which at the time was about 6 percent. The United States could further agree to ISA participation in international commodity agreements. And it was suggested that some of the revenues from seabed mining should be used for adjustment assistance to land-based producers of the minerals in question.[29]

This was not Kissinger's last contribution. When the fifth session of UNCLOS III met in New York later the same year the secretary of state was again present. On September 1 he stated:

> . . . I propose on behalf of the U.S. Government that the
> United States would be prepared to agree to a means of
> financing the Enterprise in such a manner that the Enter-
> prise could begin its mining operation either concurrently
> with the mining of state or private enterprises or within
> an agreed timespan that was practically concurrent.[30]

What we have seen is that the United States not only accepted the parallel system; it made proposals designed to contribute to making that system operational. The first major question in connection with seabed mining policy therefore is this: why did the United States so actively support the parallel system from about 1975? This policy was quite different from the original simple licensing proposal.

The second major policy change with respect to seabed mining that will be studied is the Carter administration's decision to support U.S. legislation in the area. Kissinger had spoken about the dangers of unilateralism:

> Eventually any one country's technical skills are bound
> to be duplicated by others. A race would then begin
> to carve out deep sea domains for exploitation. This
> cannot but escalate into economic warfare, endanger the
> freedom of navigation, and ultimately lead to tests of
> strength and military confrontations.[31]

The Carter administration did not support unilateral U.S. legislation at the outset. The administration's special representative for the law of the sea negotiations, Elliot L. Richardson, stated before the House Merchant Marine and Fisheries Committee on April 27, 1977: ". . . we reaffirm our intention to seek agreement on a comprehensive treaty which protects our interests. . . . I believe this is a realistic objective. We do not, therefore, suggest legislation now."[32]

Legislation might upset the coming sixth session of UNCLOS III, it was suggested. But Richardson also said that the administration would review its position after that session. The review followed and on October 4, 1977, Richardson suggested to the same committee that "Congress should continue to move forward with legislation." Certain conditions for administration support of legislation were stated. Legislation should be interim until a treaty was agreed upon, and it should contain provisions for harmonizing U.S. regulations with those of other, so-called reciprocating states. It should assure environmental protection, sound management, and financial benefits for the international community. On the other hand, it should not be specific with regard to the assignment of mining sites, not require that processing take place in the United States, nor offer U.S. mining companies financial guarantees against adverse effects of a treaty. A final condition was that legislation should leave high seas freedoms undisturbed. [33]

So the administration changed its policy. On June 28, 1980, President Jimmy Carter signed the Deep Seabed Hard Mineral Resources Act. The act established a national regulatory mechanism that was said to be interim. It would be superseded when a law of the sea treaty enters into force for the United States. And, emphasized the White House statement, "no permit for commercial recovery will be effective sooner than January 1, 1988." According to the Carter administration, this would give UNCLOS III "ample time to complete its work and to prepare for implementation of the treaty before commercial recovery under American law would actually take place." [34]

Had President Carter been reelected in 1980, it might have worked out as suggested. However, President Reagan took U.S. policy one big step further. If the Carter administration had flirted with unilateralism, the Reagan administration decided in favor of unilateralism. On July 9, 1982, President Reagan announced that the deep seabed mining part of the convention adopted by UNCLOS III did not meet U.S. objectives: "For this reason, I am announcing today that the United States will not sign the convention. . . ." [35]

Despite former Secretary of State Kissinger's warning against unilateralism, a Republican administration had chosen to go it alone. Twelve years after the rather internationalist proposals of the Nixon administration, the United States concluded that it could do without an international agreement. The first question is obviously: why? But the decision is so significant from the point of view of world order politics that we will have to consider its implications as well. The United States is a major maritime power. Can it—and should it be allowed to—undermine the world's effort to create a just and lasting legal order for 71 percent of the surface of the earth?

For students of world order the law of the sea negotiations represent an important case. A widely accepted international sea treaty could limit conflicts about access to ocean resources, including fish, offshore oil and gas, and the minerals of the deep ocean floor. A treaty setting up an International Seabed Authority with powers to regulate and tax the exploitation of manganese nodules on the deep seabed could increase international equity and provide an independent source of revenue for the U.N. system. Stipulations about limitation and reduction of ocean pollution could contribute to improving the health of the global ecosystem. International standards in respect to the exploitation of the oceans' living resources could increase the likelihood of an optimal use of an important source of protein. World order values such as peace, economic well-being, social justice, and ecological balance, therefore, could all be enhanced by an international treaty approach to ocean law.[36] And yet, the Reagan administration begged to differ. Did it have a different factual basis or different values?

NOTES

1. Wolfgang Friedmann, The Future of the Oceans (New York: Braziller, 1971), p. 3.

2. Robert O. Keohane and Joseph S. Nye, Power and Interdependence: World Politics in Transition (Boston: Little, Brown, 1977), pp. 90-92.

3. "Proclamations Concerning United States Jurisdiction over Natural Resources in Coastal Areas and the High Seas," Department of State Bulletin 13 (September 20, 1945), pp. 484-87. See also Friedmann, The Future of the Oceans, p. 7.

4. Friedmann, The Future of the Oceans, pp. 6-7.

5. Department of State Bulletin 13 (September 20, 1945), pp. 485-86.

6. Ann L. Hollick, "The Origins of 200-Mile Offshore Zones," American Journal of International Law 71 (1977):494-500. See also Jorge A. Vargas, "Latin America and Its Contribution to the Law of the Sea," in Finn Laursen, ed., Toward a New International Marine Order (The Hague: Martinus Nijhoff Publishers, 1982), pp. 51-70.

7. Shigeru Oda, International Law of the Ocean Development: Basic Documents, vol. I (Leiden: Sijthoff, 1976), p. 21. See also Lewis M. Alexander, "New Approaches to Control of Ocean Resources," in Robert G. Wirsing, ed., International Relations and the Future of Ocean Space (Columbia, S.C.: University of South Carolina Press, 1974), pp. 67-82.

8. Keohane and Nye, Power and Interdependence, p. 94.

9. Arvid Pardo, The Common Heritage: Selected Papers on Oceans and World Order 1967-1974 (Malta University Press, 1975), p. 8.

10. Friedmann, The Future of the Oceans, pp. 20-21.

11. U.N. General Assembly Resolution 2749 (XXV): 17 December 1970, adopted by 108 votes to none, with 14 abstentions. Text in Oda, International Law of the Ocean Development, vol. I, p. 44.

12. "Sea Law—'A Rendezvous with History,'" U.N. Chronicle, 19 June 1982, pp. 3-22; and U.N. Press Release SEA/514, 10 December 1982.

13. For accounts of this and earlier policies, see Lawrence Juda, Ocean Space Rights: Developing U.S. Policy (New York: Praeger, 1975); and Ann L. Hollick, "United States Ocean Policy: 1948-1971" (Ph.D. diss., Johns Hopkins University, 1971).

14. The continental margin includes the continental shelf plus the steeper continental slope and at least a part of the continental rise, the part where the margin flattens out to meet the oceanic abyss or deep ocean floor.

15. Richard Nixon, "United States Policy for the Seabed," Department of State Bulletin 62:1616 (June 15, 1970), pp. 737-41, at 737.

16. Ibid., p. 738.

17. John R. Stevenson, "U.S. Defines Position on 200-Mile Economic Zone at Conference on the Law of the Sea," Department of State Bulletin 71:1832 (August 5, 1975), pp. 232-36, at 235.

18. Ibid., p. 234.

19. John R. Stevenson, "Department Discusses Progress Toward 1973 Conference on the Law of the Sea," Department of State Bulletin 66:1715 (May 8, 1972), pp. 672-79, at 676-77.

20. For some background, see Nancy W. Graham, Fisheries Law: Unilateral or Multilateral Formulation, Technical Report WHOI-76-113, Woods Hole Oceanographic Institution, 1976 (Springfield, Va.: National Technical Information Service, Doc. no. PB 264 266).

21. "Draft Articles on the Breadth of the Territorial Sea, Straits, and Fisheries," Report of the Committee on the Peaceful Uses of the Sea-Bed and the Ocean Floor Beyond the Limits of National Jurisdiction, U.N. General Assembly, Official Records, 26th Sess., Suppl. #21 (A/8421), 1971, p. 242.

22. "Department Opposes Unilateral Establishment of 200-Mile U.S. Fisheries Zone," Department of State Bulletin 73:1896 (October 27, 1975), pp. 623-27, at 623.

23. Ibid., p. 625.

24. Ibid., pp. 625-26.

25. See, for instance, Christopher H. Phillips, "Statement," Department of State Bulletin 63:1626 (August 24, 1970), p. 212.

26. See, for instance, Stevenson's Statement to Committee I, included in "U.S. Gives Position on Seabed Regime, Scientific Research, Straits, and Economic Zone at Law of the Sea Conference," Department of State Bulletin 71:1839 (September 23, 1974), pp. 402-06.

27. Henry Kissinger, "International Law, World Order, and Human Progress," Department of State Bulletin 73:1889 (September 8, 1975), pp. 353–62, at 357.

28. Henry Kissinger, "The Law of the Sea: A Test of International Cooperation," Department of State Bulletin 74:1922 (April 26, 1976), pp. 533–42, at 540.

29. Ibid., pp. 540–41.

30. "Secretary Kissinger Discusses U.S. Position on Law of the Sea Conference," Department of State Bulletin 75:1944 (September 27, 1976), pp. 395–403, at 398.

31. Kissinger, "Law of the Sea: A Test," p. 538.

32. "Administration Gives Views on Proposed Legislation on Deep Seabed Mining," Department of State Bulletin 76:1978 (May 23, 1977), pp. 524–27, at 525.

33. "Review of the Law of the Sea Conference and Deep Seabed Mining Legislation," Department of State Bulletin 77:2004 (November 21, 1977), pp. 751–56, at 754–55.

34. "Deep Seabed Hard Mineral Resources Act: White House Statement, July 3, 1980," Department of State Bulletin 80:2043 (October 1980), pp. 73–74.

35. "U.S. Votes Against Law of the Sea Treaty: President's Statement, July 9, 1982," Department of State Bulletin 82:2065 (August 1982), p. 71.

36. On world order values, see Robert C. Johansen, The National Interest and the Human Interest (Princeton: Princeton University Press, 1980).

2

ANALYTICAL PERSPECTIVES
AND HYPOTHESES

STATIST GOALS

An important tradition within international relations and foreign policy scholarship centers on the role of the nation-state as an
autonomous, rational, and unitary actor that pursues national interests that are often defined in terms of power. Hans Morgenthau,
who exemplifies this tradition, called his contribution a realist theory of international politics.[1] Although a number of scholars have
been questioning various assumptions of realism over the last decade
or so, the theory is far from dead.[2] On the contrary, various efforts have lately been made to reassert some of the arguments and
conclusions arrived at by earlier proponents of realism.[3] One of
the more compelling efforts to reformulate some of the central
tenets of this intellectual tradition has come from Stephen Krasner,
according to whom the state, defined as consisting of "central
decision-making institutions and roles," remains an autonomous
actor. These central institutions, mainly the White House and the
State Department, pursue policies that "cannot be reduced to some
summation of private desires." They are said to have a "high degree of insulation from specific societal pressures and a set of
formal and informal obligations that charge them with furthering the
nation's general interests."[4]

The classical realist school approached the question of public
goals in a logical-deductive fashion. According to Morgenthau,
nation-states pursue "interests defined in terms of power." That
conclusion was derived from the notion that "politics, like society
in general, is governed by objective laws that have their roots in
human nature." It is the existence of such objective laws that
makes it possible to develop a rational theory of foreign policy and
international relations. Applied to foreign policy, the concept of
national interest "infuses rational order" to the subject matter. It

15

will help us to explain the "astounding continuity in foreign policy which makes American, British, or Russian foreign policy appear as an intelligible, rational continuum, by and large consistent within itself, regardless of the different motives, preferences, and intellectual and moral qualities of successive statesmen."[5]

When it comes to defining the national interest in more concrete terms, realists have tended to put territorial and political integrity first. Said Morgenthau: "In a world where a number of sovereign nations compete with and oppose each other for power, the foreign policies of all nations must necessarily refer to their survival as their minimum requirements."[6] The fact that other values were seen as conditioned by considerations of national survival and political independence explains the central concern for security, balance of power, and other aspects of "high politics" in the writings of realists.[7]

Such a definition of the national interest does not answer the question asked by students of foreign economic policies. Although one could imagine a deductive approach to economic and resource issues, Krasner arrives at the subject of raw materials policy inductively. He asks: what preferences by U.S. central decision makers have had the highest ranking over time, and has there been a consistent and persistent ranking? On the basis of a series of case studies, he concluded that central or statist actors have pursued three basic aims in raw materials policy: (1) to increase competitive economic behavior; (2) to ensure security of supply; and (3) to promote broad foreign policy objectives.[8]

The broader foreign policy objectives, according to Krasner, have included both material interests and ideological objectives. Many U.S. leaders have pursued a Lockean vision of liberalism and worked for a nonrevolutionary development of the international order. Krasner maintains that this ideological component is essential for distinguishing statism from structural Marxism. He holds that ideology has led to nonlogical behavior, such as the U.S. involvement in Vietnam, which cannot be explained by pressures from within the capitalist societal structures. It was anticommunist ideology at work.[9]

Any theory ultimately must face a dual test, namely, questions of logical consistency as well as of consistency with experience. However, by approaching his subject inductively, Krasner has created problems for a logical critique. We will have to ask whether it is possible to generalize on the basis of his findings. Can one make predictions about raw materials policy or, for that matter, other foreign economic policies? It seems that applications of a statist approach should make such assumptions if the approach has aspirations of attaining a predictive and ipso facto explanatory capacity.[10] It should be possible to state the rationale for the policies pursued. If it is not, generality and predictive capacity cannot be attained, and statism will have no explanatory power; it will not really go beyond historical description. We will then have to ask the important question: do facts really speak for themselves?

For the purpose of this study we will rely mainly on the Morgenthau approach. But since ocean politics is concerned both with security and access to resources the classical view will be supplemented with aspects of Krasner's restatement. We will assume the primacy of security goals but add resource goals in the order proposed by Krasner. This suggests the following hypotheses, which will be tested empirically:

A major issue in ocean politics for central U.S. policy makers has been the free use of ocean space for the military.
Rationale: An important part of U.S. strategic deterrent capacity consists of submarine-launched ballistic missiles. Further, the U.S. Navy has important conventional superpower missions: sea control, projection of force ashore, and "showing the flag." In carrying out these tasks, the navy depends on the right to emplace listening devices on the seabed to detect foreign submarines. Since these missions are directly related to the survival of the territorial and political viability of the United States, they should have highest priority.

With respect to resources, U.S. decision makers are likely to be concerned about avoiding the development of international cartels like the Organization of Petroleum Exporting Countries (OPEC); they want to ensure security of supply of ocean minerals, such as the oil and gas resources of the continental margins and the manganese nodules of the deep seabed.
Rationale: The economic well-being and political stability, and possibly the political survival of the United States, depend on energy resources and vital strategic minerals, such as the nickel, copper, cobalt, and manganese contained in the deep seabed nodules.

Statist goals do not rule out international cooperation or the emergence of international regimes. But according to Morgenthau, "common political action" among sovereign states is the result of the interests that these states "may have in common." International cooperation can come into being through conquest or through "consent based upon the mutual recognition of the national interests of the nations concerned." The states are calculating and maximizing; ". . . no nation will forego its freedom of action if it has no reason to expect proportionate benefits in compensation for that loss."[11]

INTERNATIONAL INTERDEPENDENCE

The statist perspective presumes a rather static national interest. The state, represented by a small group of rather insulated
decision makers, is seen as autonomous and unitary. It is presumed that power is a usable instrument in international relations.
These and other premises may not hold. The static character of
the national interest suggests problems when the model is used to
explain policy change. Since change is central for our concern we
should be looking for alternative models—rival theories—that might
better be able to explain aspects of U.S. ocean policy.

The literature on international interdependence contains some
useful insights and suggestions. This perspective, developed
largely by Robert O. Keohane and Joseph S. Nye, questions some
of the central assumptions of the realist view of international relations, such as the unitary nature and dominant influence of nation-
states in world politics, the usability of force, and the predominance
of "high politics" over "low politics." According to Keohane and
Nye, international politics increasingly approaches a situation
characterized by multiple channels between societies, making it
impossible for states to act coherently as units. Further there is
an absence of hierarchy among issues; military force plays a minor
role.[12]

All states—even superpowers—are sensitive to policies of
other states and foreign groups. An example of U.S. sensitivity is
the cost, for U.S. society, of increasing oil prices during the 1970s.
The extent to which the United States depends on smaller foreign
countries varies with respect to different resources, but this sensitivity often provides smaller countries with power that makes it
possible for them to extract concessions from larger countries.[13]

The translation of power into outcomes is accomplished
through a bargaining process, which is conditioned by different
dynamics such as agenda setting, learning, and linkage strategies.
The outcome of the process may, under certain circumstances, be
an international agreement.[14] For an international agreement to
emerge, the negotiators must develop a perception of joint gain. It
has been the premise of the package deal approach to UNCLOS III
that such joint gain would be possible in respect to ocean uses.

What are the sensitivities of the United States with respect to
the ocean, and what kind of predictions can be made on the basis of
such knowledge and the suggested dynamics of international negotiations?

Various standards of sensitivity can be examined, and much
depends on the policies of other states, which can be difficult to
predict. In terms of import figures for oil and minerals, there was

a degree of sensitivity that explains the U.S. interest in access to these ocean resources. The United States imports most of its nickel, cobalt, and manganese. It is also a net importer of fish products, but here substitutions are easier. However, knowledge about sensitivities does not provide an answer to the question of whether access is best arrived at multilaterally or unilaterally. Since the United States has important offshore resources of oil and fish, as well as the technology to exploit deep seabed minerals, it has a unilateral option with respect to exploitation of these resources. Exercising that option, however, could have certain costs: it might hurt the interests of U.S. tuna and shrimp fishermen, who have traditionally taken an important part of their catch off the coasts of Latin American countries. Furthermore, it would be difficult to predict the reaction of foreign countries who are dependent on access to U.S. coastal areas if they had to decrease their catch or to leave U.S. coastal areas completely. The Soviet Union and Japan might accept having to reduce their fishing off U.S. coasts if a 200-mile fishing zone was introduced as part of an international package deal; but they might not accept it if such zone was introduced unilaterally by the United States. These uncertainties and risks could therefore be minimized by the added legitimacy that a widely accepted international agreement could provide. With respect to deep seabed minerals, an international agreement would provide the guaranteed access sought by U.S. industry; security of tenure would be more difficult to arrive at unilaterally, since a majority of states did not accept unilateral access to those minerals.

There was a further reason for the United States to adopt the multilateral route: national sensitivities concerning navigation and military uses of the oceans. If coastal states introduced broad territorial seas (thereby restricting navigational rights), or closed some international straits, serious economic and military costs could result. In such a situation the United States would have the option of trying to defend navigational rights by the use of naval power. However, that would certainly involve diplomatic costs, and it could have military costs as well. Since Third World countries have been increasing their naval capabilities in recent years, a better way of securing navigational rights might be through a widely accepted international ocean treaty; this would be worth certain concessions in other areas. On the basis of this kind of reasoning, I would offer the following hypotheses:

International interdependence in the ocean area calls for a multilateral treaty approach.
Rationale: Through an internationally negotiated package deal, the United States would secure its most important interests—freedom

of navigation and reasonable access to resources—without the costs that a unilateral approach might entail.

The most important linkage in UNCLOS III negotiations is between navigational rights and deep seabed mining.

Rationale: The coastal nations of the world, which have the unilateral option with respect to coastal zone resources and the potential capacity to create obstacles for navigational rights, are for the most part Third World countries that do not have the technology or capital to exploit deep seabed minerals. In return for agreeing to guaranteed freedom of navigation, they are able to ask for a quid pro quo from the technologically advanced maritime powers: an operational international seabed authority that could help them get a share of the resources and revenues from deep seabed mining.

This perspective then suggests the likelihood of an international bargain being struck. To the extent that the negotiation process can be controlled by rational and pragmatic negotiators, it should be possible to generate enough trade-offs to create a perception of mutual advantages. In other words, it is the linkage aspect of international interdependence that is important.

BUREAUCRATIC POLITICS

International interdependence scholars were not the first to question some of the assumptions of the realist perspective. Mainly the notion of the state as a unitary actor was questioned earlier by advocates of a bureaucratic politics perspective. Graham Allison has put it as follows:

> The "leaders" who sit on top of organizations are not
> a monolithic group. Rather, each individual in this
> group is, in his own right, a player in a central,
> competitive game. The name of the game is politics:
> bargaining among players positioned hierarchically
> within the government.[15]

The national leaders involved in bargaining games, according to Allison, are political leaders as well as leaders of major bureaucratic agencies. They form a circle of central players. Because central players disagree, decisions and actions result from a political process. Governmental action thus is a political outcome—not deliberately chosen, but resulting from "compromise, conflict, and confusion of officials with diverse interests and unequal influence."[16]

There is a problem with Allison's model from the point of view of understanding the dynamics of the political process. It includes bureaucrats, presidents, legislators, and representatives of interest organizations. Since different motivations and forces are involved, the model's predictive capacity will be limited, at best.[17] For the purpose of this study, the importance of "bureaucrats," in the sense of career officials, will be the central element of the bureaucratic politics model. The suggested limitation follows from the reasoning that motivations of bureaucrats, as defined here, are different from the motivations of legislators and presidents. A bureaucratic politics model makes sense if policy positions taken by officials can be predicted from their positions in the bureaucracy. That is what Morton Halperin had in mind when he said, "Where an individual sits in the process determines in large part the faces of the issue that he sees and helps to determine the stakes that he sees involved and hence the stand that he takes."[18]

Most organizations, including national bureaucracies, have missions to perform. It ought to be possible to predict policy positions of various bureaucracies from their missions, or from the interpretation of those missions given by the dominant group in the organization. A general proposition of importance for the bureaucratic politics model, then, is that bureaucratic officials will try to enhance the missions of their organization. For this reason, they will tend to favor policies and strategies that they consider to be important for their agency, but will be rather indifferent to policies that do not affect their missions. They will struggle for the capabilities and functions they view as necessary for carrying out their missions, and they will resist efforts to take them away.[19]

For the purposes of the present study, the central question, then, is the following. On the basis of the above propositions about bureaucratic behavior, how will various federal departments and agencies be involved in the formulation of U.S. ocean policy?[20] The following hypotheses will be offered:

The State and Defense Departments will work toward an international agreement.
Rationale: Central to the missions of the State Department is an interest in harmonious international relations and good bilateral relations with other countries. The Defense Department will be concerned about the free military use of ocean space. Stopping "creeping jurisdiction" through a widely accepted international treaty would be safer than doing so through the use of naval power.

Resource-related agencies will support their "client" industries: the Interior Department will work for the interests of the oil industry, and the fishing and deep seabed mining industry will have found support in the Commerce Department.

Rationale: The Interior Department is in charge of offshore oil leasing, and the Commerce Department is involved in a number of ocean activities, including fisheries and deep seabed mining, through the National Oceanic and Atmospheric Administration (NOAA). By promoting their "client" industries, these agencies will enhance their missions.

A major problem with the bureaucratic politics model is its inability to predict the outcome of a conflict between security and resource-related agencies. In isolation, the prediction would be incoherence, infighting, or stalemate. Coordination of policy requires executive leadership, which may not always be forthcoming. In order to make predictions in these situations, it is necessary to go beyond the bureaucratic agencies and study wider societal forces. Such wider forces may lend weight to the arguments of particular agencies, and may thus be rather decisive.

DOMESTIC POLITICS

Wider societal forces may influence bureaucratic agencies directly. Often, however, they will be channeled through the political system via Congress. Members of Congress are influenced by public opinion and the lobbying of interest organizations. A fourth model will focus on the domestic politics of foreign policy making. According to William Quandt, "Congress often becomes the vehicle through which domestic groups try to achieve their goals, and lobbying, electoral battles, and struggles between the legislative and executive branches of government are part of the foreign policy process."[21]

Quandt talks about a domestic politics perspective and suggests that "in a democratic polity, foreign policy is inevitably influenced by domestic realities."[22] The label "democratic politics model" is used by authors such as Wilfrid Kohl[23] and Stephen Cohen.[24] They seem to have similar processes in mind. However, because of the value connotations of "democratic," I will use the term "domestic" politics.

Domestic political variables should be singled out in a special model because the dynamics are different from those of the bureaucratic system. This has been stated very explicitly by Cohen:

> In sharp contrast to career civil servants' job security, all members of Congress face reelections. The economic health of their constituents is a matter of great import. At times their self-interests require congressmen to play the role of ombudsman to assure

that the executive branch policy does not become insufficiently responsive to the needs and demands of
key groups within the domestic sector. [25]

The view of domestic politics applied in this study accepts the
pluralistic nature of modern Western societies. But it differs from
the benign view of pluralism still accepted by many Western scholars.
The view advocated here sees fragmentation, extreme particular-
ism, pork barrel, and poorly informed public opinion. It is more
in the Lippmann tradition:

> The unhappy truth is that the prevailing public opinion
> has been destructively wrong at the critical functions.
> The people have imposed a veto upon the judgements
> of informed and responsible officials. They have com-
> pelled the governments, which usually know what would
> have been wiser . . . to be too late with too little . . .
> or too intransigent. [26]

Among social scientists this more pessimistic view of domestic politics, and in particular of pluralism, finds support in the
writings of E. E. Schattschneider. [27] According to Schattschneider
the pressure system is biased. It is "skewed, loaded, and unbalanced in favor of a fraction of a minority."[28] Domestic groups can
distort the process of representation through "inside" connections,
lobbying, campaign contributions, etc., thereby shortchanging the
natural interest."[29]

Compared with the statist model, the domestic politics model
suggests a low degree of insulation of national decision makers.
According to Theodore Lowi, it is only in crisis situations that the
makers of foreign policy are "truly separated and insulated from
broad publics."[30]

The major question about which we are trying to formulate
hypotheses concerns the extent to which various domestic groups
actively lobbied for their interests, and the extent to which the interests of constituents influenced members of Congress to get involved in the process of formulating U.S. ocean policy.

Among the different interests involved in ocean policy, it is
resource interests that tend to dominate domestic politics. These
include fishing, offshore oil exploitation, mining of deep seabed
minerals, commercial navigation, marine scientific research,
environmental protection, and so forth. From the point of view of
the voter and the member of Congress, some of these interests
have been more salient than others. If we limit the discussion to
fishing and deep seabed mining, the following points can be made.

With respect to the former, there are important regional differences. In some areas (Alaska, Washington, Oregon, and New England) fishing is mainly coastal. In others, it includes important distant-water fishing (California and the Gulf Coast). Since U.S. fishing is predominantly coastal, however, this part of the industry might be expected to build a winning coalition. Some coastal stocks were being overfished, coastal fishermen therefore used the argument of conservation in their efforts to have a 200-mile fishing zone introduced, thus diminishing foreign fishing off U.S. coasts. Concerning deep seabed mining, there is a presumption of low salience. The average voter is not concerned about manganese nodules. Nor has the mining industry been able to use the conservation argument in its coalition-building efforts. More lobbying was therefore necessary in this area than in that of fishing in order to get Congress to act.

The domestic politics model focuses on "constituency jobs and real estate."[31] Since these aspects are of greater popular concern in the case of fishing than of seabed mining, a domestic politics model can be expected to have more explanatory power in the former case than in the latter; at the least, it may explain the different timing of the two policy subprocesses.[32]

The central premise of this study in respect to domestic politics is that a structural bias exists in favor of subnational or parochial interests. Forces speaking for mankind, or what Robert Johansen has called the "human interest," will be very weak.[33] Because of this structural bias of the system, world order type policies will often be frustrated. The following hypotheses are offered:

Coastal fishermen will work for national enclosure of coastal resources through unilateral legislation; this implies a de-linkage of coastal fishing issues from the international negotiations. The mining industry will also lobby for protection of its interests through national legislation. It will be against, or very skeptical about, the idea of an international authority that will regulate its activities.
Rationale: Domestic interests are more likely to trust national administration than international administration of resource rights.

Members of Congress will be responsive to demands from constituents. Members from states with special fishing or mining interests will provide leadership in building the necessary coalitions for congressional action.
Rationale: Members of Congress fear "retribution at the polls."[34] They will usually work actively for the interests of constituents.

The timing of congressional action will not depend solely on the salience of the issues; presidential involvement is very important. Im order to survive, the multilateral approach will usually need active presidential support. The perspective of domestic politics, however, suggests that presidents—especially when seeking reelection—may follow the views of domestic groups instead of the dictates of statism or international interdependence.

SUMMARY AND EXTENSIONS

Four models have been suggested for this study. Each model singles out important structures, processes, and actors. Table 2 provides an overview.

TABLE 2

Perspectives on the Making of U.S. Ocean Policy

Model	Structure	Actors	Processes
Statism	Autonomy of state	President State Department	Presidential leadership
International interdependence	Sensitivities and vulnerabilities of states	Other states International organizations	Agenda setting Learning Linkage strategies
Bureaucratic politics	Autonomy of bureaucratic agencies	Bureaucrats	Pulling and hauling
Domestic politics	Capitalist economy Fragmented political power	Constituents Interest groups Congress	Electoral battles Lobbying Logrolling Congressional leadership

Source: Compiled by the author.

The central objective of this study is to try to explain selected aspects of U.S. ocean policy making. It is a premise that explanation is a fundamental social science endeavor. It is further an assumption that explanation takes place via certain conceptual frameworks or models. The models used are less than grand theories, but they are not devoid of content: they give certain concepts and inference patterns as well as notions of which variables are important. Without such notions we would be confronted by a bewildering world, not knowing where to look for what and why. In other words, it is a premise that facts do not really speak for themselves. By emphasizing certain variables, and preferably stating the rationale for the importance of those variables, models reduce the risk of overdetermination, although they will not be able to eliminate this phenomenon, which remains a fundamental problem of social science research.[35] Models can be seen as systematic speculation about which variables should be expected to be important, thus systematically excluding other variables. They can be more or less useful analytical tools. Their usefulness depends mainly on their capacity to suggest testable hypotheses.[36]

The study is seen as a case study of foreign policy making. The models used could be used to study other foreign policy decisions and processes, both of the United States and of other countries. One can presume that the same variables will be operative in other cases or countries, but with different coefficients. However, this study does not try to make cross-country comparisons in an explicit way, even if it is admitted that such comparisons could strengthen our inferences by the added controls they would introduce. So a loss in generality is admitted. The corresponding gain, it is hoped, is one of accuracy, specificity, and in-depthness.[37] This being said, however, it is argued that case studies can be useful in establishing knowledge of a more general nature. Logically one cannot generalize on the basis of one case. But the moment that certain theories have been suggested it becomes possible to test them through case studies. To the extent that a theory—or an inference pattern of one of the models applied—compels a specific case interpretation, a noncorrespondence of a case with that interpretation should at least raise serious questions about the theory. So should correspondence in cases where one would not expect correspondence.[38]

The four models are expected to complement each other. But it is an objective of the study to arrive at conclusions about the relative weight of the variables singled out by the models. The applied methodology is in line with Donald Kinder and Janet Weiss when they speak of "pockets of understanding," and suggest: "A loosely coupled collection of subtheories may be the most promising way of dealing with the full scope of so complex a phenomenon" as decision making.[39]

NOTES

1. Hans Morgenthau, Politics Among Nations: The Struggle for Power and Peace, 5th ed. (New York: Knopf, 1973).

2. Cf. R. Harrison Wagner, "Dissolving the State: Three Recent Perspectives on International Relations," International Organization 28 (Summer 1976):435-66.

3. See David J. Sylvan, "The Newest Mercantilism," International Organization 25 (Spring 1981):375-93.

4. Stephen Krasner, Defending the National Interest: Raw Materials Investments and U.S. Foreign Policy (Princeton: Princeton University Press, 1978), pp. 5-13.

5. Morgenthau, Politics Among Nations, pp. 4-11.

6. Morgenthau, "Another 'Great Debate': The National Interest of the United States," American Political Science Review 46 (December 1952):961-88, at 973.

7. See Fred A. Sonderman, "The Concept of the National Interest," Orbis 21 (Spring 1977):121-38.

8. Krasner, Defending the National Interest, pp. 13-14.

9. Ibid., pp. 14-17.

10. For the purpose of this study, the symmetry between prediction and explanation is being assumed. See Carl G. Hempel and Paul Oppenheim, "The Covering Law Analysis of Explanation," in Leonard I. Krimerman, ed., The Nature and Scope of Social Science (New York: Appleton-Century-Crofts, 1969), pp. 54-58.

11. Morgenthau, "Another 'Great Debate,'" pp. 968, 973.

12. Robert O. Keohane and Joseph S. Nye, Power and Interdependence: World Politics in Transition (Boston: Little, Brown, 1977), pp. 23-29. Only selected aspects of Keohane and Nye's models are applied in this study.

13. Ibid., pp. 8-19.

14. See also Ernst B. Haas, "Why Collaborate? Issue-Linkage and International Regimes," World Politics 32 (April 1980): 357-405.

15. Graham Allison, Essence of Decision (Boston: Little, Brown, 1971), p. 144.

16. Ibid., p. 162.

17. For critiques, see, for instance, Amos Perlmutter, "The Presidential Political Center and Foreign Policy: A Critique of the Revisionist and Bureaucratic-Political Orientations," World Politics 27 (October 1974):87-106; and Jerel A. Rosati, "Developing a Systematic Decision-Making Framework: Bureaucratic Politics in Perspective," World Politics 33 (January 1981):234-52.

18. Morton Halperin, Bureaucratic Politics and Foreign Policy (Washington, D.C.: Brookings Institution, 1974), p. 17.

19. Ibid., pp. 39-40.

20. For an early effort to explain U.S. ocean policy from a bureaucratic politics perspective, see Ann L. Hollick, "Bureaucrats at Sea," in Ann L. Hollick and Robert E. Osgaard, New Era of Ocean Politics (Baltimore and London: Johns Hopkins University Press, 1974), pp. 1-73.

21. William B. Quandt, Decade of Decisions: American Policy Toward the Arab-Israeli Conflict (Berkeley: University of California Press, 1977), p. 15.

22. Ibid.

23. Wilfrid Kohl, "The Nixon-Kissinger Foreign Policy System and U.S.-European Relations: Patterns of Policy-Making," World Politics 28 (October 1975):1-43.

24. Stephen D. Cohen, The Making of United States International Economic Policy (New York: Praeger, 1977), pp. 93-95.

25. Ibid., p. 62.

26. Walter Lippmann, The Public Philosophy (Boston: Little, Brown, 1955), p. 20; quoted from Kenneth N. Waltz, "Electoral Punishment and Foreign Policy Crisis," in James N. Rosenau, ed., Domestic Sources of Foreign Policy (New York: Free Press, 1967), pp. 263-93, at 265.

27. Theodore J. Lowi, "Making Democracy Safe for the World: National Politics and Foreign Policy," in Rosenau, ed., Domestic Sources of Foreign Policy, pp. 295-331, at 295-96.

28. E. E. Schattschneider, The Semisovereign People (Hensdale, Ill.: Dryden Press, 1975), p. 35.

29. See also Norman J. Ornstein and Shirley Elder, Interest Groups, Lobbying and Policymaking (Washington, D.C.: Congressional Quarterly Press, 1978), pp. 14-16.

30. Lowi, "Making Democracy Safe for the World," p. 324.

31. Terms used in the chapter on "Congress and Foreign Policy," in Barbara Hinckley, Stability and Change in Congress (New York: Harper & Row, 1971), p. 155.

32. For recent studies on Congress and foreign policy, see Thomas M. Franck and Edward Weisband, Foreign Policy by Congress (New York and Oxford: Oxford University Press, 1979); and Robert A. Pastor, Congress and the Politics of U.S. Foreign Economic Policy, 1928-1976 (Berkeley: University of California Press, 1980).

33. See Robert Johansen, The National Interest and the Human Interest: An Analysis of U.S. Foreign Policy (Princeton: Princeton University Press, 1980).

34. John W. Kingdon, Congressmen's Voting Decisions (New York: Harper & Row, 1973), p. 59.

35. For the concept of overdetermination, see Adam Przeworski and Henry Teune, The Logic of Comparative Social Inquiry (New York: Wiley, 1970).

36. See Henry Teune, "Models in the Study of Political Integration," in Philip E. Jacob and James V. Toscano, eds., The Integration of Political Communities (Philadelphia and New York: J. B. Lippincott, 1964), pp. 283-303.

37. See Henry Teune, "A Logic of Comparative Policy Analysis," in Douglas E. Ashford, ed., Comparing Public Policies: New Concepts and Methods, Sage Yearbooks in Politics and Public Policy, vol. IV (Beverly Hills: Sage Publications, 1978), pp. 43-55.

38. For a useful discussion of case studies, see Harry Eckstein, "Case Study and Theory in Political Science," in Fred I. Greenstein and Nelson W. Polsby, eds., Handbook of Political Science, vol. 7 (Reading, Mass.: Addison-Wesley, 1975), pp. 79-137.

39. Donald R. Kinder and Janet A. Weiss, "In Lieu of Rationality: Psychological Perspectives in Foreign Policy Decision Making," Journal of Conflict Resolution 22 (December 1978):707-35, at 732.

3

THE POLITICS OF SECURITY

THE FEAR OF CREEPING JURISDICTION

We recall the statist hypothesis: "A major issue in ocean politics for central U.S. policy makers has been the free use of ocean space for the military." How correct was this hypothesis?

Security interests did play a primary role in the considerations of U.S. decision makers, at least until the advent of the Reagan administration. Although defined by representatives of the U.S. Navy, security interests were accepted as most important by central decision makers during the Nixon, Ford, and Carter administrations. The early proposals made by the United States in the U.N. Seabed Committee and at UNCLOS III fit the hypothesis quite well.

But the politics of security had an element of bureaucratic politics, too. The Department of the Interior in particular felt that the Department of Defense had too much influence in U.S. ocean policy during the early 1970s.

A number of naval officers as well as scholars who had been associated with the navy have written about the law of the sea and although their articles often carry the disclaimer that the views expressed are not necessarily those of the U.S. Navy or Defense Department, there is good reason to believe that these writings contain more or less the same views as those advocated by military representatives in the policy-making process. Indeed, there is little dispute about the major security interests in the law of the sea. They center on a fear of what has become known as "creeping jurisdiction."

In 1967 the U.S. Navy asked the Center for Naval Analysis to study how the changing law of the sea might affect the navy's role in national security. The resulting study, of which a shortened version has been published, was done "primarily from the standpoint of

31

the Navy."[1] In the section discussing the navy and the delimitation of the continental shelf, the authors stated: ". . . the U.S. Navy is not bound to defense strategy placing primary emphasis on nearshore defense. It is more concerned with the right to operate world-wide with minimum restrictions upon its freedom. It has therefore preferred narrow claims."[2]

The study reviewed the changes in the law of the sea that had followed the Truman Proclamations in 1945 and were codified in the 1958 Geneva Conventions. As we have seen, these developments had introduced the exploitability test of the outer edge of the continental shelf. The term "creeping jurisdiction" was not used, but this was clearly the danger perceived by the authors. They also singled out the major bureaucratic opponent of the Department of Defense (DOD) in the continental shelf area as being the Department of the Interior. In its administration of the Outer Continental Shelf Lands Act, the Interior Department had taken "actions which might be misinterpreted." It had "extended its authority over considerable stretches of sea bottom." It had already gone beyond the 200-meter isobath in its leasing policy, but actual exploitation had not gone beyond that line. It was predicted that other countries would follow a similar policy of going further out, but not necessarily limiting jurisdiction to oil and gas exploitation. "There is some reason to fear that in the extreme, median lines in the ocean may someday be national borders," sounded the dire prediction from the Center for Naval Analyses.[3]

A specific concern that appeared early in the writings by navy-associated authors was the right of free transit of straits used for international navigation. This problem was singled out by Captain Geoffrey E. Carlisle of the U.S. Navy in 1967 as the most important navy interest in relation to the changing law of the sea. As mentioned earlier, the first two U.N. Conferences on the Law of the Sea in Geneva in 1958 and 1960 had failed to solve the problem of the breadth of the territorial sea. In 1960 the United States had worked for a six-mile territorial sea combined with an additional six-mile fisheries zone, but the proposal had not been adopted. Afterward the chief U.S. negotiator, Arthur H. Dean, had stated that the United States would continue to claim a three-mile territorial sea and not recognize wider claims.[4] But more and more states introduced wider territorial seas in the 1960s. And domestically there were increasing pressures for a wider U.S. fishing zone. The result was that the U.S. Congress enacted legislation extending exclusive U.S. fishing rights to 12 miles in October 1966. The U.S. Navy had continued to oppose such a step until June 1966. Said Rear Admiral Wilfred A. Hearn in testimony before the Congress: "We believe that our security interests are best served when nations are limited to narrow territorial seas. . . ."[5]

However, analyzing the trend, Captain Carlisle concluded that U.S. opposition to a 12-mile territorial sea was becoming increasingly unrealistic. The United States should accept it on the condition of a guaranteed right of passage through and over international straits. Said Carlisle:

> It is my conclusion that the prime U.S. defense interest is on the right to sail our warships and fly our aircraft through and above those territorial sea and high sea areas long recognized as international straits. The right as regards warships is in serious and imminent danger. The right for airplanes should be procured. [6]

To put this special navy concern about territorial seas and straits into perspective, it is necessary to look a little at the concept of "innocent passage," without going into details about the legal debate that has been going on for decades about its proper interpretation.

The 1958 Convention on the Territorial Sea and the Contiguous Zone establishes the then existing regime of innocent passage. Passage was and is innocent "so long as it is not prejudicial to the peace, good order or security of the coastal State." [7] Since an increasing number of straits would fall under overlapping territorial seas of the coastal states if the territorial sea is extended from three to six or twelve miles, a relevant question from a navy point of view was whether warships have a right of innocent passage.

The International Law Commission that prepared the 1958 Law of the Sea Conference had first suggested in its 1954 report that the passage of warships should be considered innocent. This view was in accordance with the ruling of the International Court of Justice in the Corfu Channel Case in 1949. [8] But in its 1955 report the International Law Commission suggested that the passage of warships should be "subject to previous authorization or notification." And a similar provision was reported out of the First Committee of the 1958 conference. But in the plenary of that conference the authorization requirement was first deleted and in the final vote an article with the notification requirement was not adopted. [9] But did this mean that warships were entitled to innocent passage? The answer remained uncertain, leaving some discretion to coastal states. However, one problem had been settled clearly by the 1958 convention: "Submarines are required to navigate on the surface and show their flag" in territorial seas. [10] This of course was a serious problem from a navy point of view.

Thus, we have seen that the law of the sea regime of the 1958 conventions contained two central concepts that were not well defined, namely, "innocent passage" and "exploitability." These concepts

were central in navy-associated writers' discussions of the changing
law of the sea. These authors considered the two concepts ambiguous and perceived a danger of "creeping jurisdiction."

NAVAL MISSIONS

To understand the navy's concern about "creeping jurisdiction"
it is useful to look at the navy's missions. They have been defined
as (1) strategic deterrence, (2) sea control, (3) projection of power
ashore, and (4) naval presence.[11]
The maintenance of a secure second-strike capability is the
central aspect of strategic deterrence, and it is often mentioned as
the most important mission of the military establishments of the
superpowers. The argument is that as long as each superpower can
expect an attack to be followed by a devastating counterattack, it
will be irrational to attack in the first place. The significance of
the Strategic Arms Limitation Talks (SALT) agreement in 1972 was
a recognition that mutual assured destruction—by enemies of the
concept called MAD—is more secure than a situation where each
power goes for a first-strike capability.[12]
The U.S. strategic deterrence is based on a triad, namely,
land-based intercontinental ballistic missiles (ICBMs), strategic
bombers (mainly B-52s), and missile-carrying nuclear submarines
(SSBNs). Of these three forces the great advantage of the SSBNs is
the relative undetectability made possible by their mobility and the
vastness of ocean space.[13] But the relative undetectability and invulnerability of SSBNs would diminish if they had to surface and show
their flag when passing through international straits. This has been
an important reason for navy advocacy of a special regime for straits
passage.[14]
But the U.S. Navy has other missions. Sea control refers to
assuring that the seas remain free for commercial and military navigation. It thus includes the freedom to support military forces engaged overseas. Projection of force ashore includes amphibious
assault and operations of the naval air forces over land. The
capability in question is that of foreign operations without the stationing of U.S. troops on foreign soil. Naval presence, finally, essentially means the capability of "showing the flag" off the shores of the
various coastal nations, thereby communicating concern and interest in some development.[15]
These conventional missions are important from the perspective of the "flexible response" doctrine—the capability to respond in
a flexible way in a crisis situation. In the postwar period we have
seen the U.S. Navy involved in such actions as interposing naval

vessels between Taiwan and China in the 1950s, projecting power ashore during the Lebanon crisis in 1958, providing logistics support in Korea and Vietnam, establishing the quarantine of Cuba during the missile crisis in 1962, and resupplying Israel during the 1973 Arab-Israeli War.[16]

To carry out these conventional missions the navy depends on the right to pass through straits. The Sixth Fleet depends on the right to pass through the Strait of Gibraltar to be present in the Mediterranean and the Seventh Fleet depends on the right to pass through the Indonesian straits of Malacca, Sunda, Lombok, and Ombai-Wetar to pass from the Pacific to the Indian Ocean, and back.[17] So Defense Department insistence on free transit of straits becomes even more understandable when we look at these conventional naval missions.[18]

The fear of "creeping jurisdiction" was not completely without foundation. By the early 1970s the following states claimed 200-mile territorial seas: Argentina, Brazil, Ecuador, El Salvador, Panama, Peru, Sierra Leone, and Uruguay.[19] But 200-mile territorial zones would completely cover the Mediterranean, the Baltic, the North Sea, the Persian Gulf, and the South China Sea. Such a situation would be unacceptable for the United States not only from the navy point of view but also from the point of view of commercial navigation. Should wider coastal resource zones be accepted it was therefore in the U.S. interest to have the high seas status of such zones accepted for navigational purposes.[20]

A special navy activity that does not usually receive official recognition as a mission, but which can be said to support the missions, is that of intelligence gathering. By its very nature this activity is surrounded by extreme secrecy. We know that surface ships and aircraft play a role; but the seabed is also used for the installation of various listening devices. The United States has used bottom-fixed sonars to monitor its coastal areas since at least the early 1950s. The present system on the U.S. continental shelf includes the publicly known Caesar program. It is said to have proven its value during the Cuban missile crisis. A Pacific Coast Caesar system was therefore projected in 1965.[21] It is known that similar systems have been installed in other parts of the world as well.[22] From the navy's point of view "continuous surveillance is required to minimize the danger of surprise attack." These activities are seen as a part of the navy's Anti-Submarine Warfare (ASW) program, "the next major mission of Naval forces" according to one Navy representative.[23] Hydrophones can also be used in floating sonobuoy fields or sown from and monitored by helicopters.[24]

Although the logic of these detection devices seems somewhat at variance with the doctrine of mutual assured destruction, since, according to this doctrine, the SSBNs should remain as undetected as possible, the U.S. Navy has worked to assure that a new legal regime for the oceans would not explicitly outlaw such activities from ocean space. In this connection it should of course also be recognized that detection devices can play a role for the conventional missions of the navy. [25] This explains why the navy has wanted to make sure that these devices remain legal. But it should be admitted that a breakthrough in the ASW area might upset the strategic balance. [26]

SEABED ARMS CONTROL

When the U.N. General Assembly decided to establish the ad hoc Seabed Committee in December 1967, "to study . . . the reservation exclusively for peaceful purposes of the seabed,"[27] it aroused some navy concern about the definition of "peaceful purposes." Some countries interpreted this to mean complete demilitarization. Pardo himself had suggested, when he introduced the seabed issue at the United Nations, that there was a danger of a new arms race in the seas. [28] Thus, the military uses of the seas seemed to be on the minds of some diplomats.

Initially the Soviet Union also supported the view that "peaceful" implied demilitarization. "Deceptively simple" was an early U.S. evaluation of the Soviet view. [29] And in the fall of 1968 a U.S. representative made the U.S. view clear at the United Nations:

> Considering that the term "peaceful purposes" does not preclude military activities generally, we believe that specific limitations on certain military activities will require the negotiation of a detailed arms control agreement. Military activities not precluded by such an agreement would continue to be conducted in accordance with the principle of freedom of the seas and exclusively for peaceful purposes. [30]

The United States proposed that the matter, because of its technical character, would be better considered by the Eighteen-Nation Disarmament Committee (ENDC) in Geneva. [31] This was accepted by the Soviet Union. The superpowers, acting as cochairmen of the ENDC, simply put the matter on the agenda in August 1968. The U.N. Seabed Committee, or the First Committee of the General Assembly, never agreed on a definition of a specific mandate, leaving this to the ENDC. [32] So the superpowers still had some influence on international agenda setting.

In the ENDC the Soviet Union at first continued to advocate complete demilitarization, possibly because of the propaganda value of such an approach. In the spring of 1969 a Soviet draft was presented that would have banned all military activity on the ocean floor beyond 12 miles. The United States responded with a draft treaty on May 22, 1969, which would have prohibited the emplacement of nuclear weapons and other weapons of mass destruction on the seabed and ocean floor beyond a three-mile territorial sea.[33] The U.S. representative to the ENDC, Adrian Fisher, told the New York Times of May 15, 1969: "The existence of submarine forces requires states to take action, in self-defense, such as establishing warning systems that use the seabed. The United States is not prepared to enter into a treaty which would throw the property of these systems in doubt."[34]

In the Seabed Committee itself the United States argued along similar lines. It was further argued that some communication and navigation aids are used for both military and nonmilitary ends. Also, military personnel are involved in much useful scientific research. The United States thus concluded that "complete demilitarization would have the effect of prohibiting certain necessary and desirable activities and might well be harmful."[35]

For some reason the Soviet Union changed policy. After intense negotiations, the Soviet Union and the United States could present a common draft treaty to the Conference of the Committee on Disarmament (CCD), as the ENDC had been renamed after enlargement. The draft foresaw the banning of nuclear weapons or any other type of weapons of mass destruction (such as chemical or biological weapons) on the seabed beyond a 12-mile contiguous zone.[36]

The Soviet-U.S. draft was criticized by members of the CCD on certain points. Some of the criticisms were taken into account by the two cochairmen of the conference, and already three weeks later, on October 24, 1969, the two superpowers could present a revised joint draft.[37] This revised draft did not satisfy its critics either. The U.N. General Assembly's First Committee sent it back to the CCD for revision and resubmission at the next General Assembly. After further revisions, some of which dealt with verification procedures, a revised Soviet-U.S. draft was presented in Geneva on April 23, 1970. Further revisions took place and a new revised text was presented on the first of September. This draft was approved by the CCD on September 4, 1970, by a vote of twenty-four to one. In December of that year the General Assembly adopted a resolution commending the draft for signature and ratification. The treaty was signed on February 11, 1971, after about two years of negotiations.[38] It went into force after having been ratified by the three depository governments, the United States, the Soviet Union, and the United Kingdom, and twenty-two others governments on May 18, 1972.[39]

The significance of the seabed arms control treaty from the point of view of this study—apart from being a case of U.S. success in agenda setting—is its limited scope. It only outlaws weapons of mass destruction emplaced on or in the seabed. So detection devices remain legal. So do naval operations in and on the water. The treaty must therefore be seen as a success from the navy point of view. It stopped "creeping jurisdiction" in the arms control area. Or to use another metaphor, the "Paper Torpedo" that could be perceived to "attempt to anchor the world's navies permanently" had itself been torpedoed.[40]

THE 1970 NIXON PROPOSAL

Having so far analyzed early indications of naval interest in the development of a new law of the sea, the rationale for this interest (namely, the naval missions), and the U.S. success in getting the question of demilitarization of ocean space off the Seabed Committee agenda, we can now study the 1970 Nixon proposal from a security point of view. We will find further evidence in support of the argument that security interests were of decisive importance in the initial U.S. ocean policy strategy.

A detailed U.S. draft convention was submitted to the U.N. Seabed Committee in Geneva on August 3, 1970.[41] It spelled out how an International Seabed Area would be established seaward of the 200-meter isobath. Article 3 provided that "the International Seabed Area shall be open to use by all States, without discrimination, except as otherwise provided."[42] Since the exceptions provided by the draft were related to exploration and exploitation of certain natural resources, this left the area open for other uses, including military ones.[43] Naval activities were not explicitly mentioned, but Article 6 specified: "Neither this Convention nor any rights granted or exercised pursuant thereto shall affect the legal status of the superjacent waters as high seas, or that of the air space above those waters."[44]

This article was clearly devised to protect security interests in the International Seabed Area. In the statement by John R. Stevenson before the Seabed Committee, when the U.S. draft was introduced, it was emphasized that the limitation of coastal state seabed resource jurisdiction to the 200-meter isobath would be a protection against the process of "creeping jurisdiction." In general it was argued that "maritime states' interests in freedom of navigation" would be served by the convention.[45]

Evidence can also be found in hearings. The May 23 Nixon proposals were presented by Under Secretary of State Elliot L.

Richardson to the Special Subcommittee on the Outer Continental
Shelf of the Senate Committee on Interior and Insular Affairs on May
27, 1970. The subcommittee was presided over by Senator Lee Metcalf (D-Mont.), who had twice postponed hearings to give the administration time to develop a unified position. Senator Metcalf had
also advised that the "United States should attempt to maximize the
quantity of continental shelf natural resources to which it is exclusively entitled."[46] As we know, the administration had not followed
Senator Metcalf's advice. Elliot Richardson argued against broad
U.S. claims, which he said would raise "indirect, but serious, national security questions."[47] He thus confirmed that security questions had had an important impact on the initial U.S. ocean political
strategy.

About a month later, on June 25, 1970, the chairman of the
Defense Advisory Group on the Law of the Sea, Leigh Ratiner, testified about the Nixon proposals before the Subcommittee on Sea-
power of the House Armed Services Committee. He talked about
"creeping jurisdiction," the restrictions of "innocent passage," and
navy and air force needs of worldwide mobility. He also talked
about the failures to establish boundaries for the territorial sea and
the continental shelf. The result, he said, had been a "continued
proliferation of claims."[48] The Nixon proposals had been worked
out in view of trying to stop this proliferation of claims and "to
rationalize the uses of the seas." Summing up the central aspects
of the Nixon policy, he said: "In short, we are asking that the exploitability test, the right to extend coastal state jurisdiction further
and further out, be abandoned in spite of the fact it is contained in
the Geneva Convention on the Continental Shelf."[49]

A little later in Ratiner's testimony it was made specific that
"coastal states would have no rights in the trusteeship zone except
those specifically delegated to it by international agreement." The
coastal state would have "few delegated powers." And those powers
could not be expanded.[50]

THE 1971 U.S. STRAITS PROPOSAL

The 1970 Nixon policy dealt with the problems of seabed politics without explicitly addressing the problem of transit of international straits. We have seen that the U.S. Navy had a special interest in this respect. In line with that special interest the United
States made it clear to the U.N. Seabed Committee that it considered freedom of transit of international straits a nonnegotiable
right, and in 1971 the United States presented draft articles that
were designed to secure such freedom.[51] According to these ar-

ticles, each state would have the right to establish the breadth of its territorial sea "within limits of no more than 12 nautical miles" on the following condition:

> In straits used for international navigation between one part of the high seas and another part of the high seas or the territorial sea of a foreign State, all ships and aircraft in transit shall enjoy the same freedom of navigation and overflight, for the purpose of transit through and over such straits, as they have on the high seas. [52]

The draft articles were introduced in the U. N. Seabed Committee on August 3, 1971, by John R. Stevenson, legal advisor of the Department of State, and U.S. representative to the committee. He explicitly referred to the security aspect, arguing that decreased naval mobility could "intensify the competition for strategic advantages." This would have a destabilizing effect and force nations to divert more attention and resources to security matters. He referred to the doctrine of "innocent passage," which he said was inadequate when applied to international straits: "Under the Territorial Sea Convention, neither aircraft nor submerged submarines have a right of innocent passage."[53]

Apart from the security argument, Stevenson also argued that free transit of straits was in the interest of international trade: "If coastal states were given a legal basis for impairing transit, virtually every country in the world would find its very economy dependent upon the political good will of some other state by virtue of geography."[54] So broader U.S. statist goals were at stake.

INTERNATIONAL DEVELOPMENTS

However, the rest of the world, especially the major straits states, were slow in buying the U.S. argument. Tanzania and Spain brought up the issue at the 1972 summer session of the Seabed Committee, arguing the coastal state point of view. The United States indicated a clear willingness to take the legitimate concerns of coastal states about navigational safety into consideration, but demanded a right of free transit and repeated that the rules of innocent passage were inadequate. These rules could be abused if a coastal state decided to interpret them subjectively. Some delegations had already concluded that "certain types of passage, for example, by nuclear-powered ships and supertankers, should be considered non-innocent per se."

It was the U.S. view that mandatory application of traffic separation schemes developed by the Intergovernmental Maritime Consultative Organization (IMCO) and strict liability in the case of accidents could solve the problems of navigational safety. Concerning submarines, the United States argued that they navigate more safely submerged than on the surface. So no special rules were needed for these vessels. And concerning transit by aircraft, the United States proposed the establishment of some procedures through the International Civil Aviation Organization (ICAO). Finally, the United States again admitted to have security reasons for its straits policy. Said Stevenson: "If we did not take into account our security requirements in these negotiations, we would be acting irresponsibly."[55]

The lack of early international support for the U.S. proposal was not appreciated in the Defense Department. In hearings in October 1972, Stuart P. French, the director of the Defense Department Law of the Sea Task Force, expressed the DOD concern in the following way:

> . . . our national security interests require submerged transit of submarines and overflight of aircraft in straits that will become territorial seas if 12 miles becomes the agreed breadth of the territorial sea.
>
> The degree of confidence we in Defense have that this treaty will indeed accommodate those objectives, at this point in time, is considerably less than that of other members of the delegation. We are not altogether optimistic.[56]

However, the United States did get the navigational freedoms it demanded into the first UNCLOS negotiating text, which emerged in 1975. When the international negotiations really got started, it turned out to be easier to solve the problems of straits passage and other navigational rights than originally expected. The moderate states on both sides, especially the United Kingdom for the maritime powers and Fiji for the straits and archipelagic states, worked out a compromise that was proposed as an element of a package deal.[57] According to the proposed rules of "transit passage," the straits state would have some regulatory authority, but regulation had to be nondiscriminatory and based on international regulations. The proposal contained nothing about prior notification for vessels or aircraft, nor were submarines required to surface and show their flag. A similar right of passage, "archipelagic sea lanes passage," was introduced for navigation between the islands of archipelagic states, such as Indonesia and the Philippines.[58]

The first negotiating text in 1975 also stipulated that there would be freedom of navigation and overflight in the economic zone beyond the proposed 12-mile territorial zone. And coastal state jurisdiction over continental margin resources would not affect the legal status of superjacent waters. Similarly the international area beyond the limits of national jurisdiction would retain its freedom of navigation. This basic compromise was retained in the 1982 Draft Convention.[59] The coastal state will get the right to establish territorial seas up to 12 nautical miles in breadth on the condition of "transit passage" rights in international straits. And the coastal state will be able to introduce 200-mile economic zones as well as exploit continental margin resources farther out in cases where the continental margin is wider than 200 miles, on the condition of freedom of navigation, overflight, and other nonresource uses. But, let us not forget that this was all part of a package deal. Third World coastal states in particular expected a quid pro quo in other areas, not the least in respect to deep seabed mining.

NOTES

1. Norman V. Breckner, Robert L. Friedheim, Leslie R. Heselton, Jr., Leo S. Mason, Stuart G. Schmid, and Robert H. Simmonds, The Navy and the Common Sea (Washington, D.C.: Office of Naval Research, 1972), p. vii.

2. Ibid., p. 140.

3. Ibid., p. 160.

4. Geoffrey E. Carlisle, "Three Mile Limit: Obsolete Concept?" U.S. Naval Institute Proceedings 93:2 (1967), pp. 24-33, at 26.

5. Quoted, ibid., p. 29.

6. Ibid., p. 33; the importance of straits was also singled out by Bruce A. Harlow, "Freedom of Navigation," in Lewis M. Alexander, ed., The Law of the Sea: Offshore Boundaries and Zones (Columbus, Ohio: Ohio State University Press, 1967), pp. 188-94.

7. Article 14(4); for text see Shingeru Oda, The International Law of the Ocean Development. Basic Documents, vol. I (Leiden: Sijthoff, 1976), pp. 3-8.

8. The Court had stated: "It is the opinion of the Court generally recognized and in accordance with international custom that states in time of peace have a right to send their warships through straits used for international navigation between two parts of the high seas without the previous authorization of the coastal State, provided that the passage is innocent." Quoted in Frederic G.

De Rocher, Freedom of Passage Through International Straits: Community Interest Amid Present Controversy, Sea Grant Technical Bulletin #23 (Coral Gables, Fla.: University of Miami Sea Grant Program, November 1972), pp. 76-77, 87.

9. Ibid., pp. 88-94.

10. Article 14(6); Oda, International Law of Ocean Development, I, p. 5.

11. Mark W. Janis, Sea Power and the Law of the Sea (Lexington, Mass.: Lexington Books, 1976), p. 1; see also Stansfield Turner, "Missions of the U.S. Navy," Naval War College Review 26 (March-April 1974):2-17.

12. See, for instance, John Newhouse, Cold Dawn: The Story of SALT (New York: Holt, Rinehart and Winston, 1973).

13. By the end of 1972 the United States had about 1,050 land-based ICBNs, 520 B-52 and FB-111 bombers, and 41 Polaris-Poseidon submarines carrying 656 missiles. The Polaris and Poseidon missiles have a range of about 2,500 miles. J. P. Marnane, "The Breadth of the Territorial Sea and Its Implications for Unrestricted U.S. Naval Operations" (M.A. thesis, Naval War College, Newport, R.I., 1972), pp. 55-56. The most recent U.S. SSBN is the Trident. It has a missile range of over 4,500 miles. See Janis, Sea Power, p. 2.

14. For a critical evaluation of the Navy view, see Robert E. Osgood, "U.S. Security Interests in Ocean Law," Ocean Development and International Law 2 (Spring 1974):1-36.

15. Janis, Sea Power, p. 2.

16. Ibid., p. 5; and Marnane, "The Breadth of the Territorial Sea," p. 67.

17. Janis, Sea Power, pp. 5-6.

18. John A. Knauss, "The Military Role in the Ocean and Its Relation to the Law of the Sea," in Lewis M. Alexander, ed., The Law of the Sea: A New Geneva Conference, Proceedings of the Sixth Annual Conference of the Law of the Sea Institute, June 21-24, 1971 (Kingston, R.I.: University of Rhode Island, 1972), pp. 77-86, at 82.

19. U.S. Department of State, Bureau of Intelligence and Research, Limits in the Seas #36, Revised, March 1, 1973.

20. Janis, Sea Power, p. 8.

21. Sven Hirdman, "Weapons in the Deep Sea," Environment 13 (April 1971):28-42, at 40.

22. Owen Wilkes, "Strategic Anti-Submarine Warfare and Its Implications for a Counterforce Strike," in Stockholm International Peace Research Institute, World Armaments and Disarmament: SIPRI Yearbook 1979 (London: Taylor and Francis, 1979), pp. 424-52, at 429-32.

23. Captain L. E. Zeni, "Defense Needs in Accommodations among Ocean Users," in Lewis M. Alexander, ed., The Law of the Sea: International Rules and Organization for the Seas, Proceedings of the Third Annual Conference of the Law of the Sea Institute, June 24-27, 1968 (Kingston, R.I.: The University of Rhode Island, 1969), pp. 334-39, at 335.

24. R. L. Garwin, "Antisubmarine Warfare and National Security," Scientific American 227 (July 1972):14-24.

25. See, for instance, Gordon J. F. MacDonald, "An American Strategy for the Oceans," in Edmund A. Gullion, ed., Uses of the Seas (Englewood Cliffs, N.J.: Prentice-Hall, 1968), pp. 163-94.

26. On this possibility see Wilkes, "Strategic Anti-Submarine Warfare," pp. 444-48.

27. "U.N. Establishes Ad Hoc Committee to Study Use of Ocean Floor," Department of State Bulletin 58:1491 (January 22, 1968), pp. 125-27.

28. Statement to the First Committee of the U.N. General Assembly, November 1, 1967, in Arvid Pardo, The Common Heritage: Selected Papers on Oceans and World Order 1967-1974 (Malta University Press, 1975), pp. 1-41, at 17.

29. David H. Popper, "The Deep Ocean Environment: U.S. and International Policy," Department of State Bulletin 59:1520 (August 12, 1968), pp. 171-77, at 176.

30. James Russell Wiggens, "U.S. Suggests Possible Steps by U.N. to Promote Peaceful Uses of the Deep Ocean Floor," Department of State Bulletin 59:1534 (November 25, 1968), pp. 554-58, at 556.

31. Ibid., pp. 556-57; see also A. Denis Clift, ". . . of Diplonauts and Ocean Politics," U.S. Naval Institute Proceedings 96 (July 1970):32-39, at 36-37.

32. Bennett Ramberg, The Seabed Arms Control Negotiations: A Study of Multilateral Arms Control Conference Diplomacy. Monograph Series in World Affairs 15:2 (Denver, Colo.: Graduate School of International Studies, 1978), pp. 25-26.

33. "Text of U.S. Draft Treaty," Department of State Bulletin 60:1564 (June 16, 1969), pp. 523-24.

34. Quoted by Norman V. Breckner in "Some Dimensions of Defense Interests in the Legal Delimitations of the Continental Shelf," in Lewis M. Alexander, ed., The Law of the Sea: National Policy Recommendations, Proceedings of the Fourth Annual Conference of the Law of the Sea Institute, June 23-26, 1969 (Kingston, R.I.: The University of Rhode Island, 1970), pp. 188-92, at 188-89; see also Adrian S. Fisher, "U.S. Submits Draft Treaty Banning Emplacement of Nuclear Weapons on the Seabed," Department of State Bulletin 60:1564 (June 16, 1969), pp. 520-23.

35. David H. Popper, "U.N. Seabed Committee Concludes Spring Session," Department of State Bulletin 60:1556 (April 21, 1969), pp. 342-45, at 343.

36. James F. Leonard, "U.S. and USSR Agree on Draft Treaty Banning Emplacement of Nuclear Weapons on the Seabed," Department of State Bulletin 61:1584 (November 3, 1969), pp. 365-68.

37. James F. Leonard, "United States Comments on Revisions in Draft Treaty Banning Emplacement of Nuclear Weapons on the Seabed," Department of State Bulletin 61:1588 (December 1, 1969), pp. 480-84; see also James F. Leonard, "U.S. Discusses Verification on Procedures Under the Draft Treaty Banning Emplacement of Nuclear Weapons on the Seabed," Department of State Bulletin 61:1586 (November 17, 1969), pp. 425-29.

38. James A. Barry, Jr., "The Seabed Arms Control Issue 1967-1971: A Superpower Symbiosis?" Naval War College Review 25 (September-October 1972), pp. 87-101, at 96-97; see also Charles W. Yost, "U.S. Discusses Progress in Arms Control," Department of State Bulletin 61:1591 (December 22, 1969), pp. 600-06; "Arms Control Measure for the Seabed," Department of State Bulletin 62 (May 4, 1970), pp. 592-94; James F. Leonard, "United States and U.S.S.R. Table Revised Draft Treaty Banning Emplacement of Nuclear Weapons on the Seabed," Department of State Bulletin 62:1613 (May 25, 1970), pp. 663-67; and James F. Leonard, "Geneva Disarmament Conference Agrees on Text," Department of State Bulletin 63:1631 (September 28, 1970), pp. 362-66.

39. U.S. Arms Control and Disarmament Agency, Arms Control and Disarmament Agreements (Washington, D.C., 1975), p. 95.

40. Cf. Clift, ". . . of Diplonauts," p. 37.

41. "Draft United Nations Convention on the International Seabed Area: Working Paper Submitted by the United States of America," in Report of the Committee on the Peaceful Uses of the Sea-Bed and the Ocean Floor beyond the Limits of National Jurisdiction, United Nations, General Assembly, Official Records, 25th Session, Supplement No. 21 (A/8021), (New York, 1970), pp. 130-76. (Hereafter cited as Seabed Committee Report 1970.)

42. Ibid., p. 133.

43. See, for instance, the interpretation in H. Gary Knight, "The Draft United Nations Convention on the International Seabed Area: Background, Description, and Some Preliminary Thoughts," San Diego Law Review 8 (May 1971):495-550, at 544-45.

44. Seabed Committee Report 1970, p. 133.

45. "Statement by Mr. Stevenson," Department of State Bulletin 63:1626 (August 24, 1970), pp. 209-10.

46. U.S. Congress, Senate, Interior and Insular Affairs Committee, Outer Continental Shelf, Part 2, Hearings, 91st Cong., 2nd Sess., April 1, May 20, 27, 1970, p. 426.

47. Ibid., p. 430.

48. U.S. Congress, House of Representatives, Armed Services Committee, Hearings on Territorial Sea Boundaries, Hearings, 91st Cong., 2nd Sess., June 25, 1970, pp. 9287-90.

49. Ibid., p. 9293.

50. Ibid., p. 9295.

51. For a critical discussion, see H. Gary Knight, "The 1971 United States Proposals on the Breadth of the Territorial Sea and Passage Through International Straits," Oregon Law Review 51 (Summer 1972):759-87.

52. States could designate corridors for transit. It was also stipulated that straits already regulated by international agreement—this would include the Turkish and Danish straits—would not be affected by the article. See "Draft Articles on the Breadth of the Territorial Sea, Straits, and Fisheries Submitted to Sub-Committee II by the United States of America," in Report of the Committee on the Peaceful Uses of the Sea-Bed and the Ocean Floor beyond the Limits of National Jurisdiction, United Nations, General Assembly, Official Records, 26th Session, Supplement No. 21 (A/8421), (New York, 1971), p. 241. (Hereafter cited as Seabed Committee Report 1971.)

53. John R. Stevenson, "Statement," Department of State Bulletin 65:1680 (September 6, 1971), pp. 261-66, at 262.

54. Ibid., p. 263.

55. John R. Stevenson, "Statement, Main Committee, Aug. 14, 1972," in U.S. Congress, Senate, Commerce Committee, Law of the Sea, Hearing, 92nd Cong., 2nd Sess., October 3, 1972, pp. 59-62.

56. Ibid., p. 26.

57. Edward Miles, "An Interpretation of the Geneva Proceedings—Part II," Ocean Development and International Law 3 (1976): 303-40.

58. "Informal Single Negotiating Text," in Third United Nations Conference on the Law of the Sea, Official Records vol. 4 (New York, 1975), pp. 137-81.

59. Third United Nations Conference on the Law of the Sea, Convention in the Law of the Sea and Resolutions I-IV, reproduced by Office of Ocean Law and Policy, Department of State, Washington, D.C., June 1982.

4

THE POLITICS OF
OFFSHORE PETROLEUM RIGHTS

THE OIL LOBBY

As the U.N. Seabed Committee started considering the development of a new law of the sea, the U.S. oil and gas industry
was fast to realize that something was going on. And if the industry
itself did not realize it, the Department of the Interior helped it
get started considering what its policy should be. In January 1968
the Interior Department requested the National Petroleum Council
(NPC) to prepare a study which should consider:

(a) whether the definition of the Continental Shelf is
    is in keeping with technological advancements in
    offshore capability,
(b) what type of regime would best assure the orderly
    development of the petroleum resources of the
    ocean floor and the time frame within which it
    might be implemented,
(c) what type of regime is best designed to assure
    conservation of the resources and protection of
    the environment, and
(d) any other points or comments deemed appro-
    priate.[1]

The NPC had been established in 1946 as an industry advisory
body to the Interior Department. The requested report was to
assist the department and other government agencies in formulating
their posture toward the development of offshore petroleum resources. The request was prefaced by the proposition that "in the
expanding search for new supplies of energy, it is clear that offshore areas are among petroleum's brightest frontiers."[2]

The NPC agreed to undertake the study. It established a 22-member Committee on Petroleum Resources Under the Ocean Floor, which subsequently set up a Technical Subcommittee to assist it. The subcommittee was chaired by Hollis D. Hedberg, Gulf Oil's exploration advisor. After about a year's work the NPC issued its first major report, Petroleum Resources Under the Ocean Floor, in March 1969. The report analyzed U.S. energy requirements. Energy consumption in the United States was said to be rising rapidly. Of this consumption three-fourths was supplied by oil and gas. Imports of petroleum had increased from 4.3 percent of the total petroleum supply in 1945 to 12.6 percent in 1965. The nation was thus becoming more and more dependent on foreign supplies. Offshore production, which had only started in 1946, should be seen in this perspective. By 1968 this production accounted for 12 percent of the oil and 10 percent of the gas production in the United States. At this time leases were purchased in 1,800 feet (549 meters) of water. Commercial oil and gas production had been established in water depths of 340 feet (104 meters).[3] Offshore production was expected to increase and move farther out; how fast would depend on technical and economic as well as legal and political factors.

The ongoing offshore production was based on the Outer Continental Shelf Lands Act (OCSLA) of 1953 and the 1958 Geneva Convention on the Continental Shelf, both of which had given the coastal state jurisdiction over the natural resources of the continental shelf without defining an exact outer limit. The NPC report therefore tried to determine such a limit by looking at the legislative history of the 1958 convention. That convention, as mentioned earlier, had spoken of "a depth of 200 meters" or beyond "to where the depth of the superjacent waters admits of the exploitation of the natural resources of the said area." At the same time the continental shelf was said to be "adjacent to the coast." Did adjacency put a real limit on exploitability? Yes, answered the NPC, but that limit was the outer edge of the continental margin. So the coastal state's exclusive jurisdiction over the natural resources of the seabed and subsoil goes out to where the abyssal ocean floor begins, including the continental shelf, slope, "and at least the landward portion of the continental rise overlapping the slope."[4]

The major point of the long legislative history that was used to support this position was that the International Law Commission (ILC), which had prepared the 1958 conference, had included exploitability because it wanted to recognize the right to exceed the limit of 200 meters if exploitation of the seabed or subsoil at depth greater than 200 meters proved technically possible.[5] Adjacency was put into the ILC report in 1956 to take account of situations

where the continent drops off abruptly from near the coastline to
the abyssal ocean floor. If the continental shelf was taken in its
technical, geomorphic meaning, such situations would give no offshore rights. Since this kind of situation exists off the west coast
of South America, a conference of the Organization of American
States at Ciudad Trujillo in 1956 had suggested to include "other
submarine areas, adjacent to the coastal state." This was what the
ILC report in 1956 did, and the 1958 conference accepted this. The
continental shelf as defined in Article 1 of the 1958 convention is a
new legal concept, not a technical, geomorphic one. The legal
regime applies to seabed areas if they are adjacent to the coast
even if they are not technically "continental shelf." This new legal
definition was achieved by choosing the words "the seabed and subsoil of the submarine areas adjacent to the coast."[6]

It was also argued by the NPC that a broad shelf definition was
the understanding of the U.S. Congress and president when the
Geneva Convention was ratified.[7] A further argument in support of
the NPC position was found in the International Court of Justice decision in the 1969 North Sea Continental Shelf Case, where the
Court had stated that

> the rights of the coastal State in respect of the area
> of the continental shelf that constitutes a natural
> prolongation of its land territory into and under the
> sea exist ipso facto and ab initio, by virtue of its
> sovereignty over the land. . . .[8]

The right to explore and exploit the continental shelf's natural resources is "an inherent right," and it is also "exclusive." It is
not necessary to go through a legal process to establish the right.
Nor does the right have to be exercised to exist.

The report also looked at the practice of states. Of 107
coastal states that had asserted jurisdiction over offshore minerals,
it was found that at least 37 had made claims to areas that appeared
to be beneath waters deeper than 200 meters.[9]

Finally, nature provided an argument. The limit "coinciding
approximately with the outer limit of the submerged continent," it
was said, "is the most distinct, the most profound, and the only
natural boundary" that could be utilized. This was so because of a
sharp change in the geological/geophysical character of the earth's
crust at this point. It was admitted, however, that there are often
transition zones that can obscure the boundary between the continental and the oceanic crust. But it didn't discourage the authors
of the report. "Scientific facts," they maintained, make it "ap-
parent that the outer edge of the continent is a far more logical

choice than the outer edge of the geological continental shelf" as the limit of the coastal state's resource jurisdiction.[10]

Having thus developed the argument that U.S. jurisdiction to offshore petroleum resources extends to the outer edge of the continental margin, the authors of the report could turn to the international situation. Here they saw a threat of "international encroachment." They referred to the Maltese proposal in the U.N. General Assembly of establishing an international regime for the oceans. Accepting a regime that would not secure U.S. sovereign rights "out to the edge of the submerged continent, irrespective of depth of water or distance from shore" would be "giving away of rights already confirmed to this Nation." The value of the resource at stake could be estimated in tens of billions of dollars at the wellhead. Obviously, important revenue in the form of taxes, bonuses, and royalties would accrue to the Federal Treasury from the exploitation of these resources.[11]

The report specifically objected to the proposal of an "intermediate zone" that had been put forward by the Commission on Marine Science, Engineering and Resources in its recently published report, Our Nation and the Sea. This proposal foreshadowed the trusteeship idea of the Nixon proposals a year later. Such intermediate zone would, according to the NPC, subject present and future lessees and operators in that zone to the hazards of the new international regime. "Retroactive boundary" proposals were said not to be in the interests of the United States.[12]

The implication of the NPC position was that other nations would have resource jurisdiction to the continental margins off their coasts. U.S. oil companies would therefore have to seek leases from other coastal nations if they want to engage in offshore operations in other parts of the world. The NPC recognized this, but preferred such a situation to having to deal with a new international organization:

> . . . recent trends within the United Nations give
> little reason for hope that American nationals would
> fare better under a regime formulated by a 126-
> nation forum in which the United States has one
> vote, than they would fare dealing with individual
> nations under their national laws.[13]

Despite all the scientific pretensions of the NPC report this was the central political choice made by the U.S. petroleum industry in 1969. The industry preferred to deal with many coastal nations rather than an international organization. The possibility that an effective cartel of oil producers might create difficulties for the

U.S. oil industry and U.S. consumers was not considered. The Nixon proposals in 1970 followed. The president had clearly not listened to the NPC—or the Interior Department.

A couple of days after the presentation of the U.S. Draft Convention in Geneva, the Interior Department again invited the NPC to give its contribution, in the form of "an article-by-article analysis" of the U.S. draft. Interior was especially interested in the NPC view of Articles 26 and 73 of the draft. These articles dealt with the seaward limit of the trusteeship zone and leasing beyond the 200-meter isobath in the interim period prior to the ratification of a seabed treaty.[14]

The new NPC report objected to "the relinquishment by the coastal state of its existing mineral resource rights in the outer continental margin," that is, the area between the 200-meter isobath and the outer limit of the margin. Creating an international organization with "residual authority" was said to be wrong. It would unduly restrict the rights of the coastal state. An international authority holding a "residuum of powers" would create instability and uncertainty. Further, the work requirements established in the appendices of the draft were unrealistic and the procedures were excessively elaborate. The resulting treaty would discourage rather than encourage exploration and exploitation.[15]

Nor did the NPC like the proposed interim policy. Even if the draft had stipulations about security of investment and coastal state compensation for losses in connection with the entry into force of a new treaty, it was the basic idea of issuing leases subject to a treaty that the NPC could not accept. It was also argued that the draft convention could be construed to authorize international production controls, to which the NPC objected.[16]

There were, however, five points in the Nixon proposal that the NPC could accept:

1. dedication of part of the revenues from outer continental margin oil exploitation to international community purposes;
2. prevention of unreasonable interference with other uses of ocean space;
3. protection of the ocean environment;
4. assurance of the integrity of investment; and
5. compulsory dispute settlement.[17]

Since presumably points two to five would have to apply in the case of exclusive national jurisdiction over outer continental margin resources, it is the first point that is most interesting. It was not revenue sharing that the U.S. petroleum industry was against. The basis of the NPC policy was a fear of an untried international authority. In the interim period the NPC wanted the leases beyond the 200-meter isobath to continue on the basis of the OCSLA of 1953. Such leases should not be affected later by a treaty.[18]

To conclude, the NPC wanted the United States to "confirm" coastal state jurisdiction over the natural resources of the entire continental margin. This would limit the international area to the deep ocean floor beyond the continental margin. Consideration or military implications of seabed use was explicitly excluded in the report; but implicit was a clear unwillingness to trade perceived resource interests for military interests.

The petroleum industry also spoke through its own interest organization, the American Petroleum Institute (API). The API position was presented forcefully in hearings before the Subcommittee on Minerals, Material and Fuels of the Senate Interior and Insular Affairs Committee, on September 23, 1970, by Luke W. Finlay. The board of directors of the API had adopted a statement of policy on November 10, 1969. Luke Finlay quoted from that statement:

> Exclusive jurisdiction over the natural resources of
> the seabed adjacent to the U.S. coasts, including the
> entirety of the submerged continent out to where it
> meets the abyssal ocean floor, is this nation's right
> as confirmed by the 1958 Geneva Convention on the
> Continental Shelf. The importance of these ocean
> floor resources to the nation's future economic growth
> and security is such that the United States should un-
> equivocally assert, in concert with other like-minded
> nations, its full rights as confirmed by that Conven-
> tion.[19]

On this basis Finlay could criticize the U.S. Draft Convention, which, he said, failed critically to protect essential U.S. national interests, and which would have a "stifling effect" on the future development of the outer continental margin areas. He reminded the Senate committee that the U.S. draft would establish "an entirely new and untried type of international arrangement." And he argued that the developing countries would try to get a "controlling voice" in such a new regime.[20]

The API could accept some revenue sharing with the international community, but it was against the "renunciation" of national rights beyond the 200-meter isobath, and with that the International Trusteeship idea. The API wanted a policy that would assure "the integrity of investments." It saw no assurance in a negotiation process that might lead to new rules. "One should not buy a pig in a poke," was the old adage proposed by Finlay. Exploitation of the outer continental margin would involve "heavy risks." The petroleum industry therefore needed "assurance that the rules of the game will remain unchanged for the life of their leases."[21]

ALLIES OF THE INDUSTRY

An early ally of the petroleum industry was the American Bar Association (ABA), which adopted a resolution on seabed resources at its 1968 annual meeting. The resolution was based on a joint report by the sections of National Resources Law, International and Comparative Law, and the Standing Committee on Peace and Law through United Nations. The resolution recommended that the 1958 Convention on the Continental Shelf be used "to the full extent permitted." The report that accompanied the resolution disagreed with the interpretation that exploitability could carry coastal state jurisdiction to the mid-ocean. Adjacency had to be taken into account, too. But, even on that basis, the ABA report could conclude that "the exclusive rights of the coastal nations with respect to the seabed minerals now embrace the submerged land mass of the adjacent continent down to its junction with the deep ocean floor, irrespective of depth."[22]

It should be mentioned that the 1968 report created some dissension in the ABA. Its interpretation of coastal state jurisdiction did not accurately reflect the views of some members. They pointed out afterward that exploitability could only mean that sovereign rights over seabed resources beyond the 200-meter isobath extend as technological progress makes actual exploitation in that area possible. Since technology did not yet make it possible to exploit the outer continental margin down to the deep ocean floor, it was erroneous to say that sovereign rights existed already.[23] This, however, was clearly only a legalistic detail. Even according to the minority view, the outer continental margin would eventually come under national jurisdiction.

The 1969 meeting of the ABA again dealt with the issue. The result was a new joint report by the same three sections, this time incorporating the minority view:

We reaffirm our opinion that the concept of adjacency contained in the present Shelf Convention should properly be interpreted to include the submerged continental land mass. In the view widely held among our members, all of the submerged continental land

mass is subject to national jurisdiction over its natural resources. In the view of a significant number of
our members any part of this land mass will come
within national jurisdiction as soon as it becomes ac-
cessible to exploitation. [24]

The sections also maintained that the United States should "assert
to the full" its rights. And the 1969 report held, as the 1968 report
had, that an international conference was unnecessary. A precise
boundary for the legal continental shelf could be established through
"parallel declarations by interested states."[25]

When the Subcommittee on Minerals, Materials and Fuels of
the Senate Interior and Insular Affairs Committee conducted hearings on the U.S. Draft Convention and related matters in September
1970 the ABA was represented by Northcutt Ely. He told the committee that the ABA policy was the reverse of the Nixon Draft Convention. And he went on to ask about the worth of the asset at
stake. The potential resources in the area between the 200- and
2,500-meter isobaths had been estimated by the U.S. Geological
Survey at more than 600 billion barrels of oil. This was six times
as much as the oil that had been produced on land in the United
States since oil production had started about 100 years ago. There
was also a question of revenues for the U.S. Treasury. By 1970
offshore royalties and bonuses had amounted to over $4 billion.
But the offshore area leased by 1970 was only about 1 percent of the
total outer continental margin area. So why make this "major component of the American mineral estate" into some kind of "common
heritage of mankind." If there was a quid pro quo involved, it was
of minimal value. [26]

Ely did not believe in creeping jurisdiction. "The dissocia-
tion of seabed jurisdiction from jurisdiction over the superjacent
waters is already assured by Article 3 of the existing convention,"
he said. Superjacent waters remain high seas. And, continuing
the speculation about the quid pro quo, he said that

if free transit of straits is the objective, it is ludi-
crous to suppose that we can obtain the acquiescence,
say, of Indonesia, in the withdrawal of her claims to
a 12-mile territorial sea which would close the Straits
of Malacca, by offering her a deal whereby she also
renounces her mineral claims in waters deeper than
200 meters. [27]

Nor did Ely believe that the U.S. Draft Convention could get Latin
American states to renounce their 200-mile claims. So the prospects of an international treaty in line with the U.S. draft were dim.

But the crux of the Ely argument was once again the unpredictability of an international authority. Such an authority could not be controlled by the United States. "Having in mind the recent history of the United Nations, it is not at all clear that this agency would be in friendly hands," he said. [28]

The American Branch of the International Law Association (ILA) was another lawyer organization that published reports with views that were largely supportive of the U.S. oil industry. In a 1968 report the ILA had come out in support of a broad shelf definition. Referring to the 1958 convention, the Committee on Deep Sea Mineral Resources of this association had stated: "As a general rule, the limit of adjacency may reasonably be regarded as coinciding with the foot of the submerged portion of the continental land mass."[29]

CONGRESSIONAL ACTION

The petroleum industry also found early congressional support, especially in the Senate Interior and Insular Affairs Committee and its Subcommittee on the Outer Continental Shelf, chaired by Lee Metcalf (D-Mont.). Other members of this subcommittee were Henry M. Jackson (D-Wash.), Frank E. Moss (D-Utah), Mike Gravel (D-Alaska), Henry Bellmon (R-Okla.), Mark O. Hatfield (R-Oreg.), and Ted Stevens (R-Alaska). This subcommittee had shown great interest in the preparation of the Nixon proposals. After extensive hearings through 1969 and 1970, it issued a report in December 1970. The report mentioned that the Interior and Insular Affairs Committee had responsibility for legislative oversight of operations under the OCSLA of 1953. The U.S. jurisdiction asserted by this act, it was argued, could only be changed by an act of Congress. The act and the 1958 Continental Shelf Convention were interpreted to establish U.S. jurisdiction beyond the 200-meter isobath, ultimately to an area encompassing the entire continental margin. [30]

The subcommittee argued for a policy that would encourage exploration and exploitation of seabed minerals. It disagreed with the Nixon policy of limiting national claims to the continental shelf:

We feel that undisputed access to the vast energy
resources (oil, in particular) located on the U.S.
continental margin is of paramount importance. Oil
is a strategic material which is absolutely essential
to fuel our industrial machine and thereby sustain a
sound economy. [31]

The interpretation that the "adjacency" limitation allows jurisdiction over the entire continental margin was held to be "the most objective, rational, and sensible" among the possible interpretations. At the same time it was argued that there was little evidence to support the notion that such resource jurisdiction would interfere with the freedom of the seas in other ways.[32]

The subcommittee was unanimous in expressing serious doubts about many of the provisions of the Nixon proposals. It was a letter from Senators Henry Jackson, Gordon Allott (R-Colo.), Lee Metcalf, and Henry Bellmon to Secretary of State William P. Rodgers that had led to certain modifications in the U.S. Draft Convention and reduced its status to a "working paper."[33] However, major changes had not been made.

In the subcommittee's conclusions, it was demanded that security of investments beyond the 200-meter isobath in the interim period until adoption of a treaty be assured through grandfather clauses in the treaty. Such clauses should stipulate that "any rights or obligations contained within any leases . . . will remain fixed insofar as the leases are concerned, after the ratification" of a treaty. In other words, a treaty could not place new obligations on the leases.[34]

The subcommittee also demanded that the United States should "retain the exclusive right to determine whether and by whom the seabed resources to the outer edge of the U.S. continental margin would be exploited." No "renunciation" should be permitted to encroach upon the heart of U.S. sovereign rights under the 1958 convention. As interpreted by the subcommittee, these rights included (1) exclusive ownership of minerals and sedentary species (2) exclusive right to control access for exploration and exploitation, and (3) exclusive jurisdiction to regulate and control such exploration and exploitation of natural resources of the entire continental margin.[35]

The policy advocated by the subcommittee implied that outer continental margin resources should not be included in the common heritage of mankind. "This mineral estate is the heritage of the American people," maintained the report.[36] The subcommittee thus came out in clear support of the U.S. petroleum industry.

INTERNATIONAL DEVELOPMENTS

Despite domestic opposition President Nixon had defined U.S. ocean goals in 1970 with primary emphasis on security and navigational rights. The United States wanted to stop "creeping jurisdiction" and set out to do so internationally.

In 1970, however, a countermovement for extensive zones of coastal state jurisdiction set in. Leadership for this enclosure movement was provided by a number of Latin American states. But other developing countries, especially African ones, accepted the argument for wider national zones and joined the movement. So did some developed countries with important offshore interests, such as Canada, Australia, New Zealand, Norway, and Iceland.

Latin American 200-milers launched the diplomatic offensive. Two Latin American declarations on the subject of coastal states' rights (the Montevideo and Lima Declarations) were adopted in 1970. Among the principles put forward in the Montevideo Declaration were:

> 1. the right of coastal States to avail themselves of the natural resources of the sea adjacent to their coasts and of the soil and subsoil thereof in order to promote the maximum development of their economies and to raise the levels of living of their peoples;
> 2. the right to establish the limits of their maritime sovereignty and jurisdiction in accordance with their geographical and geological characteristics and with the factors governing the existence of marine resources and the need for their rational utilization.[37]

In its Preamble, the Montevideo Declaration talked of "the right of States to extend their sovereignty and jurisdiction to the extent necessary to conserve, develop and exploit the natural resources" of the coastal areas of the oceans. It was in accordance with this view that the signatory states had extended "their sovereignty or exclusive rights of jurisdiction over the maritime area adjacent to their coasts, its soil and its subsoil to a distance of 200 nautical miles." Although the declaration talked of sovereignty, and stated that the coastal state would have the right to adopt regulatory measures, this should not prejudice the "freedom of navigation by ships and overflying by aircraft of any flag."[38] This meant that the jurisdiction claimed was less than the jurisdiction associated with territorial seas. The concept of an economic zone was not fully developed yet, but the idea of some separation of resource rights and navigational rights was present already in the Montevideo Declaration. Other declarations making the same distinction were to follow. Also many proposals put forward at the U.N. Seabed Committee made the same distinction.[39]

The international trend in 1970-71 was predominantly toward wider zones of national jurisdiction. From the perspective of the Nixon proposals, this was not very promising. But for domestic

U.S. forces working for wider U.S. claims to ocean space, it was. Two congressional staff members, Merrill Englund, administrative assistant to Senator Lee Metcalf, and Charles F. Cook, Jr., minority council of the Senate Committee on Interior and Insular Affairs, attended the July-August 1971 session of the U.N. Seabed Committee. Afterward they reported to their committee that there was little chance that the Nixon proposals would be accepted internationally:

> Most coastal nations favored a seaward limit of exclusive national jurisdiction extending to the outer edge of the submerged continental land mass, or to 200 miles from shore, whichever comprises the larger area. . . .[40]

The international trend which emerged in 1971 kept developing in 1972. Both a Latin American and an African group of states made major new proposals in that year. In June 1972 a group of Central American and Caribbean states produced the influential Santo Domingo Declaration. Later the same month an African States Regional Seminar on the Law of the Sea in Yaounde, Cameroon, produced a series of recommendations.

The Central idea of the Declaration of Santo Domingo was the concept of a "patrimonial sea":

> 1. The coastal state has sovereign rights over the renewable and non-renewable natural resources, which are found in the waters, in the sea-bed and in the subsoil of an area adjacent to the territorial sea called the patrimonial sea.
> 3. The whole area of both the territorial sea and the patrimonial sea, taking into account geographic circumstances, should not exceed a maximum of 200 nautical miles.[41]

The coastal state would also have powers to regulate scientific research and marine pollution in the patrimonial sea. However, all states would enjoy the right of freedom of navigation and overflight beyond the territorial sea of a maximum of 12 nautical miles. There would also be freedom to lay cables and pipelines beyond the territorial sea. For the continental shelf reference was made to the exploitability criterion, so the possibility of coastal state jurisdiction over continental shelf resources beyond the 200-mile patrimonial sea was not excluded. But the declaration was less explicit on this point, suggesting a study of the advisability of a fixed limit, "taking into account the outer limits of the continental rise."[42]

The Yaounde Report recommended an economic zone of unspecified extent:

> The African States have . . . the right to establish beyond the Territorial Sea an Economic Zone over which they will have an exclusive jurisdiction for the purpose of control, regulation and national exploitation of the living resources of the sea and their reservation for the primary benefit of their peoples and their respective economies, and for the purpose of the prevention and control of pollution.[43]

There would still be freedom of navigation and overflight in the zone. Although the introductory part only referred to living resources, the report later stated that the economic zone embodied "all economic resources comprising both living and non-living resources such as oil, natural gas and other mineral resources."[44]

Kenya was one of the prime movers of the Yaounde recommendations. It was also Kenya that introduced the first document in the U.N. Seabed Committee clearly defining the concept of an economic zone.[45]

That the concept of an economic zone was receiving increasing support in 1972 was noticed at the spring session of the Seabed Committee by the two Senate Interior Committee observers. This time Englund was accompanied by David P. Stang, the deputy director of the Interior Committee's National Fuels and Energy Study. One of the conclusions of their report was that a major objective of most developing coastal nations was to extend their exclusive jurisdiction over fisheries, seabed minerals, and scientific research "in areas adjacent to their coasts and in other parts of high seas."[46]

The idea of an economic zone was further consolidated in 1973, the final year of the Seabed Committee. Fourteen African states now introduced draft articles on the "exclusive economic zone."[47] And many other economic zone proposals were made.

Thus, as the start of UNCLOS III came closer, there could be no doubt about the broad international support for wider coastal state jurisdiction over economic resources. There were still many points of disagreement about specifics, including the exact definition of coastal state jurisdiction in the economic zone, and the question of whether continental shelf jurisdiction could go beyond the 200 nautical miles. But the trend was clear.

ACCEPTANCE OF ENCLOSURE

Under attack at home and abroad, central U.S. decision makers had to reconsider the U.S. ocean strategy. Flexibility was indicated in 1972, and in 1973 the energy crisis gave U.S. policy a big push. It was in 1972 that the United States first indicated a willingness to accept "broad coastal state economic jurisdiction in adjacent waters and seabed areas beyond the territorial sea as part of an overall law-of-the-sea settlement." However five conditions were set up:

1. International treaty standards to prevent unreasonable interference with other uses of the ocean;
2. international treaty standards to protect the ocean from pollution;
3. international treaty standards to protect the integrity of investment;
4. sharing of revenues for international community purposes; and
5. compulsory settlement of disputes. [48]

The United States still expressed some concern about the idea of a 200-mile economic zone. Would such a zone lead to creeping jurisdiction and interfere with navigation and military uses? The proposed international treaty standards were clearly demanded to put checks on coastal state jurisdiction.

A further step was taken in 1973 when the United States introduced "draft articles for a chapter on the rights and duties of states in the coastal sea-bed economic area" in the U.N. Seabed Committee. Some of the language of the economic zone idea was now creeping into U.S. policy. The proposal would give the coastal state "exclusive right to explore and exploit and authorize the exploration and exploitation of the natural resources of the sea-bed and subsoil" of this coastal seabed area, the extent of which was not yet specified. The above international treaty standards were spelled out, and it was explicitly stated:

Nothing in this chapter shall affect the rights of freedom of navigation and overflight and other rights to carry out activities unrelated to sea-bed resource exploration and exploitation in accordance with general principles of international law, except as otherwise specifically provided in this convention. [49]

The draft articles provided nothing otherwise concerning military activities. Thus they were not affected by the proposed coastal state jurisdiction.

Why did the United States drop the trusteeship idea? John Norton Moore, councilor on international law for the Department of State, gave the following explanation in hearings in June 1973: The concept had not been "warmly embraced by most of the coastal nations participating in the negotiations." Admitting this, however, Norton Moore maintained that the United States still had the Nixon proposals of 1970 "on the table as our primary proposal."[50]

But Charles N. Brower, acting legal advisor of the State Department, admitted that there was "a change in emphasis" in U.S. policy. He further explained:

> The reason for it, I think, in large part is the realization of the negotiating imperatives. . . . We think it is more acceptable to a larger number of states if it is emphasized as international standards and as a zone of broad coastal management jurisdiction, rather than being treated as a more international area in its basic essence.[51]

Brower was saying that the U.S. policy had changed because the United States wanted an international treaty. This must be what "negotiating imperatives" referred to. So the changes, which we have seen so far, were tactical, the objective being to safeguard central U.S. interests in the law of the sea through an international treaty.

As we have seen, the United States did not suggest an exact outer limit for the coastal zone in 1973. Upon the introduction of that U.S. proposal, John Stevenson, chairman of the U.S. delegation to the U.N. Seabed Committee, referred to both the Santo Domingo Declaration and the Yaounde Declaration, and he stated that the United States had noted that 200 miles was a preponderant view. But he added that "a sizeable number of delegations would appear to prefer" a regime with coastal state jurisdiction over the entire continental margin where it extends beyond 200 miles.

> It should be clear, however, that if the outer boundary of coastal State economic resource jurisdiction is to include the entire continental margin, a precise method of delimitating that area will have to be found.[52]

The "if" of this statement implied that the United States did not exclude the possibility of coastal state jurisdiction over seabed resources of the entire continental margin. This, it will be recalled, was what the U.S. petroleum industry had demanded. But the international demand for such extensive jurisdiction was much less widespread than the demand for a flat 200-mile solution. Both the group of African states and the landlocked and geographically disadvantaged states resisted coastal state jurisdiction beyond 200 miles. It therefore looked as if the administration was about to give in to a domestic demand on this point. The domestic politics of the energy crisis were beginning to have an impact.

Stevenson admitted in September 1973 that there was international opposition in the idea that broad shelf states had "acquired rights" to continental shelf resources beyond 200 miles. Landlocked and other geographically disadvantaged states "strongly opposed" the idea, he said.[53] And yet, the United States seemed to be moving on this point in the summer of 1973. There can be no doubt that the energy crisis, which hit the world in 1973, had strengthened the bargaining position of the U.S. petroleum industry. In November 1973 John Norton Moore, who was now chairman of the NSC Interagency Task Force on the Law of the Sea, could say about the July 1973 U.S. draft on the coastal seabed economic area: "We believe this policy is substantially consistent with the recommendations of the National Petroleum Council."[54]

The May 1973 NPC report on the law of the sea had no disagreements with the U.S. policy. Something had changed since 1970.[55] Although the notion of an energy crisis mainly became widespread with the Arab oil embargo in October 1973, U.S. shortages had developed earlier that year.[56] As a matter of fact at least one book entitled The Energy Crisis had been published in 1972.[57] Energy shortages quickly affected U.S. offshore policy. On April 18, 1973, President Nixon directed the Secretary of the Interior to triple the amount of offshore oil leasing.[58] By the time of the summer session of the U.N. Seabed Committee, the Interior Department had already issued a call for nominations for offshore areas beyond the 200-meter isobath.[59]

The 1973 changes in U.S. continental margin policy were crowned by a November 5 notice in the Federal Register that leases beyond the 200-meter isobath would no longer require provisions subjecting them to future international agreements.[60] Secretary of the Interior, Rogers C. B. Morton, referred to a feeling in Washington that the 1970 policy "was not accepted by the majority of the nations"; but he also suggested that "our own national interests" had perhaps changed.[61] Statist goals, it would seem, depend on wider societal phenomena. And they may change.

By the end of 1973 the United States was so close to the idea of a 200-mile economic zone that it cannot have come as a surprise that the United States announced a conditional acceptance of the concept at the Caracas session of UNCLOS III in the summer of 1974.[62] A central condition was a coastal state duty to "prevent unjustifiable interference with navigation, overflight, and other non-resource uses and to respect international environmental obligations." The coastal state would also have seabed resource jurisdiction over the entire continental margin where it extends beyond 200 miles. However, some revenue sharing with the international community might be accepted for the outer part of the continental margin.[63]

What the oil industry wasn't able to get in 1970 it was now getting: U.S. jurisdiction over the entire U.S. continental margin. Since only about 45 states out of a total of 149 states supported such jurisdiction at Caracas, it is not possible to explain this part of U.S. policy by international negotiating imperatives.[64] Let us not forget that the United States is a broad margin state. According to one source, about 23 percent of the U.S. continental margin is situated beyond 200 miles.[65] Central decision makers now realized that this piece of submerged land might contribute to U.S. security of supply of a vital resource in the future.

NOTES

1. National Petroleum Council, Petroleum Resources under the Ocean Floor (Washington, D.C., March 1969), p. 85.
2. Ibid., p. 85.
3. Ibid., pp. 15-19.
4. Ibid., p. 57.
5. Ibid., p. 59.
6. Ibid., p. 60.
7. Ibid., p. 61.
8. Ibid., p. 62. See also North Sea Continental Shelf Judgment, I.C.J. Reports, p. 23.
9. Petroleum Resources under the Ocean Floor, p. 63.
10. Ibid., pp. 65-67.
11. Ibid., pp. 69-70.
12. Ibid., pp. 71-72.
13. Ibid., p. 72.
14. National Petroleum Council, Petroleum Resources under the Ocean Floor: A Supplemental Report (Washington, D.C., March 1971), pp. 1-2.
15. Ibid., pp. 15-16.
16. Ibid., pp. 16-17.

17. Ibid., pp. 6, 16.

18. Ibid., p. 20.

19. U.S. Congress, Senate, Interior and Insular Affairs Committee, Outer Continental Shelf, Part 3, Hearings, 91st Cong., 2d Sess., September 22-23, 1970, pp. 43-69, at 45.

20. Ibid., p. 46.

21. Ibid., pp. 48-50. The statement is also available as Luke W. Finlay, "The Draft United Nations Convention on the International Seabed Area—American Petroleum Institute Position," Natural Resources Lawyer 4 (January 1971):73-83.

22. Inserted in U.S. Congress, Outer Continental Shelf, Part 3, pp. 97-107, quotation at 99.

23. "Non-Living Resources of the Sea (A Critique)," Natural Resources Lawyer 2 (November 1969):412-41, at 429.

24. Ibid., p. 430.

25. Ibid., p. 430.

26. Outer Continental Shelf, Part 3, p. 9.

27. Ibid., p. 10.

28. Ibid., p. 11.

29. Committee on Deep Sea Mineral Resources of the American Branch of the International Law Association, "Interim Report," July 19, 1968, inserted as appendix E in U.S. Congress, Senate, Interior and Insular Affairs Committee, Outer Continental Shelf, Report, 91st Cong., 2d Sess., December 21, 1970, pp. 69-99, quotation at 80. This report had one dissenting view, viz. that of Professor Louis Henking, who found the report parochial and short-sighted. He was particularly troubled by the proposed extension of the continental shelf. That recommendation was "without foundation in the 1958 Convention, either in its language or in its history. Ibid., p. 91.

30. Ibid., p. 3.

31. Ibid., p. 5.

32. Ibid., pp. 16-17.

33. Ibid., p. 25.

34. Ibid., p. 28.

35. Ibid., p. 29.

36. Ibid. p. 31.

37. For full text, see Shigeru Oda, The International Law of the Ocean Development: Basic Documents, vol. I (Leiden: Sijthoff, 1976), pp. 347-48.

38. Ibid.

39. For details see Barry Buzan, Seabed Politics (New York: Praeger, 1976); and Shigeru Oda, The Law of the Sea in Our Time— II: The United Nations Seabed Committee 1968-1973 (Leyden: Sijthoff, 1977).

40. U.S. Congress, Senate, Interior and Insular Affairs Committee, The Law of the Sea Crisis, Print, 92d Cong., 1st Sess., December 1971, p. 2.

41. Full text in Shigeru Oda, The International Law of the Ocean Development: Basic Documents, vol. II (Leiden: Sijthoff, 1975), pp. 32-36, quotation at 34.

42. Ibid.

43. Full text in Oda, The International Law of the Ocean Development, II, pp. 23-25.

44. Ibid., p. 24.

45. Buzan, Seabed Politics, p. 190.

46. U.S. Congress, Senate, Interior and Insular Affairs Committee, The Law of the Sea Crisis: An Intensifying Polarization, Print, 92d Cong., 2d Sess., May 1972, pp. 7-8.

47. Algeria et al., "Draft Articles on Exclusive Economic Zone," in Report of the Committee on the Peaceful Uses of the Sea-Bed and the Ocean Floor Beyond the Limits of Jurisdiction, United Nations, General Assembly, Official Records, 28th Sess., Supplement No. 21 (A/9021), Vol. III (New York, 1973), pp. 87-89. (Hereafter cited as Seabed Committee Report 1973, III.)

48. John R. Stevenson, "U.S. Calls for Prompt International Action to Settle Problems of Law of the Sea," Department of State Bulletin 67:1736 (October 2, 1972), pp. 382-86, at 383-84.

49. Article 4, "Draft Articles for a Chapter on the Rights and Duties of States in the Coastal Sea-Bed Economic Area," Seabed Committee Report 1973, III, pp. 75-77.

50. U.S. Congress, Senate, Foreign Relations Committee, U.S. Oceans Policy, Hearing, 93d Cong., 1st Sess., June 19, 1973, p. 17.

51. Ibid., p. 17.

52. John Stevenson, "Statement, Subcommittee II, July 18," Department of State Bulletin 69:1787 (September 24, 1973), pp. 397-402, at 398.

53. U.S. Congress, Senate, Interior and Insular Affairs Committee, Status Report on Law of the Sea Conference, Hearing, 93d Cong., 1st Sess., September 19, 1973, p. 12.

54. Ibid., p. 100.

55. National Petroleum Council, Law of the Sea: Particular Aspects Affecting the Petroleum Industry (Washington, D.C., May 1973).

56. James W. McKie, "The United States," in Raymond Vernon, ed., The Oil Crisis (New York: W. W. Norton, 1976), pp. 72-90, at 81.

57. Lawrence Rocks and Richard P. Runyon, The Energy Crisis (New York: Crown Publishers, 1972).

58. U.S. Congress, House, Judiciary Committee, Outer Continental Shelf Oil and Gas, Hearings, 93d Cong., 2d Sess., January 24 and 30, February 7, March 6 and 14, 1974, p. 76.

59. Senate, Interior and Insular Affairs Committee, Status Report, September 19, 1973, p. 132.

60. "Outer Continental Shelf Leasing Beyond 200 Meters," Federal Register 38 (November 5, 1973), p. 30457.

61. Judiciary Committee, Outer Continental Shelf Oil and Gas, p. 27.

62. John R. Stevenson, "U.S. Defines Position on 200-Mile Economic Zone at Conference on the Law of the Sea," Department of State Bulletin 71:1832 (August 5, 1974), pp. 232-36.

63. Ibid., p. 235.

64. See David Stang's report in U.S. Congress, Senate, Interior and Insular Affairs Committee, Status Report on Law of the Sea Conference, Part 2, Hearing, 93d Cong., 2d Sess., September 17, 1974, p. 835. Forty states can be considered to have broad continental margins, depending on measurement systems. See for instance Lewis M. Alexander, "Indices of National Interest in the Oceans," Ocean Development and International Law Journal 1 (Spring 1973):21-49, or John King Gamble, Jr., Global Marine Attributes (Cambridge, Mass.: Ballinger Publishing, 1974), pp. 18, 72-75.

65. Joseph Martray, A qui appartient l'océan? (Paris: Editions Maritimes et d'Outre-Mer, 1977), pp. 356-58.

5

THE POLITICS OF FISHING

THE SPECIES APPROACH

We have seen that the 1970 Nixon policy came under attack both domestically and internationally. The U.S. petroleum industry advocated a system of national jurisdiction over oil and gas resources to the outer edge of the continental margin. Internationally the Nixon proposals for a 200-meter isobath limitation on national jurisdiction and an intermediate "trusteeship zone" received very little support.

But where was the voice—or voices—of the U.S. fishing industry in all this? Internationally, fishing rights had been an important determinant behind claims for wider zones of coastal state jurisdiction. When the enclosure movement had started in Latin America after World War II, this had been the decisive preoccupation.[1] When it reached Europe, in connection with successive Icelandic extensions of fishery limits, fishing rights had also been decisive.[2] Fishing was also very much on the mind of the leaders of the African states after they gained their independence. They wanted to aid their economic development by reserving coastal fishing for their own nationals.[3]

Let it be recalled that the United States had a 12-mile fishery limit by the time of the formulation of the Nixon proposals. It should further be mentioned that these proposals were not very specific on fishing policy. They contained only one specific reference to fisheries, namely, Article 28(f), which provided that the "Trustee Party may, in its discretion . . . decide whether and by whom the living resources of the seabed shall be exploited."[4]

The 1958 Convention on the Continental Shelf had included sedentary species, that is, "organisms which, at the harvestable stage, either are immobile on or under the seabed or are unable to move except in constant physical contact with the seabed or the subsoil," among the resources over which the coastal state has "sovereign rights" for the purposes of exploration and exploitation.[5] So there was nothing new in the U.S. policy in this point.

On the fishing regime for the waters above the continental shelf, the 1970 U.S. draft was silent. It was only a proposal for a seabed policy, not a complete law of the sea policy. But in 1971, the United States introduced an article on fisheries in connection with the articles on territorial waters and international straits. The 1971 draft article on fisheries constituted what has become known as a "species approach." It was proposed to treat three kings of fish stocks in three different ways. The general idea was to maintain a regulatory role for "appropriate international (including regional) fisheries organizations." These organizations would determine the allowable catch for different species. For coastal stocks there would be a coastal state preference: "The percentage of the allowable catch of a stock in any area of the high seas adjacent to the coastal State that can be harvested by that State shall be allocated annually to it."[6] But for highly migratory species (mainly tuna) international regulation was prescribed in such a way that there would be no coastal state preference.

Finally, concerning anadromous species (mainly salmon) it was stipulated that: "The percentage of the allowable catch of an anadromous stock that can be harvested by the State in whose fresh waters it spawns shall be allocated annually to that State."[7] In the case that it turned out to be impossible, or if it was deemed unnecessary, to establish an international or regional organization to regulate the catch of highly migratory species, regulation of these should take place through agreement or consultation among the states concerned. For coastal species, the coastal state could, in the case of nonagreement internationally, go ahead unilaterally and establish the allowable catch and its own percentage thereof. No distance for this authority was specified. But for an anadromous stock the host state had this regulatory authority "throughout its migratory range."[8]

The U.S. proposal tried to combine these provisions with some notion of historic rights by saying that "any other State whose nationals or vessels exploit or desire to exploit a regulated species have an equal right to participate without discrimination."[9] Concerning enforcement the U.S. draft foresaw flag state authority. "Each State Party shall make it an offence for its nationals and vessels to violate the fishery regulations adopted pursuant to this Article."[10] Binding dispute settlement was also foreseen.[11]

The species approach was an effort to reconcile conflicting domestic fishing interests and, at the same time, to secure U.S. navigational interests internationally. Lack of a fixed geographic zone of coastal state sovereignty as well as compulsory settlement of disputes were suggested as means to secure U.S. navigational interest. At the same time, Howard W. Pollock, deputy administrator of the National Oceanic and Atmospheric Administration (NOAA), argued that the proposal

> would allow [U.S.] coastal fisheries resources to be allocated principally to the U.S. fisheries and U.S. fishermen. It would reserve virtually all U.S. salmon for our exclusive use. . . . [And it] would prevent other nations from exercising the unilateral or exclusive control over tuna. [12]

In other words, California tuna fishermen could continue to take tuna within Ecuador's 200-mile zone. The United States could stop Japanese salmon fishing in the North Pacific, and gradually secure a greater percentage of the coastal stocks off the coasts of New England, Oregon, Washington, and Alaska to U.S. fishermen. But the proposal did not completely discard the notion of historic rights, as we have seen. That notion was a way to try to safeguard some of the U.S. shrimp fishery in the Gulf of Mexico, Caribbean, and northeastern South American waters.

Although representatives from all sections of the U.S. fishing industry had been involved in working out the species approach in 1971, it was not well received by coastal fishermen. Talking about the U.S. proposal's notion of historic rights, Jacob Dykstra of Point Judith Fisherman's Cooperative Association, Rhode Island, stated in the autumn of 1971:

> The coastal fisheries didn't like that position simply because it goes back to a common property resource. The fish belong to everyone or no one, and we feel that this is the fisheries position of the Department of Defense. . . . But we're pretty unhappy with this position.
> . . . The U.S. position at the moment seems to be at the conservative end of the spectrum as far as coastal fisheries go. [13]

A year earlier, that is, before the U.S. draft article had been worked out, Jacob Dykstra had spoken in favor of a regime that would "give the coastal State control or make the fish over the shelf the property of the coastal State." Criticizing European distant-water fishing nations for overfishing several species in the North Atlantic, he suggested that a new policy should contribute to gradually phasing out such fisheries. [14]

That the North Atlantic fisheries faced increasing problems from the late 1960s was admitted by the State Department. In June 1970, William Sullivan of the Oceanography and International Organizations Office talked about overfishing of at least haddock, yellowtail flounder, herring, and salmon in the North Atlantic area. He also admitted that the International Commission for the Northwest Atlantic Fisheries (ICNAF) had been too slow and inefficient in doing something about this. ICNAF and other international fisheries commissions were based on the rule of unanimity. This rule made it possible for distant-water fishing nations to dominate and hinder radical reductions of fishing efforts on the high seas. Sullivan summed up the problem this way: "As long as the rule of unanimity prevails, and that shows no sign whatsoever of changing, the Commissions can not be fully effective. They must operate on the level of the lowest common denominator, not the level of the greatest good."[15]

Sullivan admitted that there were increasing domestic and international pressures for a new policy to deal with the situation:

Most fishermen in the United States and throughout the world are coastal . . . and they are increasingly pressing for extended jurisdiction to solve their problems. The New England fishermen in large part do not consider ICNAF to have served their interests very well. . . . The resources on which they depend have been depleted under ICNAF, they point out, by actions of large distant water fleets which can then move on to other coasts.[16]

This was the kind of problem that the species approach was to deal with, while at the same time safeguarding U.S. navigational interests. But as we have already seen, some U.S. coastal fishermen were afraid that this approach might also be too inefficient.[17] Only the U.S. tuna fishing industry strongly supported the species approach.[18] Important U.S. tuna fishing grounds are located in Latin American coastal waters.[19] In 1972, for instance, the annual U.S. catch of tuna in the Pacific was estimated to be in the neighborhood of $70 million, of which between $20 and $25 million were estimated to have been taken off the coasts of Ecuador and Peru.[20]

In 1972 the United States introduced a revised draft on fisheries in the U.N. Seabed Committee. It maintained the species approach, but was a little more specific on some points. Most importantly, it proposed to give the coastal state increased authority: "The coastal State shall regulate and have preferential rights to all coastal living resources off its coast beyond the territorial sea to the limits of their migratory range."[21] The general tone of the draft was clearly one of increasing coastal state authority. Reduction of traditional foreign fishing was explicitly foreseen, and the possibility of foreign fishing fleets paying fees to get access to resources not utilized by the coastal state was now directly mentioned. Further, the coastal state could inspect and arrest vessels for fishing in violation of its regulations. [22]

Upon introduction of this revised fishery proposal, on August 4, 1972, Donald L. McKernan, alternate U.S. representative to the Seabed Committee, called it "another step in seeking a widely agreeable solution to the fisheries problems." He said that the U.S. delegation had listened to the statements by other representatives and "diligently tried to accommodate" U.S. fisheries interests to those of other states. But the United States remained committed to the concept that "both sound conservation and rational utilization must be linked directly to the biology and distribution" of the stocks involved. Hence a reemphasis on the species approach. But he admitted that the new U.S. draft strengthened the rights of the coastal state. [23]

The species approach went hand in hand with an effort to limit the catch of certain species through ICNAF. In 1972 the 15 member states of the commission agreed for the first time to national quotas. In the 1950s ICNAF had only used minimum mesh sizes for various species, and this had been a sufficient regulation device, because the fishing effort was still not too high. The commission did have authority to set overall catch quotas, if the members could agree, but it did not have the authority to allocate quotas nationally. This was the authority that it finally got in 1972 through an amendment of the convention establishing the ICNAF. This only happened after a U.S. threat to withdraw from the organization. An ICNAF meeting was now suddenly able to turn out 23 regulatory proposals in ten days. [24]

Could it be that the species approach would survive after the introduction of national quotas? There is no doubt that central U.S. decision makers hoped so, and that they still remained opposed to the idea of an exclusive economic zone. Said John Stevenson, legal advisor of the Department of State, in hearings in April 1972:

> Exclusive coastal state economic jurisdiction tends to disregard the existence of international community interests in the area, particularly as regards other uses such as freedom of navigation, overflight and scientific research. There is a danger that exclusive economic jurisdiction may be expanded to interfere with such other uses. [25]

So the fear of "creeping jurisdiction" still had a decisive influence on U.S. fishing policy in 1972.

VOICES OF U.S. COASTAL FISHERMEN

The U.S. fishing industry had been a little slow to realize that negotiations affecting its interests were going on.[26] This was due both to a lack of knowledge and internal disagreements within the industry between coastal and distant-water fishermen. Coastal fishermen were also badly organized. By 1972, however, they were starting to speak up individually or through local organizations.[27] Timing therefore was becoming a real problem for central U.S. decision makers. The problem came up in a number of hearings. The administration tried to buy time by introducing a High Seas Fisheries Conservation bill (H.R. 4760), which had the objective of improving fisheries management without taking unilateral steps against foreign fishing. The bill would authorize the Secretary of Commerce to promulgate fishing regulations in the U.S. 12-mile fishing zone as well as on the high seas for U.S. and foreign vessels. In the latter case, however, they had to be "vessels of a party to an international fishery agreement with the United States."[28]

The bill was based on the doctrine of the freedom of the seas. Foreign fishing could therefore only be limited through flag state consent, that is, through treaties and negotiations. Concerning domestic fisheries management, the administration argued that there was a "split jurisdiction" problem. Within the three-mile territorial sea the states had management authority, but there was no legislative authority to regulate U.S. fishing within the contiguous nine miles fisheries zone or on the high seas beyond. The bill would authorize federal regulation of U.S. vessels in all waters beyond the territorial sea.[29]

Many members of Congress felt that the result of the proposed legislation would be more regulation of U.S. fishing, but little regulation of foreign fishing off U.S. coasts. Congressman Gerry E. Studds (D-Mass.) told NOAA Administrator Dr. Robert M. White that the city he represented, New Bedford, was "a seriously depressed city." He could not understand the administration's approach: "Given the frustrations of the American fishermen, to come to us with a bill, the guts of which proposes to give our Government further authority to arrest American fishermen, strikes me as absurd, frankly."[30] And Congressman William S. Cohen (R-Maine) told administration representatives:

> I do not think there is anyone who is more fiercely in-
> dependent than the New England fisherman. Yet, on
> one item they seem completely unanimous and that is
> their lack of trust and faith in what this Government
> is doing to protect their interests. I have never seen
> a greater unanimity among fishermen than the need to
> have a 200-mile limit. [31]

A similar hope for 200-mile legislation was expressed by other
congressmen from states with coastal fishing. Pressures from constituents were clearly behind what was happening now. Congressman William Cohen explicitly admitted this: "There are many of us
here in Congress who have fishermen as constituents. We have
voices but because we have not been using our voices to speak up
for them, those constituents doubt the legitimacy of our own repre-
sentations as their Congressmen." [32]

But the State Department was not easy to convince. "We happen to be a law-abiding nation," said Donald McKernan, coordinator
of Ocean Affairs and special assistant for Fisheries and Wildlife to
the secretary of state. He tried to educate the impatient congressmen a little about the risks of unilateralism by suggesting that a
unilateral extension of the U.S. fishing limit to 200 miles "would
wipe out completely the tuna fishermen, the shrimp fishermen, and
our fishermen who are fishing off the coast of Canada." [33]

CONGRESSIONAL ACTION (1973-75)

Coastal fishermen of the United States did not buy the administration's argument against unilateralism. They put increasing
pressure on their representatives in Congress. A number of bills
that would extend U.S. fishing jurisdiction to the 200-mile limit
were now introduced. Senator Warren G. Magnuson (D-Wash.) introduced his bill (S. 1988) in the Senate on June 13, 1973, and Congressman Gerry Studds introduced the companion bill (H.R. 8665)
in the House of Representatives. The domestic forces for extended
U.S. fisheries jurisdiction had established themselves clearly by
1973. Whereas the oil industry had found bureaucratic support in
the Interior Department for its demand for coastal state jurisdiction
over oil and gas resources of the entire continental margin, the
coastal fishermen felt that they received less bureaucratic support
from "their" Commerce Department. They therefore went to their
representatives in Congress.

The Senate Commerce Committee had already started hearings on the Magnuson bill at about the time that UNCLOS III was meeting for its first organizational session in New York in December 1973. And hearings on the House bills started in May 1974, before the Caracas session of UNCLOS III.[34] So there was now a race going on between the multilateral approach pursued internationally by the administration and the unilateral approach demanded by coastal fishermen. Would Congress and the president eventually accept the argument for unilateralism?

This argument was developed by coastal fishermen and their allies in the hearings. It was largely stated in terms of conservation. A number of species off U.S. coasts were said to be over-fished, and that mainly by foreign distant-water fleets. Coastal fishermen were joined by sports fishermen and a number of environmental and conservation groups, which supported the unilateral introduction of the 200-mile limit to protect threatened species. Some of these organizations also had branches in noncoastal states, which put some pressure on members of Congress from those inland states. Opposition came from tuna fishermen and shrimp fishermen as well as some salmon fishermen who feared that Japan might retaliate by no longer respecting the so-called abstention principle, according to which they did not catch salmon east of the 175° west longitude in the Pacific.[35]

Congressional frustration with the administration became clear at a number of points during the hearings. Said Senator Magnuson at one point, "it's the Navy first, then the merchant marine, and then they throw in fish after they're all through."[36] And frustration was occasionally turned against those who testified against the proposed 200-mile bill. When a representative from the National Shrimp Congress suggested that Congress should wait until the conclusion of UNCLOS III, Senator Magnuson told him that he sounded as if the State Department had cleared his speech.[37]

As an alternative to unilaterally introducing a 200-mile fishing zone, some representatives from opposing sections of the fishing industry and Samuel R. Levering from the U.S. Committee for the Oceans suggested the application of Article 7 of the 1958 Convention on Fishing and Conservation of the Living Resources of the High Seas. That article stipulated:

> Any coastal State may, with a view to the maintenance
> of the productivity of the living resources of the sea,
> adopt unilateral measures of conservation appropriate
> to any stock of fish or other marine resources in any
> area of the high seas adjacent to its territorial sea,
> provided that negotiations to that effect with other

States concerned have not led to an agreement within six months.[38]

However, the use of Article 7 was ruled out by the administration representative, Acting Secretary of State Kenneth Rush. Japan and the Soviet Union had not ratified the 1958 Fisheries Convention, so they would not accept such a procedure, it was argued. Said Kenneth Rush: "We would have another Iceland situation."[39]

The administration claimed to have achieved significant progress within ICNAF and in bilateral talks with Japan. The enactment of the Magnuson-Studds bill, however, would have "serious foreign policy implications which would create political tensions internationally." It could "seriously prejudice the achievement" of a satisfactory law of the sea treaty, and it would be "a violation of international law."[40]

But the senators from the New England states and the Pacific Northwest did not accept the administration view. They went ahead with their bill, which was first reported favorably by the Commerce Committee on August 8, 1974, about three weeks before the end of the Caracas session of UNCLOS III. The report mentioned that it was likely that UNCLOS III would adopt a 200-mile fisheries or economic zone, although there was uncertainty about the exact scope of such coastal state jurisdiction. It reiterated the increasing fishing effort by foreign fleets off U.S. coasts and the alleged threat of depletion of many species. It especially mentioned the declining U.S. share of the Atlantic Ocean catch. In 1960 the U.S. share had been 92.9 percent of the total catch. In 1972 it had been reduced to 49.1 percent. The report further claimed that U.S. imports of seafood had grown from 23.4 percent in 1950 to over 60 percent in 1972. The United States, which has about 6 percent of the world population, consumes about 7 percent of the world catch of fish, but it was only catching 2.5 percent of the world's total catch in 1972. This resulted in an adverse balance of payments of $1.3 billion in fish and fisheries products. This of course introduced a kind of mercantilist argument that was different from the conservation argument, which had been so central during the hearings. But the report also mentioned the alleged failure of international fishery agreements to protect fish stocks. The report further depicted the United States as predominantly a coastal fishing nation. Of the U.S. catch, coastal species accounted for 82.5 percent in quantity and 68.2 percent in value in 1972.[41] (See Table 3.)

The Magnuson bill then went to the Foreign Relations Committee. New England Senators Edmund S. Muskie (D-Maine) and Claiborne Pell (D-R.I.) testified in its support. But John Norton Moore, chairman of the NSC Interagency Task Force on the Law of the Sea, stated five reasons why the administration opposed the bill:

1. it would be counter to U.S. policy of resisting unilateral claims to ocean space, which could interfere with other U.S. interests;
2. it would be seriously harmful to important foreign relations interests;
3. it was not compatible with international law, in particular with the 1958 Convention on the High Seas;
4. it would pose serious risks for U.S. fisheries interests, in particular the U.S. distant-water fishing interests; and
5. it could seriously undercut efforts to conclude the law of the sea treaty. [42]

TABLE 3

Landings and Value of U.S. Fish and Shellfish
by Major Groupings, 1972

Fishery	Quantity (million pounds)	Percent	Value (million dollars)	Percent
Coastal species	4,037.7	82.5	522.1	68.2
Anadromous species	216.7	4.4	62.8	8.2
Migratory species	524.4	10.7	120.6	15.8
Coastal species off foreign coasts	111.3	2.4	60.0	7.8
Total	4,894.1	100.0	765.5	100.0

Source: Senate Commerce Committee, Emergency Fisheries Protection Act of 1974, Report 93-1079, August 8, 1974, p. 15.

On September 23, 1974, the Foreign Relations Committee reported the Magnuson bill (S. 1988) unfavorably by a tight, split decision of eight yeas against nine nays. Secretary of State Henry Kissinger wrote Senator J. W. Fulbright (D-Ark.) afterward, expressing his appreciation that a majority of the committee members had opposed passage of S. 1988. [43]

However, surprisingly enough, S. 1988 fared better in the Senate Armed Services Committee, despite opposition from the chairman of the Joint Chiefs of Staff (JCS), General George S. Brown. Senator John C. Stennis (D-Miss.), however, singled out the political problem, "there is a lot of membership in the Senate that come from these seacoast States."[44] So, despite the fact that President Gerald Ford also had indicated his opposition in letters of September 24, 1974, to Senate Majority Leader Mike Mansfield (D-Mont.), Senate Minority Leader Hugh Scott (R-Pa.), and House Minority Leader John J. Rhodes (R-Ariz.),[45] the Armed Services Committee reported the bill favorably by an eight-to-six margin, on November 27, 1974. A leading spokesman for passage on the Committee was Senator Henry M. Jackson (D-Wash.).[46]

S. 1988 then went to the Senate floor. It passed on December 11, 1974, by a 68-27 vote, a clear defeat for the administration.[47] However, the companion House bill, H.R. 8665, failed to reach the floor in the House of Representatives. So the Emergency Marine Fisheries Protection Act died with the closing of the Ninety-third Congress.[48]

THE FISHERY CONSERVATION AND MANAGEMENT ACT (1976)

Senator Magnuson reintroduced his 200-mile fisheries bill, now referred to as the Energency Marine Fisheries Protection Act of 1975 (S. 961), in the Ninety-fourth Congress, on March 5, 1975. The bill had 18 cosponsors, 12 of whom represented New England and Pacific Northwest states.[49]

When hearings started on S. 961 on June 6, 1975, that is, after the Geneva spring session of UNCLOS III, Senator Magnuson could say that "S. 961, or something like it, will be passed by the Congress sometime this year." So the hearings of the Commerce Committee were really not so much about whether S. 961 should pass, but mostly about timing and implementation. At the same time, Magnuson wanted to put the executive branch on notice that his legislative proposal was serious: "Now that another session of the Law of the Sea Conference has ended without resolving the fishery conservation question, we here in Congress must do the job. And we must prepare to do it both effectively and efficiently."[50]

Senator Packwood told about the many letters that he received from his constituents—over 400 in the past two weeks—demanding immediate and effective action to protect the U.S. fishing industry.[51] Senator Muskie said that there had been too little progress in Geneva. He referred to how serious the situation was in Maine, noting that "so many Maine residents depend on . . . fish stocks for their living." But since 1966 Maine's whiting catch had declined by 90 percent, sea herring by 75 percent, ocean perch by 61 percent, cod by 30 percent, pollock by 42 percent, and haddock by no less than 97 percent; and this despite the fact that the United States was party to 22 international fishing agreements. Major fishing nations of the world hadn't shown much sense of responsibility, so the United States had to introduce a 200-mile fisheries management zone unilaterally. Said Senator Muskie, "The 200-mile limit has become a symbol—a rallying cry for fishermen who see the livelihood of generations threatened by rapacious foreign competition."[52]

The executive branch had not completed its post-Geneva policy review. So David Wallace, associate administrator for Marine Resources, NOAA, had to be a little careful in expressing his sympathy for S. 961. He mentioned that NOAA had to coordinate through the Office of Management and Budget (OMB) on such legislation, to which Senator Magnuson harshly asked: "What do they know about fishing down there?" And he added: "If they say no, that is fine; then we will take a look at their 'no' and override them and go ahead."[53]

When the Commerce Committee continued its hearings on S. 961 on September 19, 1975, the administration had completed its policy review and Carlyle E. Maw, State Department under secretary for Security Affairs, could tell the committee: "The President has decided to continue to oppose unilateral legislation, such as S. 961."[54] He argued that UNCLOS III had made "substantial progress" and mentioned various expected costs of unilateral action: broader claims by other nations that could interfere with U.S. navigation and freedom to pursue scientific research, possible confrontation with other nations, and negative impact on U.S. tuna, shrimp, and salmon fishing. In the meantime, the administration was increasing its efforts to find interim solutions through negotiations within existing international fisheries commissions and through bilateral agreements. The aim of the administration's approach was to achieve "the functional objective of a 200-mile fisheries zone," through what was referred to as "phased negotiations." The State Department had created a special task force under the chairmanship of Thomas Clingan to implement this program.[55]

But the senators present were not impressed. "It is just a little late now," said Senator Ted Stevens (R-Alaska). Senator John O. Pastore (D-R.I.) said that fishermen in Massachusetts and Rhode Island were "up in arms."[56] Also Senator Lowell O. Weicker (R-Conn.) referred to the problems faced by his constituents:

> For those of us who have fishing industries in our
> States, this is not an academic matter to be bounced
> around by the State Department. You people have
> put my people out of business for failure to go ahead
> and act. That is what worries me about the State

Department. It is a world by itself. But its impact
is clearly felt on people.[57]

Once again the Commerce Committee did not buy the administration's argument. On October 7, 1975, it recommended passage
of S. 961 with an amendment, namely, the establishment of a national fishery management program, including seven Regional Fishery Management Councils, to be supervised by the Secretary of Commerce. The committee's report gave the following arguments for
passage:

—International fishery agreements had failed to conserve several stocks. The normal negotiating process was too time consum-
ing, and the resulting measures were insufficient.
—The world community was ready to adopt the 200-mile limit,
but final international agreement would only come after a long delay.
—Existing international agreements had not been effectively en-
forced because of the flag state enforcement system.
—The United States was predominantly a coastal fishing nation.
But coastal species were increasingly taken by foreign fleets at a
time when domestic consumption was increasing. Since the U.S.
catch had remained static this had led to an increasing import of
fisheries products.
—There was a need for a national management program in an
extended fisheries zone.
—The fears expressed by segments of the salmon industry were
exaggerated. It was not likely that Japan would respond by abrogat-
ing the International North Pacific Fisheries Treaty and start fishing salmon inside the abstention line. S. 961 excluded highly migratory species from coastal state authority within the 200-mile zone.
They would have to be managed through international agreements.
—In the long run 200-mile zones would remove a source of international conflict and contribute to world order.[58]

From the Commerce Committee, S. 961 went to the Foreign
Relations and Armed Services Committees. The Foreign Relations
Committee held a hearing on October 31, 1975. Testimonies in
favor of S. 961 were given by Senator Magnuson and Congressmen
Gerry Studds, Joel Pritchard (R-Wash.), and Don Young (R-Alaska).[59]
Testimonies against S. 961 followed from the administration
represented by Under Secretary of State Carlyle E. Maw and chair-
man of the NSC Interagency Task Force on the Law of the Sea, John
Norton Moore. Under Secretary Maw mentioned Secretary of State
Henry Kissinger's speech at the annual meeting of the American Bar
Association in Montreal on August 11, 1975, in which Kissinger had

said that "unilateral action is both extremely dangerous and incompatible with the thrust of the Law of the Sea negotiations." Reference was also made to an unprecedented message from President Ford to the delegates at the ICNAF meeting in Montreal in September, in which the president had stated that he was "strongly opposed to unilateral claims by nations to jurisdiction on the high seas."[60]

According to the administration, the ICNAF meeting had been successful. A 23 percent reduction of catch quotas had been agreed to. It had also been decided to close a large area of the Georges Bank for the taking of groundfish. Further, a system of national registration of vessels had been agreed to. These agreements constituted a step toward reaching the administration's objective of achieving the functional equivalent of a 200-mile fishing zone. The emerging UNCLOS consensus on the economic zone had created a new negotiating climate in multilateral and bilateral fisheries negotiations, it was said.[61] More importantly, the U.S. share of the catch in the ICNAF area actually increased from 17 to 25 percent, and in volume from 189,550 to 211,600 tons between 1972 and 1975.

The greatest surprise during the Foreign Relations Committee hearing was that Senator Mike Gravel (D-Alaska), who had been a cosponsor of S. 961, had changed his mind. Despite the fact that his constituents were overwhelmingly in favor of S. 961, he now opposed it. He argued that the State Department had been very successful, not only in the ICNAF negotiations, but also in bilateral talks with Japan and the Soviet Union. There had been a 20 percent reduction in the total bottom fish quota for the Northeast Pacific.[62]

But Senator Gravel went further than that. He went on to talk about congressional misperceptions about UNCLOS and international negotiations. UNCLOS III had in only 20 weeks of actual negotiations arrived at a single negotiating text, which he claimed represented 90 percent agreement on the issues. This was a great accomplishment, he said. But Congress did not understand: "That is because we are operating from our perception and our experience. We legislate from a basis of sovereignty. In the international community, you don't legislate from a basis of sovereignty. You legislate from a basis of consensus."[63]

He reminded the Senate that Congress had taken several years to agree on social security and Medicare. And he added an internationalist argument for giving UNCLOS III a chance, an argument not often heard in the Congress: "We have before us in the law of the sea the first time in the history of the human race the ability to bring about international sovereignty over two-thirds of the surface of this planet."[64] Such sovereignty could grow "and from that we will have world peace." But, said Senator Gravel, "that is what our great country is going to flick over because of a frustrated, immature act by the Congress."[65]

The internationalist chairman of the Subcommittee on Oceans and International Environment, Senator Pell, who was presiding, was impressed with the argument. "Quite startling," he said. But he had seen his "own area's fish being vacuumed off the floor," so he had to be for the passage of S. 961.[66] Eventually, however, the Foreign Relations Committee reported S. 961 unfavorably by the narrowest possible margin, thus repeating its performance from the year before.[67]

The hearing conducted by the Armed Services Committee on November 19, 1975, had no similar surprises. Admiral James L. Holloway III, chief of Naval Operations, Admiral Max Morris, special assistant to the chairman of the JCS for law of the sea matters, and General David C. Jones, chief of staff of the U.S. Air Force, all told the Committee that passage of S. 961 would be detrimental to U.S. security interests. And John Norton Moore argued that recent multilateral and bilateral fisheries negotiations had been so successful that there was no longer any rationale for S. 961. ICNAF reductions had been 42 percent over the past three years, increasing U.S. quotas from 21 to 35 percent in the same period. "The biomass will be increasing in that area as of now," he said. And the situation had also improved significantly in the Northeast Pacific.[68] But the Armed Services Committee reported S. 961 favorably on December 8, 1975.[69]

At this time the companion House bill, H.R. 200, which had been reintroduced by Representative Gerry Studds and 24 other members of the House on January 14, had already passed. The Merchant Marine and Fisheries Committee held hearings through March 1975,[70] and reported the bill favorably on August 20, 1975, by a 36-to-3 vote.[71] The House International Relations Committee held a special oversight hearing on H.R. 200 on September 24, 1975,[72] and decided to advise against passage on October 7, 1975, by a 15-to-5 vote.[73] But the House passed the bill on October 9, 1975, with 208 yeas against 101 nays.[74]

On the Senate side, the final vote on the Magnuson bill came on January 28, 1976. The preceding floor fight for S. 961 was led by Senators Magnuson and Ted Stevens, and the fight against the bill was led by Alan Cranston (D-Calif.) and Robert Griffin (R-Mich.), supported by Senator Gravel. The floor debate was a repetition of familiar arguments, centering around the need for conservation versus the dangers of unilateralism. The opposition to S. 961 suggested the application of Article 7 of the 1958 Convention on Fishing and Conservation of the Living Resources of the High Seas. But this approach was called "totally unacceptable" by the Magnuson coalition. In reality they were not only conservationists as they tended to claim; they wanted to increase U.S. fishing and decrease foreign fishing.

So Article 7, which prescribed a nondiscriminatory approach to conservation, was rejected. However, foreign fishing had actually been decreasing off U.S. shores since 1972 (see Table 4). The fact that ICNAF had made important progress was mentioned in the debate, but it did not convince Senators Magnuson, Stevens, Muskie, Kennedy, and so forth. They showed determined leadership and were able to build the necessary coalition. Senator Magnuson's membership on the Appropriations Committee was not without importance from a logrolling perspective.[75] Even if the conservation argument was of doubtful validity at this point, too few members of Congress had incentives to support the multilateral approach. Structurally the system was biased against international interests, especially because of lack of presidential leadership for the multilateral approach. After a final warning by Senator Adlai E. Stevenson, III (D-Ill.) against the Magnuson bill's "flagrant disregard of solemn international commitments" the Senate accepted the House bill (H.R. 200) which had been amended to contain the provision of S. 961, as amended on the floor. The vote was 77-19, the 19 nays being cast by a group of liberal senators who accepted the internationalist argument presented by the State Department and a group of conservative senators, who were probably more impressed by the security argument presented by the Defense Department.[76] The following senators cast the 19 nay votes:[77]

Dewey F. Bartlett (R-Okla.)	Roman L. Hruska (R-Neb.)
Lawton Chiles (D-Fla.)	Jacob K. Javits (R-N.Y.)
Dick Clark (D-Iowa)	James A. McClure (R-Idaho)
Alan Cranston (D-Calif.)	William Proxmire (D-Wisc.)
John C. Culver (D-Iowa)	Hugh Scott (R-Pa.)
Hiram L. Fong (R-Hawaii)	Adlai E. Stevenson, III (D-Ill.)
John Glenn (D-Ohio)	Richard (Dick) Stone (D-Fla.)
Mike Gravel (D-Alaska)	John Tower (R-Tex.)
Robert P. Griffin (R-Mich.)	John Tunney (D-Calif.)
Gary Hart (D-Colo.)	

The minor differences between the House and Senate versions of the bill were then resolved by conference between the managers of the two versions. The conference compromise set March 1, 1977, as the effective date of the bill.[78] The conference report was agreed to by the Senate on March 29 by voice vote, and on March 30 by the House, by a 346-52 roll call vote.[79]

TABLE 4

Total U.S. Fish Catch and Foreign Catch in
U.S. 200-Mile Zone Area
(in metric tons)

Year	Total U.S. Catch	Foreign Catch in U.S. 200-Mile Area
1970	2,810,000	3,079,342
1971	2,875,200	3,535,546
1972	2,759,700	3,292,824
1973	2,796,000	3,206,427
1974	2,846,594	3,123,217
1975	2,842,070	2,781,837
1976	3,054,478	2,480,102
1977	2,980,296	1,783,014
1978	3,417,559	1,767,480
1979	3,510,854	1,624,452

Sources: (U.S. catch): Food and Agriculture Organization of the United Nations, Yearbook of Fishery Statistics: Catches and Landings, vol. 48, 1978 (Rome, 1980), p. 37.

(Foreign catch): Letter from William H. MacKenzie, Senior Policy Analyst, National Oceanic and Atmospheric Administration, U.S. Department of Commerce, to the author, April 3, 1981. The catches include foreign catches of tuna over which the United States does not assert management authority.

THE PRESIDENT'S SIGNATURE

Now the bill only needed the president's signature. It came in the middle of the fourth session of UNCLOS III, on April 13, 1976, despite opposition from the NSC and the Defense, Justice, and State Departments.

The final Senate vote, we recall, was January 28. At this time the president was concerned about the upcoming New Hampshire primary, where he faced a tough and important battle with Governor Ronald Reagan. [80] Asked about the 200-mile limit at a news conference in New Hampshire on February 8, 1976, 16 days before the primary, President Ford said: "If the [UNCLOS] negotiators dilly

dally, don't do something affirmatively, then they ought to recognize
the United States feels it is vitally important that we do something to
protect not only our game fish but our commercial fish."[81] If sufficient progress was not coming soon "then the United States ought to
move unilaterally."[82] The president soon decided that UNCLOS
negotiators did not do enough.

President Ford admitted to be concerned about four specific
problem areas of H.R. 200 when he signed it:

impediments for existing treaty and agreement obligations of the
   United States;
the stipulated jurisdiction over anadromous species beyond the 200-
   mile zone;
enforcement, including possible seizure of unauthorized fishing vessels; and
encroachment "upon the exclusive province of the Executive relative
   to matters under international negotiations."[83]

But, despite these concerns, the president had his official reasons
for signing the bill. He referred to the slow pace of the international
negotiations and the need to do something about foreign overfishing
off U.S. coasts. The bill was also "generally consistent with the
consensus emerging" at UNCLOS.[84]

What the president did not say was that this was an election
year. So H.R. 200 became Public Law 94-265, known as the Fishery Conservation and Management Act of 1976. It extended U.S.
jurisdiction over 2.2 million square miles of ocean. The United
States was enclosing about 10 percent of the world's fishery resources, the largest fishery resource of any nation in the world,
under its control.[85]

There were about 161,400 fishermen in the United States in
1974. Of these many were employed part-time only. Even if all
U.S. fishermen lived in Alaska, they would still be a minority group.
The coastal fishermen, although the majority, constituted the least
organized part of the industry. Tuna and shrimp fishermen were
much better organized. So the success of the coastal fishermen
cannot be explained purely by numbers or organization.[86] Instead,
the wide sympathy that they met in the press and the wider public
turned out to be very important. It made it easier for the congressional leaders who wanted the 200-mile bill passed to get the necessary support. The conservation argument had its impact. This was
a period of growing concern for resources in general. The importance
of the support for the 200-mile zone concept from conservation and
environmental groups, as well as vocal sport fishermen, should not
be underestimated. But the broad sympathy had a nationalist flavor

to it: "Let's stop those foreigners from taking our fish!" The Soviet factory ships could be seen from the shore. And there was a somewhat romantic component, too. Fishermen have a tough and difficult job; but they are free. They, more than any other group, fit an old American dream of freedom. The Soviet factory ships, on the other hand, were owned by the state. For these reasons, and because of lack of presidential leadership for the multilateral approach, the members of Congress from the coastal states could secure the necessary support from inland states. Logrolling was part of the story. Senator Magnuson was an influential senator. Not supporting a bill that he strongly wanted passed could have its cost. Support, on the other hand, could well have future benefits.[87]

The NCS had prepared a bill based on the Article 7 approach in late 1974. But this approach was blocked in the State Department for over a year. Presumably the nonratification of the 1958 Fisheries Convention by important distant-water fishing nations, such as Japan and the Soviet Union, was a reason for concern in the Legal Advisor's Office. It could explain the bureaucratic inertia. Only shortly before the Senate's final action did the State Department recommend the application of Article 7 to the president. But the president refused to take any action, even informally.[88] The dictates of election year domestic politics turned out to be decisive.

NOTES

1. See, for instance, Ann L. Hollick, "The Origins of 200-mile Offshore Zones," American Journal of International Law 71 (July 1977):494-500.

2. See, for instance, Bruce Mitchell, "Politics, Fish, and International Resource Management: The British-Icelandic Cod War," The Geographical Review 66 (April 1976):127-38.

3. See Evelyne Peyroux, "Les états africains face aux questions actuelles du droit de la mer," Revue générale de droit international public 78 (Juillet-septembre 1974):623-48.

4. "Draft United Nations Convention on the International Sea-Bed Area: Working Paper Submitted by the United States of America," in Report of the Committee on the Peaceful Uses of the Sea-Bed and the Ocean Floor beyond the Limits of National Jurisdiction, U.N. General Assembly, Official Records, 25th Sess., Suppl. No. 21 (A/8021) (New York, 1970), pp. 130-76, at 140. (Hereafter cited as Seabed Committee Report 1970.)

5. Article 2(4); for text see Shigeru Oda, The International Law of the Ocean Development: Basic Documents vol. I (Leiden: (Sijthoff, 1976), p. 21.

86 / SUPERPOWER AT SEA

6. Article III (2c), "Draft Articles on the Breadth of the Territorial Sea, Straits, and Fisheries," in Report of the Committee on the Peaceful Uses of the Sea-Bed and the Ocean Floor beyond the Limits of National Jurisdiction, U.N. General Assembly, Official Records, 26th Sess., Suppl. No. 21 (A/8421) (New York, 1971), p. 242. (Hereafter cited as Seabed Committee Report 1971.)

7. Article III (2D), ibid.

8. Article III, ibid., p. 243.

9. Article III (1), ibid., pp. 241-42.

10. Article III (4A), ibid.

11. Article III (7), ibid., pp. 244-45.

12. Howard W. Pollock, "The Outlook for Fisheries and Scientific Research," Law of the Sea Reports 1971 (Washington, D.C.: Marine Technology Society, 1972), pp. 129-34, at 131.

13. Jacob Dykstra, "The Prospects of Coastal Fisheries," Law of the Sea Reports 1971, pp. 171-74, at 172.

14. Jacob J. Dykstra, "Remarks," in Lewis M. Alexander, ed., The United Nations and Ocean Management, Proceedings of the Fifth Annual Conference of the Law of the Sea Institute, 1970 (Kingston, R.I.: University of Rhode Island, 1971), pp. 49-52.

15. W. Sullivan, "A Warning—The Decline of International Cooperative Fisheries Management Looking Particularly at the North Atlantic Ocean," in ibid., pp. 43-48, at 46.

16. Ibid., p. 46.

17. See also Frank Grice, "The Northeast Atlantic Fisheries Crisis," in Lewis M. Alexander, ed., The Law of the Sea: A New Geneva Conference, Proceedings of the Sixth Annual Conference of the Law of the Sea Institute, 1971 (Kingston, R.I.: University of Rhode Island, 1972), pp. 212-13.

18. August Felando, "The Prospects for Distant Water Fisheries," Law of the Sea Reports 1971, pp. 175-79, especially at 178.

19. Dale G. Broderick, "Law of the Sea Negotiations and the Tuna Fishery," in Alexander, ed., The Law of the Sea: A New Geneva Conference, pp. 213-16.

20. U.S. Congress, House, Foreign Affairs Committee, Fishing Rights and United States-Latin American Relations, Hearing, 92nd Cong., 2d Sess., February 3, 1972, pp. 13-14.

21. United States of America, "Revised Draft Fisheries Article," in Report of the Committee on the Peaceful Uses of the Sea-Bed and the Ocean Floor beyond the Limits of National Jurisdiction," U.N. General Assembly, Official Records, 27th Sess., Suppl. No. 21 (A/8721), (New York, 1972), pp. 175-79, at 175. (Hereafter cited as Seabed Committee Report 1972.)

22. Ibid., pp. 176-78.

23. Donald L. McKernan, "Statement," inserted in U.S. Congress, Senate, Commerce Committee, Law of the Sea, Hearing, 92nd Cong., 2d Sess., October 3, 1972, pp. 48-49.

24. William L. Sullivan, Jr., "The Northwest Atlantic Fisheries," in Lewis M. Alexander, ed., The Law of the Sea: Needs and Interests of Developing Countries, Proceedings of the Seventh Annual Conference of the Law of the Sea Institute, 1972 (Kingston, R.I.: University of Rhode Island, 1973), pp. 105-06.

25. John Stevenson, "Statement," in U.S. Congress, House, Foreign Affairs Committee, Law of the Sea and Peaceful Uses of the Seabeds, Hearings, 92nd Cong., 2d Sess., April 10-11, 1972, p. 7.

26. See, for instance, Ann L. Hollick, "Bureaucrats at Sea," in Ann L. Hollick and Robert E. Osgood, New Era of Ocean Politics (Baltimore: Johns Hopkins University Press, 1974), p. 44.

27. See, for instance, H. Gary Knight, "Comments on U.S. Ocean Policy and the International Law of the Sea Negotiations," in U.S. Congress, Senate, Commerce Committee, Law of the Sea, Hearing, October 3, 1972, pp. 79-86, at 85.

28. H.R. 4760, Sec. 3(a), in U.S. Congress, House, Merchant Marine and Fisheries Committee, Territorial Seas, Hearings, 93rd Cong., 1st Sess., May 17, July 30, 1973, p. 2.

29. Ibid., passim.

30. Ibid., p. 32.

31. Ibid., p. 34.

32. Ibid., p. 64.

33. Ibid., pp. 55-59.

34. U.S. Congress, Senate, Commerce Committee, Interim Fisheries Zone Extension and Management Act of 1973, Part I, Hearings, 93rd Cong., 2d Sess., May 10, June 7 and 22, July 12, August 9 and 10, September 13, October 4, 5, and 18, 1974.

35. U.S. Congress, Senate, Commerce Committee, Interim Fisheries Zone Extension and Management Act of 1973, Part 2, Hearings, 93d Cong., 2d Sess., February 11 and 14, March 29, 30, 31, and April 1, 1974, passim.

36. Ibid., p. 268.

37. U.S. Congress, Senate, Commerce Committee, Interim Fisheries Zone Extension and Management Act of 1973, Part 3, Hearings, 93d Cong., 2d Sess., April 18, 19, 26, May 3, 13, 14, and June 14, 1974, p. 657.

38. Quoted, ibid., p. 697. For full text of Convention, see, for instance, S. Houston Lay, Churchill and Nordquist, eds., New Directions in the Law of the Sea, vol. I, pp. 353-60.

39. Commerce Committee, Interim Fisheries Zone Extension, Part 3, p. 819.

40. Ibid., p. 791.

41. U.S. Congress, Senate, Commerce Committee, Emergency Marine Fisheries Protection Act of 1974, Senate Report 93-1079, 93d Cong., 2d Sess., August 8, 1974.

42. U.S. Congress, Senate, Foreign Relations Committee, Emergency Marine Fisheries Protection Act of 1974, Hearing, 93d Cong., 2d Sess., September 5, 1974, pp. 49-51.

43. U.S. Congress, Senate, Foreign Relations Committee, Emergency Marine Fisheries Protection Act, Report, 93d Cong., 2d Sess., September 23, 1974, pp. 7-8.

44. U.S. Congress, Senate, Armed Services Committee, Extending Jurisdiction of the United States over Certain Ocean Areas, Hearings, 93d Cong., 2d Sess., October 8, 9, 11, 1974, pp. 38-45.

45. Inserted, ibid., p. 258.

46. U.S. Congress, Senate, Armed Services Committee, Emergency Marine Fisheries Protection Act of 1974, Senate Report 93-1300, 93d Cong., 2d Sess., November 27, 1974.

47. For roll call vote, see Congressional Record, vol. 120, part 129, p. 39105; for preceding floor debate, ibid., pp. 38965-39105, passim.

48. See H. Gary Knight, "International Fisheries Management without Global Agreement: United States Policies and Their Impact on the Soviet Union," Georgia Journal of International and Comparative Law 6 (Winter 1976):119-42.

49. "S. 961," in U.S. Congress, Senate, Commerce Committee, Emergency Marine Fisheries Protection Act of 1975, Part 1 Hearing, 94th Cong., 1st Sess., June 6, 1975, p. 2.

50. Ibid., p. 1.

51. Ibid., pp. 29-32.

52. Ibid., pp. 53-57.

53. Ibid., pp. 33-34.

54. U.S. Congress, Senate, Commerce Committee, Emergency Marine Fisheries Protection Act of 1975, Part 2, Hearing, 94th Cong., 1st Sess., September 19, 1975, p. 91.

55. Ibid., pp. 91-98.

56. Ibid., pp. 94, 97.

57. Ibid., p. 103.

58. U.S. Congress, Senate, Commerce Committee, Magnuson Fisheries Management and Conservation Act, Report 94-416, 94th Cong., 1st Sess., October 7, 1975, especially pp. 10-17.

59. U.S. Congress, Senate, Foreign Relations Committee, Two-Hundred-Mile Fishing Zone, Hearing, 94th Cong., 1st Sess., October 31, 1975, pp. 74-100.

60. Ibid., pp. 150-53.

61. Ibid., pp. 152-56.

62. U.S. Congress, Senate, Foreign Relations Committee, Two-Hundred-Mile Fishing Zone, Hearing, 94th Cong., 1st Sess., October 31, 1975, pp. 101-07.

63. Ibid., p. 105.

64. Ibid., p. 112.

65. Ibid.

66. Ibid., pp. 145-46.

67. U.S. Congress, Senate, Foreign Relations Committee, Fisheries Management and Conservation Act, Senate Report 94-459, 94th Cong., 1st Sess., November 18, 1975.

68. U.S. Congress, Senate, Armed Services Committee, Emergency Marine Fisheries Protection Act of 1975, Hearing, 94th Cong., 1st Sess., November 19, 1975, pp. 1-37.

69. U.S. Congress, Senate, Armed Services Committee, Fisheries Management and Conservation Act, Senate Report 94-515, 94th Cong., 1st Sess., December 8, 1975.

70. U.S. Congress, House, Merchant Marine and Fisheries Committee, Fisheries Jurisdiction, Hearings, 94th Cong., 1st Sess., March 10-14, 18-20, and 27, 1975.

71. U.S. Congress, Merchant Marine and Fisheries Committee, Marine Fisheries Conservation Act of 1975, House Report 94-445, 94th Cong., 1st Sess., August 20, 1975.

72. U.S. Congress, House, International Relations Committee, Potential Impact of the Proposed 200-Mile Fishing Zone on U.S. Foreign Relations, Hearing, 94th Cong., 1st Sess., September 24, 1975.

73. U.S. Congress, House, International Relations Committee, Potential Impact of the Proposed 200-Mile Fishing Zone on U.S. Foreign Relations, Special Oversight Report 94-542, October 8, 1975.

74. For the roll call vote, see Congressional Record, vol. 121, part 25 (October 9, 1975), pp. 32602-03; for preceding floor debate, ibid., pp. 32532ff.

75. Congressional Directory 1977 (Washington, D.C.: U.S. Government Printing Office, 1977), p. 251.

76. Congressional Record, vol. 122, part 1, pp. 121-1309, passim. See also "Senate Approves Extension of the U.S. Fishing Zone," Congressional Quarterly Weekly Report 34 (January 31, 1976):206-07.

77. Ibid., part 2 (January 28, 1976), p. 1309.

78. U.S. Congress, Senate, Fishery Conservation and Management Act of 1976: Report of the Committee of Conference on H.R. 200, Report 94-711, March 24, 1976.

79. Congressional Record, vol. 122, part 7, pp. 8550-59. See also David M. Maxfield, "Congress Approves 200-Mile Fishing Zone," Congressional Quarterly Weekly Report 34 (April 3, 1976): 750-51.

80. See Ron Nessen, It Sure Looks Different from the Inside (New York: Simon and Schuster, 1978), pp. 196-201.

81. The Presidential Campaign 1976, vol. 2, part 1: President Gerald Ford (Washington, D.C.: U.S. Government Printing Office, 1979), p. 114.

82. Ibid.

83. Gerald R. Ford, "Statement by the President upon Signing H.R. 200 into Law," Weekly Compilation of Presidential Documents, vol. 12, no. 16 (April 13, 1976):644; reprinted in U.S. Congress, Senate, Commerce Committee, A Legislative History of the Fishery Conservation and Management Act of 1976, Print, 94th Cong., 2d Sess., October 1976, pp. 34-45.

84. Ibid.

85. "NOAA and the Marine Fisheries Conservation Act," Marine Fisheries Review 38 (August 1976):27.

86. For figures, see U.S. Dpartment of Commerce, U.S. Ocean Policy in the 1970's: Status and Issues (Washington, D.C.: U.S. Government Printing Office, 1978), pp. III-2.

87. These conclusions have benefited from talks with various U.S. officials and representatives of nongovernmental organizations in Washington, D.C., October 1978, March 1979, and February-March 1981. See also Warren G. Magnuson, "The Fishery Conservation and Management Act of 1976: First Step toward Improved Management of Marine Fisheries," Washington Law Review 52 (July 1977):427-50.

88. John Norton Moore, "Foreign Policy and Fidelity to Law: The Anatomy of a Treaty Violation," American Journal of International Law 70 (October 1976):802-08; see also David Binder, "Senate Approves a 200-Mile Limit on Fishing Rights," New York Times, January 29, 1976, pp. 1 and 10; and Leslie Gelb, "Ex-U.S. Aide Accuses Government of Neglecting Sea Law Negotiations," New York Times, July 20, 1976, p. 4.

6

THE POLITICS OF
DEEP SEABED MINING

THE NIXON PROPOSAL AND THE
MINING INDUSTRY

The U.S. Draft Convention that was introduced in the U.N. Seabed Committee in August 1970 stipulated the creation of the International Seabed Area, which would start at the 200-meter isobath. This area, we recall, was to be divided into a Trusteeship Zone, which would comprise the continental margin part of the area, and an international area beyond. For the former the coastal state would act as a trustee for the international community. For the latter a new International Seabed Resource Authority (ISRA) would have the administrative authority.

For the deep seabed area, the proposed ISRA would have the authority to issue licenses to companies sponsored by member states ("Sponsoring Parties") and collect revenues from the exploitation of the area's mineral resources, mainly the manganese nodules, which contain various quantities of manganese, copper, nickel, cobalt, and other minerals. Licenses were to be issued for a certain area ("block") and for a certain period. The ISRA should prescribe rules for the protection of the environment. Scientific research would remain free. Exploration or exploitation of the seabed should not affect the high seas status of the superjacent waters. The area would be part of the common heritage of mankind, and it would be open to use by all states without discrimination (except as provided by the convention). It would be "reserved exclusively for peaceful purposes."[1] We recall that "peaceful purposes," according to the United States, did not preclude the deployment of military equipment or personnel.[2]

The principal organs proposed for the ISRA were an assembly, a council, a tribunal, and three commissions. The assembly was to be composed of all member states, each having one vote. The assembly would elect the council, which would have 24 members. The 24 were to include the "six most industrially advanced Contracting Parties" and 18 additional members of which at least 12 should be developing countries "taking into account the need for equitable geographical distribution." It was further stipulated that at least 2 of the 24 members should be landlocked or shelf-locked countries.[3]

The council was to appoint and supervise the three commissions, composed of five to nine members, namely, a Rules and Recommended Practices Commission, an Operations Commission, and an International Seabed Boundary Review Commission. The Operations Commission was the one that was to be in charge of issuing licenses for deep seabed mineral exploration and exploitation. It would supervise the licensees but not itself engage in exploration or exploitation.[4] So this was a clear limitation of the powers of the ISRA.

Finally, the tribunal was to be composed of five, seven, or nine independent judges. It was to decide all disputes and advise on all questions relating to the interpretation and application of the convention. It could also request advisory opinions from the International Court of Justice.[5]

The council was no doubt expected to be the most important body in this institutional setup. It would appoint and supervise the commissions, establish procedures for the coordination of their activities, and determine the terms of office of their members. It could also establish subsidiary organs and issue emergency orders. It would appoint the secretary general of the Authority and submit proposed budgets to the assembly for its approval.[6]

Whereas the assembly would normally take decisions by a majority of the members present and voting, a system of weighted voting was prescribed for the council. Decisions by the council would take "a majority of all its members, including a majority of members in each of the two categories," namely, the six most industrially advanced and the eighteen additional members.[7] This system of concurrent majorities meant that three of the six most industrially advanced states could collectively veto a decision of the ISRA. In an appendix it was specified that the most industrially advanced countries were those having "the highest gross national product."[8]

The U.S. hard minerals industry was less violent in its attacks on the Nixon proposals than the oil industry was. But it had its points of criticism, too. And as time went without an international agreement, the industry became increasingly critical of the administration's policy, also because the administration went further in trying to accommodate international demands than it liked.

The U.S. Draft Convention was analyzed critically by the American Mining Congress (AMC) in a long statement in January 1971.[9] The AMC, which is the trade association representing most U.S. companies that are involved in the metals and minerals industry, proposed the following as a central guiding idea: "The most serious needs are to establish the secure investment climate for the commitment of substantial funds to ocean mining and to provide for security of tenure beyond the limitation of national jurisdiction."[10] The AMC made proposals both concerning the interim period until a treaty might be agreed to by the United States and concerning the provisions of such a treaty, often mixing up the two, because the industry's basic demands for the interim period were also those which the industry wanted realized in the longer run. The possibility of change at an unspecified time would create the kind of uncertainties that investors do not like. So the Nixon proposal was criticized for the suggested transition measures.

Although the draft had stipulated that there would be due protection of investments in the interim period, it had also specified that licenses issued after July 1, 1970, should be converted into licenses under the ISRA within five years after its establishment. This, according to the AMC, posed "serious uncertainties," since no one knew what license provisions would ultimately be included in the final text of a treaty. The AMC wanted licenses existing at the time of the entry into force of a treaty to remain valid for the period for which they had been issued. There should be no imposition on an operator of ex post facto requirements.[11]

The AMC found the proposed ISRA "unnecessarily elaborate": "It is feared that this type of organization will encumber the exploration and exploitation of marine mineral resources through administrative red tape and the imposition of financial burdens."[12] It should not come as a surprise that the AMC wanted to keep fees, rentals, and bonuses at a minimum level. Front end payments should be abolished. However, in order to avoid speculators from seeking licenses and keeping blocks for later times, the AMC wanted to increase the minimum work requirement from the $100,000 per year suggested in the Nixon draft to somewhere in the range of $500,000 to $1 million per year, and to substantially shorten the time limit for relinquishment of blocks from the proposed fifteen to possibly four years. With such requirements the licensee would have to put the "money in the ground" and develop the mineral resources more rapidly.[13]

A further complaint by the AMC about the Nixon Draft Convention concerned the proposed reporting provisions:

> Industry should not be required to supply proprietary
> information, trade secrets, interpretations of data,
> or any processes, methods and techniques utilized at
> sea or in land-based operations. Complete disclosure
> will place the operators in a disadvantageous position
> due to the very competitive nature of the business. [14]

The tax payable should be related to the economic success of the venture. It was proposed that the tax rate should be lower than the one existing for land-based mining because of the more hazardous nature of deep seabed mining. Why not even introduce a tax holiday for the first five years to "encourage venture capital" asked the AMC. [15]

The general tone of the industry view can be summarized this way: security of investments and security of tenure were necessary to get this new industrial activity started. Some legal framework was needed, but such a framework should give the U.S. industry as much freedom as possible. And costs should be as low as possible. The International Seabed Authority should be as weak and simple as possible. [16]

As an alternative to waiting for an international treaty, the AMC suggested U.S. legislation. The purpose would be to assure the security of investment and protect the miner against the risk of interference from others and the lack of security of tenure. It was agreed that such legislation could only regulate U.S. citizens, but it could also "provide a basis for reciprocal agreements with like-minded states during the interim period." The legislation should establish a U.S. authority to issue licenses, which would give exclusive rights to the licensee to explore and exploit a defined area of the deep seabed over a certain time period as well as establish other conditions, including work requirements. Reciprocating states, forming eventually a kind of mini-OECD through parallel legislation, would agree to respect each other's licenses, which would be issued on a first come, first served basis. To avoid different reciprocating states issuing licenses for the same areas, an international registry clearinghouse should be established. It was also proposed that the reciprocating states should establish an escrow fund to become available for assistance especially to developing countries. However, it should also be possible to withdraw money from the fund to cover losses suffered because of interferences by nonreciprocating states or their citizens. [17]

If representatives of the oil industry tended to criticize the Defense Department for its creeping jurisdiction argument, it was as if the hard minerals industry feared the "creeping jurisdiction" of a new international organization. One industry-associated author,

Northcutt Ely, called the proposed ISRA a "new supersovereignty," when he spoke at the Offshore Technology Conference in Houston, Texas, in April 1971. He said:

> Once the principle is conceded that an agency of the
> United Nations shall have the inherent power to deny,
> grant, condition and revoke a nation's power to use the
> bed of the sea for production of minerals, it becomes
> difficult to say why, on principle, the international
> authority should not have similar competence to grant
> or deny use of the seabed for all purposes, including
> peaceful military uses, and, indeed, to grant or deny
> use of the water column itself. [18]

Ely suggested that a registry of national claims would be sounder and sufficient. The proposed machinery of the ISRA was said to be "wholly disproportionate to any business that it ought to be transacting." The problem was not one of structuring "a police force to maintain order in a gold rush" but to "provide the incentives" that would induce people to risk their money to get those minerals up from the bottom of the sea. [19]

THIRD WORLD MAXIMALISM

The debate concerning an international seabed regime for the area beyond national jurisdiction, which took place in the Seabed Committee after the introduction of the U.S. Draft Convention in 1970, gradually became more and more polarized between industrialized and developing countries. The industrialized countries favored some kind of international licensing and a seabed authority with limited powers and weighted voting, which would give them a kind of veto. The developing countries, on the other hand, had concluded that a strong International Seabed Authority (ISA) would be necessary to give the common heritage concept meaning. They felt that a simple licensing system would favor the technologically advanced states, which would thus get the lion's share of the deep seabed minerals. [20]

The developing countries came to the conclusion that the only way in which they could participate in deep seabed mining would be through an ISA that would itself engage directly in exploration and exploitation of these resources. They realized that they did not have the technology or the capital needed for such activity individually. But they hoped to solve these problems collectively through a strong ISA over which they did not want to lose control. For this reason they rejected any system of preferential or weighted voting. They did not want another Security Council type organization. They advocated the application of the "one state, one vote" principle and claimed that all states are equal.[21]

These basic ideas were spelled out in some concrete proposals. An important proposal was made by Tanzania in 1971. Under the Tanzanian proposal, the ISA would have comprehensive powers. It would be empowered

to explore the international seabed area and exploit its resources directly,

to issue licenses to states or private companies,

to provide for equitable sharing,

to establish measures designed to minimize and eliminate price fluctuations of land-based minerals because of seabed production,

to encourage and assist technological research,

to enhance the application of scientific techniques for seabed exploration and exploitation,

to foster exchange of scientific and technical information,

to promote and encourage the exchange and training of scientists and experts in the field of seabed mining,

to establish oceanographic institutions on a regional basis,

to provide technical assistance to developing countries in oceanography,

to establish safeguards against the military use of materials, services, equipment, facilities, and information made available by the ISA,

to establish standards for the protection of the marine environment,

to establish any facilities useful in carrying out of these functions, and

to take any action necessary to give effect to the convention's provisions.[22]

This of course was a rather comprehensive list. However, by including licenses to states or private companies, the proposal could lead to what later became known as a parallel system. Among the other powers mentioned we should especially notice the power to control prices of the minerals in question. This idea was intended to calm the fears of the countries having land-based production of nickel, copper, cobalt, and manganese. (For a list, see Table 5.) We should further notice the importance attached to transfer of technology.

The Tanzanian proposal also stipulated that the ISA should contribute to the furthering of worldwide disarmament and that the benefits from seabed mining should be allocated in such a manner

TABLE 5

Approximate 1971 Value of Mineral Production
(in millions of dollars)

	Cobalt	Copper	Manganese	Nickel	Total	Percent of World Production
Group of 77						
Chile		790			790	11.0
Zambia	10	718			728	10.0
Zaire	65	449	4		518	7.0
Peru		235			235	3.0
Philippines		230			230	3.0
China		110	12		122	2.0
Mexico		70	2		72	1.0
Cuba	8			27	35	.5
Brazil			29		29	.4
Gabon			20		20	.3
India			20		20	.3
Indonesia				18	18	.3
Morocco	5				5	.1
Ghana			7		7	.1
Not Group of 77						
United States		1,522		9	1,531	22.0
Canada	11	720		186	917	13.0
Soviet Union	8	680	76	80	844	12.0
Australia	2	195	11	22	230	3.0
South Africa		174	36	9	219	3.0
Japan		133	2		135	2.0
Poland		99			99	1.0
France				71	71	1.0
Rhodesia				9	9	.1
Finland	6				6	.1
Greece				9	9	.1
Total	115	6,125	223	445	6,908	96.3

Source: U.S. Congress, Senate Interior and Insular Affairs Committee, Ocean Manganese Nodules. Print. Prepared by the Congressional Research Service, 94th Cong., 1st Sess., June 1975, p. 45. (Data from UNCTAD and U.S. Department of the Interior documents.)

that the interests and needs of the developing countries were taken into particular consideration.[23] The principal organs of the proposed ISA would be an assembly, a council, and a secretariat headed by a secretary general. The assembly would be composed of all member states, each having one vote. The more important council would consist of 18 members elected by the assembly "with due regard to geographic distribution." Three of them would be landlocked states. Substantive decisions would be taken by two-thirds majorities.[24] But no weighted or chambered voting was foreseen.

A more "radical" proposal was introduced by 13 Latin American states, namely, Chile, Colombia, Ecuador, El Salvador, Guatemala, Guyana, Jamaica, Mexico, Panama, Peru, Trinidad and Tobago, Uruguay, and Venezuela. The Latin American proposal would introduce a unitary system that would only allow private companies to mine the deep seabed through joint ventures with the ISA. Article 15 of the proposal stipulated:

> The Authority shall itself undertake exploration and exploitation activities in the area; it may, however, avail itself for this purpose of the services of persons, natural or juridical, public or private, national or international, by a system of contracts or by the establishment of joint ventures. . . .[25]

The ISA would also have jurisdiction over scientific research and pollution control. And it would have the power to fix prices and aid developing countries, financially and technically.[26]

The principal organs of the ISA according to the Latin American proposal would be an assembly, a council, an International Seabed Enterprise, and a secretariat. The "Enterprise" was a Latin American contribution to the law of the sea debate. Article 33 stipulated: "The Enterprise is the organ of the Authority empowered to undertake all technical, industrial or commercial activities relating to the exploration of the area and exploitation of its resources (by itself, or in joint ventures with juridical persons duly sponsored by States)."[27] Exactly how this Enterprise would be set up was not specified. Concerning the other organs only these points were delineated: The assembly would consist of all member states, and decisions would be taken by a majority of the members present and voting; the council would have 35 members, and substantive decisions would require a two-thirds majority.[28]

By 1973 about 70 states were on record as favoring a Seabed Authority with direct powers over exploitation. These states included the 42 members of the Organization of African Unity which, in its "Declaration of 1973 on the Issues of the Law of the Sea," had stated that the ISA machinery

. . . shall be invested with strong and comprehensive
powers. Among others it shall have the right to explore and exploit the area, to handle equitable distribution of benefits and to minimize any adverse economic
effects by the fluctuation of prices of raw materials resulting from activities carried out in the area; to dis-
tribute equitably among all developing countries the pro-
ceeds from any tax (fiscal imposition) levied in connection with activities related to the exploitation of the area;
to protect the marine environment; to regulate and conduct scientific research and in this way give full meaning to the concept of the common heritage of mankind. [29]

Also the group of Caribbean states had demanded a strong ISA in
their Santo Domingo Declaration in 1972. [30]

There were also a few industrialized countries that had expressed conditional support for an ISA with powers of direct exploitation by 1973. The group included such countries as Austria, Denmark, the Netherlands, New Zealand, Australia, Canada, Spain,
and Yugoslavia. Most of these countries supported some mixed or
parallel system. The opposition in the Seabed Committee against a
directly operating ISA came mainly from the United States, the
United Kingdom, France, Japan, Italy, and the Soviet bloc. [31]

Third World countries argued against the Nixon proposal and
similar proposals from other industrialized countries. They feared
that a weak international regime would allow the rich and developed
countries to appropriate what they considered belonged to everybody.
The common heritage resolution adopted by the United Nations was
not without legal meaning. It prescribed certain kinds of solutions.
Technology as such should not give special rights. The result would
be that the poor and underdeveloped countries would be presented
with a fait accompli. The common heritage would be exploited by
the few. The developing countries therefore had to demand strong
international machinery, which could carry out exploration and exploitation directly on their behalf. [32]

The confrontations that had begun during the Seabed Committee
sessions continued within UNCLOS III. At Caracas in 1974 an overwhelming majority of the states participating declared their support
for an ISA with the powers to engage directly in deep seabed mining. [33]

THE PARALLEL SYSTEM

It was at the Geneva session of UNCLOS III in 1975 that the
United States started moving away from the simple licensing proposal.

The United States suggested a two-area system whereby an applicant for a contract should propose two alternative areas for possible exploitation. The ISA would then let the applicant have one area and keep the other one. The applicant should, if some basic conditions were fulfilled, have one area. The ISA would have full discretion over the exploitation of the other area. It could, for instance, be retained for later exploitation. This was referred to as a "banking system."[34]

The more important negotiations on deep seabed mining at Geneva took place within the Working Group of Committee I, which had been set up at Caracas toward the end of the session, and which was chaired by Christopher Pinto of Sri Lanka. But the negotiations were made difficult because of internal problems within the Group of 77 (G-77). Some developing countries had clear substantive interests in the outcome of the negotiations because they were land-based producers of some of the minerals that were contained in the manganese nodules. This included countries like Peru, Chile, Zaire, and Zambia. Other countries in the group were less concerned directly about the substance of the matter, but some countries used the issue as a test of the work for a new international economic order (NIEO). Some authors have referred to these countries as the "radicals." Mentioned are usually Algeria, Tanzania, and China. And it is argued that they were especially "ideological" about it.[35] Whether the "radicals" had substantive interests would of course depend on whether revenues for international sharing would be generated. This financial aspect, however, was not well analyzed at the time.[36]

In an effort to channel the negotiations in a constructive direction, the chairman of the Working Group, Pinto, introduced a paper entitled "Basic Conditions of Exploration and Exploitation" (CP/cab. 12/C. 1), on April 9, 1975. The paper tried to borrow from the different proposals made so far, both from G-77 proposals and proposals from the United States, the Soviet Union, Japan, and the EEC countries. The central idea of the Pinto text was that the ISA would "enter into a contract, joint venture or any other such form of association," with applicants, whether they be states or companies. But the Pinto paper also included the U.S. two-area proposal:

> Each applicant with respect to activities of evaluation
> and exploitation shall be required to propose to the
> Authority two alternative areas of equivalent commer-
> cial interest for the conduct of operations under con-
> tract. The Authority shall determine one such area
> to be a reserved area. . . .[37]

The Pinto text had stipulations about transfers of technology to developing countries as well as security of tenure. Although it looked as if the ISA would have full discretion over the 50 percent retained as "reserved areas," it did not mention direct exploitation by the ISA or an operative arm, the Enterprise, as demanded by G-77.

At Caracas the United States had insisted on detailed rules and regulations. Now, however, the United States agreed to give up that insistence and accept the Pinto paper as a basis for negotiations if it were modified on two points. The United States wanted it specified that the ISA was not the owner of the common heritage, but its trustee. Secondly, the United States wanted specified when the title to the minerals would pass to the contractor. It was necessary for the firms to know this if they were to be able to borrow capital for investment.[38] This conditional U.S. acceptance of the Pinto paper was a concession on the part of the United States in the hope of moving the negotiations.

However, a number of G-77 countries preferred the original G-77 proposals. After a series of internal deliberations they announced that they wanted to maintain the "direct and effective control of the Authority at all times," and that they were opposed to the concept of reserved areas. However, the group wanted to continue negotiations. It was prepared to discuss objective criteria governing the relationships between the ISA and contractors.[39]

The U.S. representative expressed disappointment. After eight years of negotiation the views of the developed countries were almost entirely rejected, he said. The United States had made concessions; but G-77 had not been willing to split the difference and meet the industrialized countries halfway. This U.S. intervention only elicited angry replies from China, Peru, and Brazil.[40]

Eventually Pinto had a revision of his paper (cab. 12/rev. 1) ready. But it was only just before the end of the session, so it was not discussed. The chairman of Committee I, Paul B. Engo (Cameroon) included it as an appendix to his part of the Informal Single Negotiating Text (ISNT), which was issued after the 1975 session of UNCLOS III.[41]

The new Pinto text was clearly more in line with G-77 demands than the original text. It had a section on the Enterprise that would "carry out directly scientific research or a general survey or exploration of the Area or operations relating to evaluation and exploitation of the resources of the Area. . . ."[42] The idea of joint ventures was retained, but all references to reserved areas had been deleted. So we can conclude that the U.S. effort to reach a compromise did not fare well at Geneva.

It was against this Geneva background that Secretary of State Henry Kissinger became involved in trying to strike a law of the sea bargain. It started with his speech at the American Bar Association meeting in Montreal in August 1975, in which he developed the U.S. support for a parallel regime. If an ISA could be created that would "insure fair adjudication of conflicting interests and security of investment," in which voting procedures would "reflect and balance the interests of the participating states," and that would "not have the power to control prices and production rates," then the United States would agree that the ISA should also have the right to conduct mining operations directly on behalf of the international community. The United States was further "prepared to explore ways of sharing deep seabed technology with other countries." Kissinger suggested that a breakdown of UNCLOS would lead to unrestrained military and commercial rivalry. The establishment of an international seabed regime, on the other hand, could "turn interdependence from a slogan into reality."[43]

The U.S. willingness to accept a parallel system and help do something about the transfer of technology could be seen as a concession to the Group of 77, and that was how U.S. decision makers perceived it. But the question was whether this was a sufficient concession, or a concession at all, from the point of view of the Group of 77. This group conceived of the common heritage of mankind in such a way that giving U.S. companies guaranteed access to deep seabed mining would be a great concession on their part.[44] And there was a problem of economic implications. In 1975 the United States had only suggested a monitoring of economic impacts, but explicitly ruled out price and production controls. It was on this latter point that a new U.S. concession followed in 1976. In an April 8, 1976, speech in New York, Secretary of State Kissinger talked about "The legitimate concerns of land-based producers of minerals," and he now said that the United States could "accept a temporary limitation, for a period fixed in the treaty, on production of the seabed minerals." Such temporary limitation was to be "tied to the projected growth in the world nickel market," which, at the time, was estimated to be about 6 percent per year.[45] But Kissinger also issued a threat: "If the deep seabeds are not subject to international agreement, the United States can and will proceed to explore and mine on its own."[46]

For a time it looked as if the Kissinger involvement was giving new momentum to UNCLOS III. The fourth session produced a Revised Single Negotiating Text (RSNT), which was much more in line with U.S. demands on deep seabed mining than the ISNT had been.[47] The RSNT included the parallel system. The Annex I on Basic Conditions reverted to what looked rather much like the original Pinto text (cab. 12). The applicant could either submit "two areas of like size and equivalent commercial value," one of which would then be designated "the contract area" by the ISA, or one area of double size, half of which would then be designated the contract area. In either case the ISA would retain an area to be exploited directly by or in association with the Enterprise. [48]

In many ways the RSNT followed the Kissinger proposals. The idea of tying seabed mining to the growth of the nickel market for a limited period, 20 years beginning in 1980 according to the RSNT, was also included. From the U.S. point of view, there were still problems to be solved concerning the council's voting system. The United States was also opposed to the idea of state quotas, which were mentioned in the text without being elaborated. Finally, there was still no consensus concerning the financing of the Enterprise until it could start generating revenue. Nor had the U.S. proposal for provisional application of the Committee I section of a treaty been accepted. But, all in all, the U.S. delegation felt that the fourth session had been fairly constructive. [49] Because of this the United States pushed for a fifth session in the summer of 1976. [50]

But U.S. optimism came too early. The RSNT had in reality been rejected by the Group of 77 at the end of the fourth session. It was the linkage to broader NIEO questions that was decisive. And it was not only "radical" G-77 members who made this linkage in the spring of 1976. In his opening statement at the fourth session, U.N. Secretary General Kurt Waldheim had talked about the new law of the sea regime as a contribution to "a more equitable global economic system." A successful outcome of the negotiations would have "a major impact on the establishment and implementation of the new international economic order." [51]

As the fifth session got started in August 1976, the Group of 77 was ready for a frontal attack on the RSNT provisions on deep seabed mining. The group would not accept the parallel system. The result was a stalemate in Committee I and a lot of procedural jockeying during the session. [52]

It was in an effort to break the deadlock that Secretary Kissinger appeared in New York at the beginning of September 1976. He now proposed that the United States would agree to help financing the Enterprise in such a way that it could "begin its mining operation either concurrently with the mining of state or private enterprises or within an agreed timespan that was practically concurrent." It was on the same occasion that Kissinger further suggested that there should be periodic review conferences, for example every 25 years. [53]

Afterward Kissinger referred to his new proposal as "a significant move." [54] This, however, was a matter of perception. Most of the concessions offered by the United States were basically economic, including the last one about financing of the Enterprise. But the Group of 77 had political goals, too. The important issue of the political control of the ISA still remained. And should the parallel system be made operational there were still many technical, especially financial, problems to be solved. But the Kissinger concessions offered a basis for further negotiations and a possible future compromise. Those more detailed negotiations fell upon the Carter administration.

CONGRESSIONAL ACTION (1971-76)

We have seen earlier that the American Mining Congress (AMC) suggested the idea of interim U.S. legislation in 1971. On November 2, 1971, Senator Lee Metcalf (D-Mont.) introduced a Deep Seabed Hard Mineral Resources Act (S. 2801), which had been drafted by the AMC. The Metcalf bill was cosponsored by Senators Henry M. Jackson (D-Wash.), Gordon Allott (R-Colo.), Henry Bellmon (R-Okla.), and Ted Stevens (R-Alaska). A companion bill, H.R. 13904, was introduced by Representative Thomas Downing (D-Va.) and 16 cosponsors on March 20, 1972. [55]

Different U.S. companies were already involved in preparing deep seabed mining. They were now lobbying members of Congress through the AMC or directly. [56] The industry argued that interim legislation was necessary to provide safeguards against various risks. It was maintained that deep seabed mining was a high seas freedom, but certain guarantees were necessary to get banks to lend the required amounts of money to the companies in question. The AMC-Metcalf bill therefore provided for safeguards against encroachment by persons subject to the jurisdiction of the United States. Citizens of the United States could only mine the deep seabed after getting a license from the Interior Department.

Protection against encroachment from companies from other developed countries was sought through the idea of reciprocating states. Such states would forbid interference by their companies and citizens through legislation comparable to the proposed U.S. legislation. Finally, protection against loss due to interference by nationals of nonreciprocating states or increased burdens because of a future treaty was sought through government insurance. [57]

The industry emphasized that it did not ask for subsidies, only insurance against certain risks. This was in keeping with the U.S. free enterprise system. The benefits to society would mainly be secure supplies of the minerals in question at reasonable prices. In other words, deep seabed mining would reduce U.S. dependence on import of these minerals and have a favorable impact on the balance of payments. [58]

The mining bills were not reported out of committee during the Ninety-second Congress. But they were reintroduced in the Ninety-third Congress. Senator Metcalf reintroduced the Senate bill on March 8, 1973, as S. 1134. The identical House bill had already been reintroduced by Congressman Downing on January 3, 1973, as H.R. 9.[59] So the leadership came from a senator from a mining state, Montana, and a representative from a state, Virginia, where one of the mining companies, Deepsea Ventures, was located, in Gloucester Point.

Initially the executive branch chose not to have an official policy in respect to the mining bills. However, on March 1, 1973, Charles N. Brower, acting legal advisor of the State Department, told the Subcommittee on Oceanography of the House Merchant Marine and Fisheries Committee that the administration had decided to oppose the enactment of H.R. 9 for the moment. The bill had "become a symbol to many countries of what they regard as defiance of the multilateral negotiating process." So, to give UNCLOS a chance, the administration was urging legislative restraint for a limited period. Timing was admitted to be essential; but the administration believed that a treaty could be ready for signature by 1975.[60]

Representatives from the mining industry were not happy about the administration's decision not to support interim legislation. Marne A. Dubs, director of the Ocean Resources Department of the Kennecott Copper Corporation, argued that H.R. 9 was "not unilateral in the pejorative sense." Its provisions would only apply to "persons subject to the jurisdiction of the United States." What else was achieved through this legislation was achieved through reciprocal relations with other states and through insurance provisions.[61]

John E. Flipse, president of Deepsea Ventures, Inc., talked about the "critical need for legislation." Because of the extensive costs of deep sea mining it was important that the particular mine site "be protected by a preferential right to the selected ore body." Tenneco (and Deepsea Ventures) had assumed risks in the development of pioneering technology. But it was "the responsibility of government to minimize the risks imposed on its citizens."[62] Tenneco also produced figures for U.S. import dependence for copper, nickel, cobalt, and manganese (see Table 6). Deep seabed mining could diversify the sources, improve the balance of payments, and give impetus to technological development.[63]

Since much of the early criticism of the mining bills focused upon international implications, Senator Metcalf introduced an amendment, No. 946, to S. 1134 on January 28, 1974, which dropped the provisions concerning reciprocating states, the proposed escrow fund, and the international clearing house. This, however, did not secure administration support. Enactment of the Metcalf bill "prior

TABLE 6

U.S. Production and Import of Minerals
Contained in Manganese Nodules
(in millions of pounds)

	U.S. Production	U.S. Consumption	U.S. Net Import	Origin of Import	Percent
Manganese (ore basis)	9	2,156	2,110	Brazil	35
				Gabon	31
				South Africa	8
				India	4
				Ghana	4
				All others	16
				Total	98
Nickel	31	320	270	Canada	70
				Norway	6
				South Africa	1
				All others	7
				Total	84
Copper	4,000	4,280	334	Chile	6
				Peru	6
				Canada	4
				South Africa	1
				All others	2
				Total	19
Cobalt	0	13	12	Zaire	52
				Belgium/Lux.	25
				Norway	6
				All others	9
				Total	92

Source: Statement of N. W. Freeman, Tenneco, Inc., in U.S. Congress, House, Merchant Marine and Fisheries Committee. Deep Seabed Hard Minerals. Hearings. March 1, 28, 29, April 3, 1973; February 26, 27, 28, 1974, at p. 84.

to the Caracas session of the Law of the Sea Conference would adversely affect progress on the deep seabeds as well as other aspects" of the law of the sea negotiations, said John Norton Moore in
hearings in March 1974.[64]

But the industry wanted a bill passed. Marne A. Dubs of
Kennecott Copper, also speaking on behalf of the American Mining
Congress (AMC), now used the OPEC analogy:

> The importance [of] promoting the development of the
> hard-mineral resources of the deep seabed has been
> strongly affirmed by recent events relating to the sup-
> ply of petroleum and by the obviously increasing ef-
> forts of foreign raw-material suppliers of all kinds to
> organize themselves so as to control the availability
> and price of minerals to the detriment of the United
> States.[65]

The AMC could accept the elimination of the escrow fund and reluc-
tantly accept the moratorium on commercial recovery before January 1, 1976, which had been included in the amended version of the
bill. However, the elimination of the reciprocating state concept
was a serious matter. "This principle tells all nations that the
United States intends to cooperate with and take into account the operations of other nations," said Marne Dubs.[66]

Early opposition against the Metcalf bill came from environ-
mentalists and internationalists. Richard A. Frank, representing
the Environmental Defense Fund, the Environmental Policy Center,
the Friends of the Earth, the Natural Resources Defense Council,
and the Sierra Club, expressed doubt that it was either necessary or
advisable to enact legislation at the time (1974). He argued that the
marine environment only could be protected through international
agreement. He also said that no objective and comprehensive study
of the environmental impact of deep seabed mining had been completed. Further, since the national stockpiles of the minerals that
could be recovered from the deep seabed were adequate there was
no pressing need for this legislation, which would prejudice international negotiating efforts.[67]

Samuel R. Levering, secretary of the United States Committee
for the Oceans, strongly opposed the passage of the Metcalf bill.
"Such unilateral action would be deeply resented by most of the nations of the world," which did not consider that the United States had
any right to take possession of the sites prior to general agreement
at UNCLOS III. It was further argued that only an international
agreement could provide the secure property rights sought by the industry.[68] But the real problem with the Metcalf bill was that it was

an expression of the kind of policies that the great powers had pursued in the nineteenth century when they "divided Africa and caused
much conflict and injustice." The world had changed since then:

> The U.S. is living in a world where much of the re-
> sources are in the hands of developing countries. It
> is likely that these resources will be available to the
> U.S. on more favorable terms if development of deep
> oceans is carried on in an orderly fashion, which is
> considered equitable and just by developing countries. [69]

But the Senate Interior Committee did not follow Sam Levering's advice. On July 15, 1974, while UNCLOS III was having its
first substantive session in Caracas, the committee unanimously
recommended that an amended S. 1134 be approved by the Senate.
The amended version had reintroduced the concepts of reciprocating
states and an international registry clearinghouse. The reported
version also provided protection for proprietary information. It
further provided for the formation of international consortia by limiting the U.S. guarantee insurance and compensation to the portion
of the interest owned by U.S. corporations. [70]

The reported S. 1134 was then referred to the Foreign Relations Committee from which it did not reappear during the Ninety-
third Congress. The Foreign Relations Committee took this course
of nonaction in support of the administration. So the mining bills
died with the close of the Ninety-third Congress. But the industry
was starting to get impatient. On November 14, 1974, Deepsea Ventures, Inc. filed a "Notice of Discovery and Claim of Exclusive Mining Rights and Requests for Diplomatic Protection of Investment"
for a mining site in the Pacific Ocean, with the relevant federal
agencies, foreign embassies, and private corporations. [71]

The State Department answered that it did not grant the kind
of rights sought by Deepsea Ventures, but also added that it considered deep seabed mining a high seas freedom: "The position of the
United States Government on deep ocean mining pending the outcome
of the Law of the Sea Conference is that the mining of the seabed beyond the limits of national jurisdiction may proceed as a freedom of
the high seas under existing international law." [72]

The deep seabed mining bills were reintroduced in the Ninety-
fourth Congress. Representative Thomas N. Downing introduced
the House bill (H.R. 1270) on January 14, 1975, and Senator Metcalf
reintroduced the Senate bill (S. 713) on February 18, 1975. [73] The
Senate Interior and Insular Affairs Committee conducted its first
hearing on deep seabed mining in the Ninety-fourth Congress on
November 7, 1975, that is, after the third session of UNCLOS III

and the publication of the first negotiating text, the ISNT, which took
a predominantly G-77 position on deep seabed mining. Industry representatives were clearly not impressed with the progress of international negotiations. John E. Flipse, president of Deepsea Ventures,
said that the deep seabed section of the ISNT "would make private investment in deep seabed mining extremely unattractive." There was
a great risk of discriminatory treatment of the industrialized countries, including the United States. In particular, reference was
made to price and production controls by the ISA, which might be
dominated by Third World land-based mineral suppliers.[74]

The industry was now at a "critical decision point," according
to Flipse. Commercial exploitation would require very large capital
investment. It was all right to be told by the administration that
deep seabed mining was a high seas freedom; but that did not provide
"sufficient assurance of continuity of the availability of the ore body,"
so it was inadequate to insure bank support. The industry was therefore now looking to the Congress for the help it needed.[75]

The Interior and Insular Affairs Committee did not act on S.
713 in 1975. But on March 18, 1976, just as the fourth session of
UNCLOS III had started in New York, the committee, by unanimous
vote of a quorum present, recommended that the Senate pass S. 713
in a slightly amended form.[76] The reported S. 713 then went to the
Commerce, Foreign Relations, and Armed Services Committees,
which conducted joint hearings on May 17 and 19, 1976, that is, after
the fourth UNCLOS III session and the publication of the Revised
Single Negotiating Text (RSNT). The administration continued its
opposition to U.S. deep seabed mining legislation.[77] But how strongly and for how long? The secretary of the interior, Thomas S.
Kleppe, seemed more ready to accept U.S. legislation than the secretary of commerce, Elliot L. Richardson.

The industry kept pressing for legislation. Northcutt Ely,
speaking on behalf of Deepsea Ventures, argued that attainment of
mineral self-sufficiency should be a top priority of U.S. minerals
policy. Secretary Kissinger's efforts to strike an international bargain were strongly criticized. The production control, which he had
agreed to, would be "absolutely fatal."[78] Ely analyzed this and
other aspects of the RSNT and concluded that Secretary Kissinger
had capitulated: "The end result is a total replacement of a freedom
of the seas with respect to seabed mining by a system that I can fairly characterize as state socialism of the deep seabeds of the world,
to be controlled by nations hostile to the American free enterprise
system."[79]

The three Senate committees did not accept the industry's plea
for legislation, at least not for the moment. The Armed Services
and Commerce Committees reported S. 713 without recommendation,

and the Foreign Relations Committee reported it adversely, recommending against passage after a voice vote on May 25, 1976. [80] Once again the deep seabed mining bills died with the end of a session of Congress. Neither S. 713 nor H.R. 1270 made it.

THE INFORMAL COMPOSITE
NEGOTIATING TEXT (1977)

The fifth session of UNCLOS III in New York, August-September 1976, did not move international negotiations further. As a matter of fact the RSNT, from the fourth session, was strongly attacked by a number of Third World countries, which argued that it went too far in trying to satisfy the industrialized countries. [81]

The question was now whether substantive negotiations would fare better at the sixth session, held in New York, May-July 1977. The Carter administration had now been inaugurated. The new president had chosen a Republican, Elliot L. Richardson, as his special representative to UNCLOS III. And, said one observer: "Richardson proved articulate, competent, and effective, and brought a new level of prestige to the difficult LOS negotiations." [82]

It had been decided to allocate the first three weeks of the sixth session to deep seabed matters. Jens Evensen of Norway, who had conducted some intersessional negotiations in Geneva on these issues, was invited by the Committee I chairman, Paul Engo, to continue the efforts as his "special co-ordinator." [83]

On the basis of the negotiations conducted by Evensen, various compromise proposals were worked out. These proposals foresaw a parallel system, but also a strong ISA that would have certain discretionary powers. Concerning production limitation Evensen first proposed a five-year limitation tied to the full increase in nickel demand and to 75 percent of that increase afterward. Since this proposal was strongly criticized by the bigger industrialized countries, he modified the proposal to a seven-year limitation to the full increase and 66.67 percent thereof afterward. [84]

Five days after the closing of the sixth session a new negotiating text, the Informal Composite Negotiating Text (ICNT), was made public. It turned out that Chairman Engo had not followed all of Minister Evensen's compromise proposals for his part of the text. According to most observers the ICNT was more favorable toward the positions of the Group of 77 than the Evensen proposals had been. [85]

The ICNT retained a kind of parallel system. Activities in the international area would be carried out by the Enterprise or by states or private companies in association with the Authority "through contractual or other arrangements." Such states or companies were

"to contribute the technological capability, financial and other resources necessary to enable the Authority to fulfill its functions."[86]

Annex II on "Basic conditions of exploitation and exploration"
retained the banking system. But it also specified: "The Authority
may require that the Contractor make available to the Enterprise
the same technology to be used in the Contractor's operations on
fair and reasonable terms and conditions. . . ."[87] Contractors en-
tering joint ventures with the Enterprise to exploit the reserved
areas would receive financial incentives. The purpose of this and
other provisions was to enable the Enterprise to engage in seabed
mining effectively from the time of entry into force of the convention.[88] By giving better conditions to companies willing to associate
directly with the Enterprise in exploration and exploitation, the ICNT
introduced a somewhat unbalanced parallel system.[89]

The ICNT also stipulated that there would be a review conference after twenty years. Should such conference fail to reach agreement within five years, activities would "be carried out by the Authority through the Enterprise and through joint ventures" afterward.
And it was specified that the Authority would "exercise effective control."[90]

Concerning production control the ICNT introduced a seven-
year interim period in which seabed mining would be limited by "the
projected cumulative growth segment of the world nickel demand."
After that period seabed mining should "not exceed 60 percent of the
cumulative growth segment of the world nickel demand."[91]

The institutional setup proposed by the ICNT was based on the
"sovereign equality" of the member states. An assembly would be
"the supreme organ." Substantive decisions of the assembly would
require a two-thirds majority. The executive organ, the council,
would have 36 members, 18 of which would be elected according to
the principle of equitable geographical distribution. There would be
four members "from among countries which have made the greatest
contributions to the exploration for, and the exploitation of, the resources of the Area, as demonstrated by substantial investment or
advanced technology. . . ." The four would include at least one
East European state. Then there would be four members from the
major importers of the minerals to be derived from the area, including at least one East European state. Next there would be four
members representing major exporters of the minerals in question,
including at least two developing countries. Finally there would be
six members from among especially poor and disadvantaged countries. Each of these members would have one vote. Substantive decisions would require a three-fourths majority.[92]

The United States responded quickly to the ICNT. Although
there had been true progress at the sixth session, there were both

procedural and substantive problems with the ICNT, said Ambassador Richardson afterward. The ICNT deviated from the Evensen text, which had been prepared "on the basis of full, fair, and open discussion." Although the Evensen text was not without problems, it was "generally viewed as a useful basis for further negotiation." But the ICNT, which was "produced in private, never discussed with a representative group of concerned nations," and released only after the session, could not be viewed "as a responsible substantive contribution to further negotiation."[93]

According to Richardson, the ICNT section on deep seabed mining was "fundamentally unacceptable." The substantive problems of the ICNT were the following:

It did not give reasonable assurance of access.
It could be read to make technology transfer by contractors a condition of access to the deep seabed.
It could be interpreted as giving the ISA the power to effectively mandate joint ventures with the Authority as a condition for access.
It failed to set clear and reasonable limits on the financial burdens to be borne by contractors.
It would set an artificial limit on seabed production.
It would give the ISA extremely broad, new, open-ended power.
It failed adequately to protect minority interests in its system of governance.
It would allow the distribution of benefits from seabed exploitation to peoples and countries not party to the convention.
It would seriously prejudice the likely long-term character of the international regime because of the possible conversion to a unitary system after 25 years.[94]

Because of these substantive problems Ambassador Richardson now had to recommend to the president that "a most serious and searching review" of U.S. ocean policy be undertaken.[95]

The Richardson reaction suggested that certain bottom line U.S. objectives had been reached. Although the industry was critical of the executive branch, the latter was in reality defending the former's interests very well. Richardson explained in an interview afterward that there should not be unfair pressure on industry to give up proprietary information, and that financial burdens should not be economically prohibitive. He also explained the reason why the ICNT's production limit was "unacceptably restrictive." Assuming a 4.5 percent average annual rate of increase in world demand for nickel, the ICNT's 60 percent limitation after the interim period would only allow twelve deep seabed mining sites by the year 2000. Since half of these would go to the Enterprise under the banking system only six would be available for states and private corporations. And this number was insufficient.[96]

The reason that the administration continued international negotiations despite the impasse on seabed mining was also explained by Richardson: ". . . significant U.S. interests may suffer from the failure to achieve a treaty." He suggested that most countries had already got what they sought through the extension of coastal state jurisdiction over living and nonliving resources. But "only a few countries had or have a vital interest in transit passage through straits, or in the preservation of high seas rights in the economic zone."[97] So navigational and military interests remained central preoccupations of the U.S. negotiators at the time of the Carter administration.

MOVING TOWARD UNILATERAL ACTION

Shortly after the sixth session of UNCLOS III, Senator Metcalf again introduced his seabed mining bill, S. 2053, on August 5, 1977. Cosponsors were Senators Henry Belmon (R-Okla.), Daniel Patrick Moynihan (D-N.Y.), and Daniel K. Inouye (D-Hawaii). On the House side the Merchant Marine and Fisheries Committee was now chaired by John M. Murphy (D-N.Y.) and its Subcommittee on Oceanography by John B. Breaux (D-La.). Murphy and Breaux had already introduced a new ocean mining bill, H.R. 3350, on February 9, 1977.[98] "Our patience in the Congress has run out," said Breaux as hearings on H.R. 3350 started in March 1977.[99]

The industry continued to argue for the passage of legislation to create the investment climate said to be necessary to raise funds to go ahead toward commercial exploitation of manganese nodules. "Time is running short for us," said Marne Dubs on behalf of the American Mining Congress and Kennecott Copper. Even if a satisfactory treaty might be the result of the international law of the sea negotiations, it would take two to ten years to get the necessary number of ratifications. Waiting so long would lead to a dissipation of effort. The industry anyhow had doubts about the likelihood of a satisfactory international treaty. Dubs quoted from an AMC resolution of September 1976, according to which the RSNT would "stifle participation by U.S. private capital in the development of deep seabed minerals."[100]

Technology was ready and the industry could accept normal business risks, said Dubs. However, there was a political risk. A treaty might significantly alter conditions. So the industry needed some guarantee against that political risk. Such guarantee was available through H.R. 3350. The enactment of that bill "would provide a considerable and immediate stimulus to ocean mining."[101]

The Carter administration started out being somewhat timid on the question of U.S. legislation. The May-July 1977 session of UNCLOS should be given a chance. The future of UNCLOS would depend much on the "group dynamics within the Group of 77," said Ambassador Richardson before that session. But even if the administration did not support legislation at the outset, Richardson had certain ideas about how legislation ought to look. It should not grant exclusive rights to a specific site. Nor should it provide compensation for loss suffered as a result of the entry into force of a treaty. But he promised that the U.S. delegation would "seek special grandfather protection for investment already made." He also said that a domestic processing requirement was unnecessary and that legislation should provide for benefits for the international community. [102]

But the industry had a good ally in the House Merchant Marine and Fisheries Committee which reported the Murphy-Breaux bill favorably on July 28, 1977, by voice vote. [103] The Senate Energy and Natural Resources and Commerce Committees held joint hearings on the Metcalf bill, S. 2053, in September and October, 1977. Now that the ICNT had been issued, Lee Metcalf talked about the "bankruptcy" of UNCLOS, and Congressman John Murphy said that after "the famous Engo text" it had become necessary for the Congress to move to protect U.S. investors who would like to mine the deep seabed. [104]

Industry representatives continued the pressure for legislation. Marne Dubs said that the ICNT was "simply not a basis for investment." So "enactment of appropriate legislation" was now "more urgent than ever." Phillips Hawkins of United States Steel Corporation said that the ICNT would make it impossible for a U.S. private enterprise operation to survive. The industry, however, was unhappy about some of the specifics of the Metcalf bill. The effective date of the bill, January 1, 1980, would create serious difficulties. The secretary was given too wide powers. The environmental protection procedures were too open ended, and the bill failed to clarify the taxation aspects. [105]

Ambassador Richardson testified on October 4, 1977. He said that the administration's review of policy had not yet been completed. But he repeated his criticism of the sixth session of UNCLOS and the ICNT. He suggested that "Congress should continue to move forward with legislation." He stated nine elements that would have to be included in ocean-mining legislation to get the administration's support. The legislation should

be interim in nature,
contain provisions for harmonizing U.S. regulations and those of
    reciprocating states,
provide for environment protection and sound resource management,

provide for international revenue sharing,
address the exploratory stage of deep seabed mining in detail, but
    only treat the framework of a regulatory regime in general terms,
not be specific with regard to the assignment of mining sites,
not require that processing plants be located in the United States,
not offer U.S. mining companies financial protection against adverse
    effects of a treaty concluded subsequent to the passage of legisla-
    tion, and
leave undisturbed the concept of high seas freedom. [106]

On the House side the Murphy-Breaux bill was reported favorably by the Interior and Insular Affairs Committee on October 26,
1977. [107] H.R. 3350 was then referred to the International Relations
Committee which had until February 10, 1978, to act. It was in a
testimony to this committee that Ambassador Richardson finally
could say on January 23, 1978:

> Since my last appearance before members of this com-
> mittee, the President has decided to support congres-
> sional efforts to develop deep seabed mining legislation
> consistent with our substantive position. The decision
> by the President to support interim deep seabed mining
> legislation is a shift from the administration's prior
> disinclination to lend its support. [108]

Three major reasons were given for the decision. First, the
administration felt that legislation would "be needed with or without
a successful law of the sea treaty." Second, the administration believed that "the orderly development of deep seabed mining should
not only be continued but also it should be encouraged." Finally,
the administration had concluded that legislation would not "negatively affect the prospects for reaching agreement at the Law of the Sea
Conference." To the latter point Richardson added: "Administration
opposition to deep seabed mining legislation could be misunderstood
as a total reliance on the Law of the Sea Conference for achievement
of our seabed objectives." [109]
    This suggests that there were both domestic and international
reasons for the change in policy. The administration wanted to encourage a new domestic industry to go forward and at the same time
signal to other countries that the United States could not agree to an
international regime like the one proposed in the ICNT. The U.S.
decision indicated that a regime of guaranteed nondiscriminatory access for private companies to seabed mining would have to be established soon if the United States should not choose the option of going
unilateral.

With the encouragement of the administration the International Relations Committee reported H.R. 3350 favorably—with amendments—on February 8, 1978. The committee's amendments followed the advice of the administration on the most essential points. [110]

Because of the tax aspect of international revenue sharing, H.R. 3350 then sent to the Ways and Means Committee. This committee decided to impose a charge of .75 percent of the total annual revenue of the ocean mining operator to be dedicated to an International Revenue Sharing Fund. [111] This figure was much lower than the various figures considered internationally.

The bill, H.R. 3350, then went to the House floor. The issue of whether the Interior Department or the Commerce Department should have primary jurisdiction over deep seabed mining was settled by a vote of 214 to 184 in favor of the Commerce Department. And on July 26, 1978, H.R. 3350 passed by a vote of 312 to 80. In its final version the House bill did not include any investment guarantee. Indeed, the bill followed the administration's substantive views to a large degree. [112]

Action was slower on the Senate side. The primus motor of S. 2053, Senator Lee Metcalf, died on January 12, 1978. This left a leadership vacuum. [113] But the Senate Committee on Energy and Natural Resources (formerly Interior and Insular Affairs) did report S. 2053 favorably, with amendments, by unanimous voice vote of a quorum, on May 2, 1978. And on August 10, 1978, the Senate Commerce, Science and Transportation Committee reported an amended version of the bill by a roll call vote of sixteen to one, the opposing vote being cast by Senator Robert Griffin (R-Mich.), who opposed the U.S. cargo preference that was included in the bill. Although the reported bills were slightly different, the two committees issued a joint report on August 18. [114]

The Senate was now in a hurry. The Foreign Relations Committee had a hearing on S. 2053 before it had received the reports from the Energy and Commerce Committees. It was confirmed in this hearing that the maritime unions were pressing strongly for the cargo preference. The director of the AFL-CIO Department of Legislation, Andrew J. Biemiller, wrote Senator John Sparkman, the chairman of the Foreign Relations Committee, the day before the hearing, explaining AFL-CIO support for S. 2053. The bill would benefit the U.S. people "in terms of supply of strategic mineral resources, tax revenues, an improved balance of payments posture, and new employment opportunities."[115] The latter point was of course especially important from an AFL-CIO point of view. On August 25, the Foreign Relations Committee reported the bill favorably, with amendments, by a vote of ten to two. The "nays" were cast by Senators Dick Clark (D-Iowa) and Robert P. Griffin. [116]

The administration's decision to support deep seabed mining legislation seems to have been the decisive event swaying the Foreign Relations Committee to support the bill.

With the overwhelming support the Metcalf bill now had in the three committees of Energy and Natural Resource, Commerce, and Foreign Relations, there was reason to expect that it could also pass the floor. However, to the surprise of many observers, it ran into problems. Senator Ted Kennedy (D-Mass.) became interested in it and placed a hold on it. He was concerned about antitrust aspects. But more importantly, Senator James Abonreszk (D-S.D.), one of the Senate's most liberal members, also was interested and placed a hold on it. His concerns were similar to the internationalist concerns of Senator Clark. And he stood firm, refusing to follow the pleas of the administration, the mining industry, the maritime unions, and many members of Congress. He even threatened to filibuster the bill. Since the Senate was in a rush to adjourn, the last thing that Majority Leader Robert Byrd (D-W.Va.) wanted was a filibuster. Senator Aboureszk thus succeeded in killing seabed mining legislation in the Ninety-fifth Congress. [117] However, since he did not seek reelection in 1978 there was reason to expect that the following session of Congress might pass deep seabed mining legislation.

THE DEEP SEABED HARD MINERAL
RESOURCES ACT (1980)

Deep seabed mining bills were reintroduced in the Ninety-sixth Congress in 1979. Senator Spark M. Matsunaga (D-Hawaii) introduced S. 493 on February 26, for himself and nine other senators, including Henry Jackson (D-Wash.), Frank Church (D-Idaho), and Russell B. Long (D-La.). On the House side, H.R. 2759 was introduced by Congressman John M. Murphy (D-N.Y.), Congressman John B. Breaux (D-La.), and ten other members of the House.

The Energy and Natural Resources, and the Commerce, Science, and Transportation Committees held joint hearings on S. 493 on March 29 and April 9, 1979. Senator Matsunaga in his opening statement gave various reasons for passage of S. 493. It would spur an early agreement at UNCLOS III, protect the U.S. lead in technology, reduce dependence on imports of minerals, "provide jobs both at sea and on land," and reduce the U.S. balance of payments deficit. [118]

The administration continued its support of legislation. However, it opposed some of the specific provisions of S. 493. According to Ambassador Richardson, the administration strongly opposed "any provisions in S. 493 that would require any or all mining, processing, or transport vessels to be documented solely in the United States." The administration was also concerned about "the provision requiring all hard-mineral resources to be processed in the United States or aboard vessels documented under the laws of the United States." A third issue concerned the so-called "grandfather rights" language. The administration agreed with expressing congressional intent on this issue, namely, the "sense of Congress that U.S. negotiators at the Law of the Sea Conference should negotiate treaty language that provides assured access and security of tenure to U.S. mining companies." However, the specific language of S. 493 could create the implication that the government had "a moral if not a legal obligation to compensate companies against loss due to treaty provisions" that might be less advantageous. [119]

The mining industry wanted legislation as soon as possible. Said Marne A. Dubs of Kennecott Copper, who also spoke on behalf of the American Mining Congress: "mining Companies cannot begin the advanced stages of mine-site development, full-scale prototype testing, or large-scale construction until a legal framework expressly sanctioning this activity is established." [120] The "grandfather rights" provision was the principal feature of this legislation according to Dubs. It would create the kind of security needed for investment decisions. The mining industry was not happy about U.S. vessel and domestic processing requirements, but could live with them. [121]

Opposing legislation were Representative Berkley W. Bedell (D-Iowa) and Samuel R. Levering of the U.S. Committee for the Oceans. They both felt that U.S. legislation could damage the international negotiations. And there was no need to hurry. "The mining itself is not likely until 1988 to 1990," said Levering. [122]

The industry, on the other hand, seemed close to having given up the hope that an acceptable agreement might be negotiated internationally. Northcutt Ely, special counsel of Ocean Mining Associates, a consortium consisting of the U.S. Steel Corporation, the Sun Company, and Union Minière, a Belgian company, stated directly: "Ocean Mining Associates could not and would not invest money under the terms of the informal composite negotiative [sic] text or under any revision of that text which has been disclosed to us to date." [123]

The Foreign Relations Committee held a hearing on S. 493 on June 13. Ambassador Richardson reported from the eighth session of UNCLOS III that "the number of major issues still to be resolved has been narrowed." [124] However, the administration still supported legislation if appropriate modifications on S. 493 could be made to meet its concerns.

On August 9, 1979 the three committees (Energy and Natural Resources; Commerce, Science, and Transportation; and Foreign

Relations) all reported S. 493 favorably with amendments.[125] On October 3, the Finance Committee reported favorably on Title V of the bill, which imposed an excise tax of 0.75 percent of the fair market value of the nodules removed, to be paid into a Deep Seabed Fund, which would be available for appropriation by Congress, including for international purposes.[126] Finally, the Environment and Public Works Committee reported S. 493 favorably, with an amendment, on October 9, 1979.[127]

The House Interior and Insular Affairs Committee held hearings on H.R. 2759 on May 1 and 23, 1979. "The Congress and the American people must now give industry a signal that we support them," said Congressman Jim Santini (D-Nev.).[128] The Merchant Marine and Fisheries Committee conducted hearings on May 22, 23, and June 7. Congressman John Murphy pressed for passage, stating that "major investment decisions by international seabed consortia are being held in abeyance pending legislation or a successful Law of the Sea Treaty. Since $200 million has already been spent but further infusion of capital is dependent on the establishment of a sound legal framework."[129]

Among testimonies supporting legislation was one from Robert L. Leggett, president of the Joint Maritime Congress, an organization of U.S. flag shipping companies. He strongly opposed "any attempt to dilute or to exclude entirely any or all provisions guaranteeing U.S. manning and vessel documentation for mining, transport and processing ships."[130] These provisions clearly served a coalition-building purpose. Jobs for the maritime industry were considered important by many members of Congress.

The Interior and Insular Affairs Committee reported H.R. 2759 favorably with an amendment on August 2, 1979.[131] The Merchant Marine and Fisheries Committee reported it favorably on August 17, with amendments.[132] Then followed the Ways and Means Committee, which recommended passage of the bill on November 2.[133]

The final committee on the House side to consider H.R. 2759 was the Foreign Affairs Committee. It held hearings on July 11, November 1, and December 19, 1979. Congressman Bedell continued to have his doubts about legislation: "I cannot see why, if we are trying to build an image of a responsible citizen in the world community, that we should be the one to step forward and say that we are going to go ahead and do this at a time when we have said we are going to negotiate in good faith."[134] The administration, however, kept supporting legislation if provisions concerning documentation of ships, grandfather rights, and effective dates could be modified. And industry, of course, kept pressing.[135]

The November 1 hearing especially addressed the issues of cargo preference and processing requirements. The administration continued its opposition to these protectionist provisions. But the maritime industry strongly supported them. The U.S. shipping companies supported the U.S. flag ship requirements in order to create jobs and avoid the use of flag of convenience ships. So did the Seafarers International Union of North America, AFL-CIO, whose vice president, John Yarmola, stated that H.R. 2759 would "provide new jobs for American workers by stimulating the development of a U.S. dry bulk and ocean mining fleet."[136]

The December 19 hearing dealt with national security implications. Ambassador Richardson argued that U.S. security interests were satisfied by the ICNT, Revision 1. Indeed U.S. security could best be satisfied through "a widely accepted body of international law for the ocean." It was because of international progress in that direction that Richardson now suggested that it would be better to delay passage of legislation until after the February-March 1980 session of UNCLOS III.[137]

The Foreign Affairs Committee reported H.R. 2759 favorably, with amendments, on May 15, 1980. The reported version included the requirements that commercial recovery and processing vessels should be documented under U.S. laws. But there was no domestic processing requirement, leaving this issue to regulations by the Secretary of Commerce. The grandfather clause took the form of a declaration of congressional intent that an international agreement should provide assured and nondiscriminatory access "under reasonable terms and conditions," and security of tenure "under terms, conditions, and restrictions which do not impose significant new economic burdens." No commercial recovery under the domestic regime would commence before January 1, 1988.[138]

The Senate version, S. 493, had already been passed by the Senate on December 14, 1979.[139] In the floor debate the bill was endorsed by Senators Russell B. Long (D-La.), Warren G. Magnuson (D-Wash.), James A. McClure (D-Idaho), Mark O. Hatfield (R-Ore.), Jesse A. Helms (R-N.C.), Lowell P. Weicker, Jr. (R-Conn.), Spark M. Matsunaga (D-Hawaii), Theodore Stevens (R-Alaska), and a few others.[140] Senator Long considered the common heritage concept to be "inimical to U.S. interests," and the ICNT "unacceptable."[141] According to McClure the ICNT was "unacceptable and offensive to the fundamental national interests of the United States." Only one senator spoke in opposition to S. 493, Senator Paul E. Tsongas (D-Mass.): "Interdependence is the reality of the future . . . we ought to devote more attention to establishing stable international regimes for interdependence."[142]

The House of Representatives considered and passed H.R.
2759 on June 9, 1980.[143] Speaking in favor, among others, were
Congressmen John M. Murphy and John B. Breaux as well as Paul
M. McCloskey (R-Calif.), Robert J. Lagomarsino (R-Calif.),
Clement J. Zablocki (D-Wis.), Jonathan B. Bingham (D-N.Y.), and
Jim Santini (D-Nev.). According to John Murphy the United States
was now importing 80 to 90 percent of over 12 metals critical to
U.S. defense and industrial needs. Three of these, manganese,
cobalt, and nickel, could be obtained from ocean mining.[144] Only
Congressman Berkley Bedell rose in opposition.

The Senate then considered H.R. 2759 and passed an amended
version on June 23.[145] The adopted version authorized commercial
recovery from January 1, 1988, thus accepting the House provision
on this point. However, the domestic processing requirement was
retained.

On June 25 the House concurred to the Senate amendments.[146]
Congressman Bedell continued to express his doubt about the advisability of passing legislation. He detected "the political pressure of
some of the mining interests" in the United States and suggested that
these interests might not correspond with the interests of the U.S.
people:

> I for one believe that if we are going to operate as we
> should as a Congress serving the people of the United
> States that we have to have the will, the power and
> the strength to stand up to those political pressures
> from special interest groups which would put their in-
> terests above the interests of the people of the United
> States.[147]

But Bedell's voice was a lonely voice. H.R. 2759 was signed by
President Carter on June 28, 1980, and became the Deep Seabed
Hard Mineral Resources Act.[148] The act claimed to be interim.
But the possibility that UNCLOS III might fail to produce an agree-
ment that could be ratified by the United States Senate was foreseen.

The administrator of the National Oceanic and Atmospheric
Administration (NOAA) could designate other states as reciprocating
states if they regulated their citizens in a compatible manner and
recognized U.S. licenses and permits.[149] A possible alternative
mini-treaty was thus foreseen.[150]

The act also put strict limits on U.S. negotiators by its grandfather rights language, which demanded that an international agreement should provide "assured and nondiscriminatory access" and
"security of tenure." No "significant new economic burdens" on

U.S. miners could be accepted.[151] Cargo preferences survived:
"No permittee may use any vessel for the commercial recovery of
hard mineral resources or for the processing at sea of hard mineral resources recovered under the permit issues to the permittee
unless the vessel is documented under the laws of the United States"[152]
The permittee should further use at least one U.S. documented transportation vessel. And, with a few exceptions to be granted by the NOAA
administrator, "the processing on land of hard mineral resources recovered pursuant to a permit shall be conducted within the United
States."[153]

National protectionism was the order of the day. By including
these vessel and processing requirements the advocates of unilateralism had been able to build a stronger domestic coalition.

NOTES

1. "Draft United Nations Convention of the International Seabed
Area: Working Paper Submitted by the United States of America,"
Report of the Committee on the Peaceful Uses of the Sea-Bed and the
Ocean Floor Beyond the Limits of National Jurisdiction, General
Assembly, Official Records, 25th Sess., Suppl. No. 21 (A/8021),
(New York: United Nations, 1970), pp. 130-76, at 132-37. (Here-
after cited as Seabed Committee Report 1970.)

2. William Palmer, "The United States Draft United Nations
Convention on the International Sea-Bed Area and the Accommodation
of Ocean Uses," Syracuse Journal of International Law 1 (October
1972):110-15, at 114.

3. Seabed Committee Report 1970, pp. 141-42.

4. Ibid., pp. 143-45.

5. Ibid., p. 146.

6. Ibid., p. 143; see also Oliver L. Stone, "The United States
Draft Convention on the International Seabed Area," Tulane Law Review 45 (April 1971):527-45, at 533.

7. Seabed Committee Report 1970, pp. 142-43.

8. Ibid., p. 176.

9. "Statement of American Mining Congress with Respect to
Working Paper of the Draft United Nations Convention on the Inter-
national Seabed Area, by T. S. Ary, January 27, 1971," reprinted
in U.S. Congress, Senate, Interior and Insular Affairs Committee,
Mineral Resources of the Deep Seabed, Hearings, 93d Cong., 1st
Sess., May 17, June 14, 15, 18, 19, 1973, pp. 144-59.

10. Ibid., p. 145.

11. Ibid., pp. 147-48.

12. Ibid., p. 148.

13. Ibid., pp. 152-53.

14. Ibid., p. 153.

15. Ibid., p. 154

16. See also T. S. Ary, Implications for the Hard Mineral Industry," in Law of the Seabed Reports 1971 (Washington, D.C.: Marine Technology Society, 1972), pp. 71-76.

17. "Statement of American Mining Congress," pp. 146-47, 156-59.

18. Northcutt Ely, "United States Seabed Minerals Policy," Natural Resources Lawyer 4 (July 1971):597-621, at 614-15. For an article antedating the Nixon proposals, see Northcutt Ely, "A Case for the Administration of Mineral Resources Underlying the High Seas by National Interests," Natural Resources Lawyer 1 (June 1968): 78-84.

19. Ely, "United States Seabed Minerals Policy," pp. 615-16.

20. R. P. Anand, Legal Regime of the Sea-Bed and the Developing Countries (Leiden: A. W. Sijthoff, 1976), pp. 220-22.

21. Ibid., pp. 222-23.

22. Tanzania, "Draft Statute for an International Sea-Bed Authority," in Report of the Committee on the Peaceful Uses of the Sea-Bed and the Ocean Floor Beyond the Limits of National Jurisdiction, General Assembly, Official Records, 26th Sess., Suppl. No. 21 (A/8421), (New York: United Nations, 1971), pp. 51-64, at 55-56. (Hereafter cited as Seabed Committee Report 1971.)

23. Ibid., pp. 56-57.

24. Ibid., pp. 57-58.

25. Chile et al., "Working Paper on the Regime for the Seabed and Ocean Floor, and Subsoil Thereof Beyond the Limits of National Jurisdiction," in ibid., pp. 93-101, at 95.

26. Ibid., pp. 95-96.

27. Ibid., p. 100.

28. Ibid., pp. 97-99.

29. Full text in Shigeru Oda, ed., The International Law of the Ocean Development: Basic Documents, vol. II (Leiden: Sijthoff, 1975), pp. 26-30, at 30.

30. Text, ibid., pp. 32-36, at 35.

31. See table in Barry Buzan, Seabed Politics (New York: Praeger, 1976), p. 171.

32. Anand, Legal Regime of the Sea-Bed and the Developing Countries, pp. 229-31.

33. Edward Miles, "An Interpretation of the Caracas Proceedings," in Francis T. Christy, Jr. et al., eds., Law of the Sea: Caracas and Beyond, Proceedings, 9th Annual Conference, Law of the Sea Institute, January 6-9, 1975 (Cambridge, Mass.: Ballinger, 1975), pp. 39-94, at 56.

34. Jon McLin, "The Third United Nations Law of the Sea Conference: Geneva," American Universities Field Staff Reports: West Europe Series 10 (May 1975):1-10, at 6.

35. Edward Miles, "An Interpretation of the Geneva Proceedings, Part I," Ocean Development and International Law 3 (1976): 187-224, at 193-94.

36. See Jean-Pierre Lévy, "Vers un nouveau droit de la mer: La politisation de processus de création juridique," Révue générale de droit international public 79 (October-December 1975):897-931, at 920.

37. Text included as appendix to Miles, "An Interpretation of the Geneva Proceedings," pp. 215-23, at 217.

38. Ibid., pp. 195-96.

39. Ibid., p. 203.

40. Ibid., pp. 204-06.

41. "Annex I," in Third United Nations Conference on the Law of the Sea, Official Records vol. IV (New York: United Nations, 1975), pp. 149-52.

42. Ibid., p. 149.

43. Henry Kissinger, "International Law, World Order, and Human Progress," Department of State Bulletin 73 (September 8, 1975), pp. 353-62, especially 355-58.

44. See, for instance, Carl Q. Cristol, "An International Seabed Authority," in Don Walsh, ed., The Law of the Sea: Issues in Ocean Resource Management (New York: Praeger, 1977), pp. 172-225, at 192-95; and Margaret E. Galey, "From Caracas to Geneva to New York: The International Seabed Authority as a Creator of Grants," Ocean Development and International Law 4 (1977):171-93.

45. Henry Kissinger, "The Law of the Sea: A Test of International Cooperation," Department of State Bulletin 74 (April 26, 1976), pp. 533-42, at 540.

46. Ibid., p. 538; see also "Kissinger Issues Warning on Sea Mining," National Journal 8 (April 17, 1976):527.

47. Larry D. Dershem and Scott J. Kaisler, "Recent Developments in the Law of the Sea 1976-1977," San Diego Law Review 14 (April 1977):718-35, at 721.

48. Doc. A/CONF.62/WP.8/rev.1, in Third United Nations Conference on the Law of the Sea, Official Records vol. V (New York: United Nations, 1976), pp. 125-201, at 140. See also Article 22 at 131.

49. T. Vincent Learson, "The March-May Session of the Law of the Sea Conference," Department of State Bulletin 74 (June 14, 1976), pp. 764-67; see also Giorgio Bosco, "La terza Conferenza delle Nazioni Unite sul diritto del mare," Trasporti (Padova) 9 (1976):55-73, at 70-71.

50. Jean-Pierre Beurier et Patrick Cadenat, "Les Sessions de New York de la troisième conférence sur le droit de la mer," Droit maritime français No. 339 (Mars 1977):131-43, at 133.

51. Quoted, Edgar Gold, "The Third United Nations Conference on the Law of the Sea: The 4th and 5th Sessions, New York, 1976," Maritime Policy and Management 4 (January 1977):171-82, at 171-72.

52. John Temple Swing (rapporteur), "Third United Nations Conference on the Law of the Sea: Report on the 1976 New York Sessions," San Diego Law Review 14 (1977):736-50, at 739; and Haight, "Law of the Sea Conference—Why Paralysis?" p. 286.

53. "Secretary Kissinger Discusses U.S. Position on Law of the Sea Conference," Department of State Bulletin 75 (September 27, 1976), pp. 395-403, at 398. See also Tullion Treves, "La Conferenza sul Diritto del Mare," Rivista di Diritto Internazionale 60 (1977): 566-78, at 574.

54. "U.S. Calls for Equitable Resolution of Law of the Sea Issues," Department of State Bulletin 75 (October 11, 1976), pp. 451-53, at 452.

55. U.S. Congress, Senate, Interior and Insular Affairs Committee, Ocean Manganese Nodules, 2d ed., Print. Prepared by the Congressional Research Service, 94th Cong., 2d Sess., February 1976, p. 66.

56. F. M. Auburn, "The Deep Seabed Hard Mineral Resources Bill," San Diego Law Review 9 (May 1972):491-513.

57. John G. Laylin, "The Law to Govern Deepsea Mining Until Superseded by International Agreement," San Diego Law Review 10 (May 1973):433-45, at 438-39.

58. Ibid., p. 44. See also John G. Laylin, "The Legal Regime of the Deep Seabed Pending Multinational Agreement," Virginia Journal of International Law 13 (April 1973):319-30; and Donald L. Humphreys, "An International Regime for the Exploration and Exploitation of the Resources of the Deep Seabed—The United States Hard Minerals Industry Position," Natural Resources Lawyer 5 (Fall 1972):731-51.

59. Senate, Interior and Insular Affairs Committee, Ocean Manganese Nodules, 2d ed., pp. 73-74.

60. U.S. Congress, House, Merchant Marine and Fisheries Committee, Deep Seabed Hard Minerals, Hearings, 93d Cong., 1st and 2d Sess., March 1, 28, 29, April 3, 1973, February 26-28, 1974, pp. 15-28.

61. Ibid., p. 66.

62. Ibid., pp. 81-82.

63. Ibid., p. 84.

64. U.S. Congress, Senate, Interior and Insular Affairs Committee, Mineral Resources of the Deep Seabed, Hearings, 93d Cong., 2d Sess., March 5, 6, 11, 1974, pp. 932-33.

65. Ibid., p. 1016.

66. Ibid., pp. 1018-19.

67. Ibid., pp. 1070-79.

68. Ibid., pp. 1080-82.

69. Ibid., p. 1085.

70. U.S. Congress, Senate, Interior and Insular Affairs Committee, Deep Seabed Hard Minerals Act, S. Rpt. 93-1116, 93d Cong., 2d Sess., August 21, 1974.

71. Senate Interior and Insular Affairs Committee, Ocean Manganese Nodules, 2d ed., pp. 83-84.

72. Quoted, R. Sebastian Gibson, "An Illusion of Camelot, the Validity of a Claim, and the Consequences of the Negotiations: The Great Nodule Spectacle," San Diego Law Review 13 (March 1976):667-706, at 690. See also Richard B. Frank and Bruce W. Jenett, "Murky Waters: Private Claims to Deep Ocean Seabed Minerals," Law and Policy in International Business 7 (Fall 1975):237-70.

73. Senate Interior and Insular Affairs Committee, Ocean Manganese Nodules, 2d ed., p. 84.

74. U.S. Congress, Senate, Interior and Insular Affairs Committee, Current Developments in Deep Seabed Mining, Hearing, 94th Cong., 1st Sess., November 7, 1975, p. 8.

75. Ibid.

76. U.S. Congress, Senate, Interior and Insular Affairs Committee, Deep Seabed Hard Minerals Act, S. Rpt. 94-754, 94th Cong., 2d Sess., April 14, 1976, especially pp. 20-21.

77. U.S. Congress, Senate, Commerce, Foreign Relations, and Armed Services Committees, Deep Seabed Hard Mineral Act, Joint Hearings, 94th Cong., 2d Sess., May 17 and 19, 1976, passim.

78. Ibid., pp. 105-07.

79. Ibid., p. 109.

80. U.S. Congress, Senate, Commerce, Armed Services, and Foreign Relations Committees, Deep Seabed Hard Minerals Act, S. Rpt. 94-935, 94th Cong., 2d Sess., June 8, 1976.

81. Part of the debate was public. See Third United Nations Conference on the Law of the Sea, Official Records, vol. VI (New York: United Nations, 1977), passim.

82. Alan G. Friedman, "The Law of the Sea Game," USA Today, May 1979, pp. 23-24, at 24.

83. "Statement made by Mr. P. B. Engo," 25 May 1977, Third United Nations Conference on the Law of the Sea, Official Records, vol. VII (New York: United Nations, 1978), pp. 74-78, at 78.

84. Denmark, Ministry of Foreign Affairs, Beretning, FN's 3. havretskonference: Mødesamlingen i New York, 23. maj.-15. juli (Copenhagen, 1977), pp. 7-9.

85. Ibid., pp. 1, 5. See also R. P. Barston, "Law of the Sea Conference: Old and New Maritime Regimes," International Relations (London) 6 (May 1978):302-10, at 306.

86. Article 151 (2), Informal Composite Negotiating Text, Third United Nations Conference on the Law of the Sea, Official Records, vol. VIII (New York: United Nations, 1978), p. 26. (Hereafter referred to as ICNT.)

87. Ibid., p. 51.

88. Ibid.

89. See, for instance, Fabrizio Bastianelli, Dalla prima alla terza conferenza delle nazioni unite sul diritto del mare—il regime giuridico delle risorse minerarie dei fondi marini con particolare riferimento ai noduli polimetallici," Bollettino della Associazione Mineraria Subalpina 14 (sett.-dic. 1977):426-40, at 433.

90. Article 153 (6), ICNT, p. 27.

91. Article 150 (1B[i]), ibid., p. 25.

92. Articles 154-160, ibid., pp. 27-30.

93. Elliot L. Richardson, "Law of the Sea Conference: Problems and Progress," Department of State Bulletin 77 (September 19, 1977), pp. 389-91, at 390.

94. Ibid., pp. 390-91.

95. Ibid., pp. 389, 391. On the ICNT, see also Nicholas Raymond, "Sea Law: The Unpleasant Options," Ocean World, January 1978, pp. 4-8, 10-12, 28.

96. "Law of the Sea: An Impasse on Seabeds. A Conversation with Ambassador Elliot Richardson," Sea Power 20 (September 1977):23-28, at 25-26. Richardson also mentioned that nonparties which might receive benefits according to the ICNT would include groups like the Palestine Liberation Organization (PLO).

97. Ibid., p. 27.

98. For background and discussion, see Dana B. Ott, "An Analysis of Deep Seabed Mining Legislation," Natural Resources Lawyer 10 (1977):591-604.

99. U.S. Congress, House, Merchant Marine and Fisheries Committee, Deep Seabed Mining, Hearings, 95th Cong., 1st Sess., March 17, 18, April 19, 26, 27, May 11 and 20, 1977, p. 1.

100. Ibid., p. 58.

101. Ibid., pp. 53-77.

102. Ibid., pp. 444-59.

103. U.S. Congress, House, Merchant Marine and Fisheries Committee, Deep Seabed Hard Minerals Act, Rept. 95-588, part 1, 95th Cong., 1st Sess., August 9, 1977, especially pp. 17-21.

104. U.S. Congress, Senate, Energy and Natural Resources, and Commerce, Science, and Transportation Committees, Mining of the Deep Seabed, Joint Hearings, 95th Cong., 1st Sess., September 19, 20, and October 4, 1977, pp. 2, 61.

105. Ibid., pp. 124-59.

106. Ibid., pp. 378-83.

107. U.S. Congress, Senate, Interior and Insular Affairs Committee, Promoting the Orderly Development of Hard Mineral Resources in the Deep Seabed, Pending Adoption of an International Regime Relating Thereto, Rept. 95-588, part 2, 95th Cong., 1st Sess., November 7, 1977, especially pp. 15-18

108. U.S. Congress, House, International Relations Committee, Deep Seabed Hard Minerals Resources Act, Hearings and Markup, 95th Cong., 2d Sess., January 23, 24, 25, 31, February 7 and 8, 1978, p. 28.

109. Ibid.

110. U.S. Congress, House, International Relations Committee, Deep Seabed Hard Mineral Resources Act, Rept. 95-588, part 3, 95th Cong., 2d Sess., February 16, 1978, pp. 1-11.

111. U.S. Congress, House, Ways and Means Committee, Explanation of Ways and Means Committee Amendment to H.R. 3350 (Deep Seabed Hard Mineral Resources Act), Print, 95th Cong., 2d Sess., June 7, 1978, p. 1.

112. Ann Pelham, "House Endorses Seabed Mining by U.S. Companies," Congressional Quarterly Weekly Report 36 (July 29, 1978):2004-05; and Pelham, "Seabed Mining Bill Awaiting Action by Senate Committee," Congressional Quarterly Weekly Report 36 (August 5, 1978):2073-74.

113. Interviews with congressional staff members, March 29, 1979.

114. U.S. Congress, Senate, Energy and Natural Resources, and Commerce, Science, and Transportation Committees, Deep Seabed Mineral Resources Act, S. Rpt. 95-1125, 95th Cong., 2d Sess., August 18, 1978, p. 58.

115. U.S. Congress, Senate, Foreign Relations Committee, Deep Seabed Hard Mineral Resources Act, Hearing, 95th Cong., 2d Sess., August 17, 1978, p. 255.

116. U.S. Congress, Senate, Foreign Relations Committee, Deep Seabed Mineral Resources Act, S. Rpt. 95-1180, 95th Cong., 2d Sess., September 11, 1978, p. 5.

117. Friedman, "The Law of the Sea Game," p. 24.

118. U.S. Congress, Senate, Energy and Natural Resources and Commerce, Science, and Transportation Committees, Deep Seabed Mineral Resources Act, Joint Hearings, 96th Cong., 1st Sess., March 29 and April 9, 1979, p. 2.

119. Ibid., pp. 112-13.

120. Ibid., p. 114.

121. Ibid., passim, especially pp. 115 and 120.

122. Ibid., p. 262.

123. Ibid., p. 178.

124. U.S. Congress, Senate, Foreign Relations Committee, Deep Seabed Hard Minerals Act, Hearing, 96th Cong., 1st Sess., June 13, 1979, p. 82.

125. U.S. Congress, Senate, Energy and Natural Resources, Commerce, Science and Transportation, and Foreign Relations Committees, Deep Seabed Mineral Resources Act, Senate Report No. 96-307, 96th Cong., 1st Sess., August 9, 1979.

126. U.S. Congress, Senate, Finance Committee, Title V of the Deep Seabed Mineral Resources Act, S. Rept. 76-357, 96th Cong., 1st Sess., October 3, 1979.

127. U.S. Congress, Senate, Environment and Public Works Committee, Deep Seabed Mineral Resources Act, S. Rpt. 96-360, 96th Cong., 1st Sess., October 9, 1979.

128. U.S. Congress, House, Interior and Insular Affairs Committee, Development of the Hard Mineral Resources of the Deep Seabed, Hearings, 96th Cong., 1st Sess., May 1 and 22, 1979, p. 55.

129. U.S. Congress, House, Merchant Marine and Fisheries Committee, Law of the Sea, Hearings, 96th Cong., 1st Sess., February 27, May 22 and 23, June 7, 1979, p. 38.

130. Ibid., p. 361.

131. U.S. Congress, House, Interior and Insular Affairs Committee, Promoting the Orderly Development of Hard Mineral Resources in the Deep Seabed, Pending Adoption of an International Regime Relating Thereto, H. Rept. 96-411, part 1, 96th Cong., 1st Sess., August 2, 1979.

132. U.S. Congress, House, Merchant Marine and Fisheries Committee, Deep Seabed Mining, H. Rpt. 96-411, part 2, 96th Cong., 1st Sess., August 17, 1979.

133. U.S. Congress, House, Ways and Means Committee, Deep Seabed Hard Mineral Resources Act, H. Rpt. 96-411, part 3, 96th Cong., 1st Sess., November 2, 1979.

134. U.S. Congress, House, Foreign Affairs Committee, Deep Seabed Hard Mineral Resources Act, Hearings and Markup, 96th Cong., 1st and 2d Sess., July 11, November 1, December 19, 1979, April 30, 1980, p. 8.

135. Ibid., especially pp. 11-13, 25-26.

136. Ibid., pp. 64-87, quotation at 76.

137. Ibid., pp. 90-99.

138. U.S. Congress, House, Foreign Affairs Committee, Deep Seabed Hard Mineral Resources Act, H. Rpt. 96-411, part IV, 96th Cong., 2d Sess., May 15, 1980, passim.

139. Congressional Record 125:179 (December 14, 1979): S18510-64.

140. Ibid., S18510-11.

141. Ibid., S18515.

142. Ibid., S18530.

143. Congressional Record 126:93 (June 9, 1980):H4631-68.

144. Ibid., H4641.

145. Congressional Record 126:104 (June 23, 1980):S7927-34.

146. Congressional Record 126:106 (June 25, 1980):H5665-68.

147. Ibid., H5667.

148. "Deep Seabed Hard Mineral Resources Act: White House Statement on H.R. 2759, July 3, 1980," Weekly Compilation of Presidential Documents 16 (July 7, 1980):1284-85.

149. See Section 118, Public Law 96-283, June 28, 1980 (94 STAT 553).

150. See Section 201, ibid.

151. Ibid.

152. See Section 102, ibid.

153. Ibid.

7

THE DRAFT CONVENTION AND
THE REAGAN REVIEW

INTERNATIONAL PROGRESS

The 1977 negotiating text, the ICNT, had been termed "fundamentally unacceptable" by Ambassador Richardson. Within a few months the U.S. administration had decided to support domestic legislation, partly to give certain assurances to industry, partly to put pressure on the international negotiations and the Group of 77 in particular.

It may appear that 1977 was a low point in UNCLOS III's history. And yet something had happened: the conflict was now not about the parallel system as such, but about its balance.[1] A "formula" had been reached. It was now a question of details. Details about production limits, financial arrangements, transfer of technology, and decision making. Gradually the positions were moving closer over the next three to four years.

The first part of the seventh session, in the spring of 1978, identified seven core issues and established a special negotiating group (NG) for each:

NG 1: System of exploration and exploitation and resource policy (chairman: Frank Njenga, Kenya).

NG 2: Financial arrangements (chairman: Tommy Koh, Singapore).

NG 3: Organs of the Authority, their composition, powers, and functions (chairman: Paul Engo, Cameroon).

NG 4: Access of landlocked and geographically disadvantaged states to the living resources of the exclusive economic zone (chairman: Satya Nandan, Fiji).

NG 5: Settlement of disputes relating to the exercise of the sovereign rights of coastal states in the economic zone (chairman: Constantine Stravopoulos, Greece).

NG 6: Delimitation of the outer edge of the continental margin (chairman: Andres Aguilar, Venezuela).

NG 7: Delimitation of maritime boundaries between adjacent and opposite states (chairman: E. J. Manner, Finland). [2]

Before the eighth session in 1979, Ambassador Richardson reported to the House Foreign Affairs Committee that UNCLOS III was "closer to the stage of a final showdown on outstanding issues."[3] After the first part of the eighth session Richardson reported "more than 20 significant improvements," which were incorporated into a revision of the ICNT. [4]

The first part of the ninth session in the spring of 1980 produced a second revision of the ICNT, and Richardson reported to Congress: "Only somewhere between 6 and 10 substantive problems remain to be negotiated."[5] The second part of the ninth session in the summer of 1980 produced more progress and a third revision of the ICNT. Richardson now reported to Congress:

> The single most important statement to be made about
> the Geneva session is that it concluded with very little
> left to be done at the 10th session, which has been
> scheduled for March 9 to April 17, 1981, with the
> possibility of extension for an additional week. [6]

According to Richardson, "most participants left Geneva believing that the Conference could and should conclude its work at the 10th session."[7] Basically four issues remained to be dealt with: the so-called three Ps: Participation, the Preparatory Commission (PrepCom), and Preparatory Investment Protection (PIP); and the issue of delimitation of continental shelves and economic zones between adjacent and opposite states. The problem in respect to participation was mainly the question of whether liberation movements such as the Palestine Liberation Organization (PLO) should be allowed to participate. The United States was strongly against that idea. The United States, however, could accept the participation of international integration organizations such as the European Community. The PrepCom would design the administrative structures and prepare the rules, regulations, and procedures of the future ISA. The actual charter of this PrepCom had still to be worked out. PIP involved "measures necessary to encourage seabed mining investment" in the interim period between the agreement on a convention and its entry into force. Delimitation, finally, was a question of reconciling, on the one hand, the states that advocated the application of the median or equidistance line and, on the other hand, the states that advocated "equitable principles."[8]

The most important accomplishment of the resumed ninth session was a seabed mining package, which included a compromise on decision-making procedures of the council of the ISA. Explained Richardson:

> The deadlock was broken by a proposal to make decisions on the most sensitive issues subject to consensus. The issues that have in fact been made subject to consensus are those concerning production policies and limitations, adoption of rules, regulations, and procedures of the Authority, and the adoption of amendments to the seabed mining part of the convention, including the relevant annexes.[9]

Other substantive decisions were made subject to a three-fourths majority vote of those present and voting or a two-thirds majority, depending on their importance.[10]

Speaking to the American Mining Congress at San Francisco on September 24, 1980, Ambassador Richardson said: "The result by any standard is an unprecedented achievement for multilateral negotiation." He tried to convince the miners that they, too, had an interest in the establishment of a universally recognized international regime. Such a regime was the only sure way of removing various threats and uncertainties.[11] Richardson suggested that investors were entitled to

assured access to the opportunity to exploit a specific mine-
    site,
a fair chance to earn a return on investment commensurate with
    the risk undertaken, and
solid protection against the arbitrary or unpredictable use or abuse
    of the Authority's power.

He went on to argue forcefully that these requirements were satisfied by the Draft Convention. The contract approval process was "fair, clear, and well-nigh automatic." If certain objective requirements were met, a "plan of work" had to be approved by the Legal and Technical Commission. Once approved by that commission a plan of work could only be disapproved by the ISA Council by consensus.[12]

The production ceiling was "not likely to bar access for any qualified miner." It was limited in duration and a "floor" had been added. There would thus be "sufficient tonnage under any reasonable set of assumptions."[13]

Concerning return of investment it was Richardson's view that
"the treaty's financial provisions are not worse than most other
tax systems." The transfer of technology provisions were "toler-
able." Transfer would be on "fair and reasonable commercial
terms and conditions." The obligation was limited to ten years
after the Enterprise began commercial production, and the obligation could only be invoked after a contract was in effect and it had
turned out to be impossible to buy the technology on the open market. Any dispute was further subject to commercial arbitration.[14]

Various provisions of the Draft Convention would protect
against the abuse of power. Most important in this respect was
"the care with which the powers and functions of the Authority have
been allocated." The three-tiered voting system would prevent the
council from "taking majority action contrary to the vital economic
interests of its seabed mining and consumer members." And the
United States had "now been effectively assured a seat in the
Council" by the new provision that gave each interest group—most
important miners, consumers, and so forth—represented on the
36-nation Council "the right to select its own representatives."[15]

THE MINING INDUSTRY STRIKES BACK

The mining industry did not buy the Richardson argument.
When President Carter lost the election on November 2, 1980 to
Ronald Reagan the industry saw a new chance. The president-elect
was bombarded by letters from various components of the industry
and their allies, including members of Congress. Actually, the
American Mining Congress had strongly criticized the Draft Treaty
in a Declaration of Policy, adopted September 21, 1980:

Under the present draft of the Treaty, access by U.S.
citizens is neither assured nor nondiscriminatory.
Broad discretionary powers would be vested in an
"International Seabed Authority," with the opportunity
for effective obstruction by a small number of nations,
including an assured veto power in the U.S.S.R. and
its satellites. A quota is imposed on access by any
one nation and on mineral production in the aggregate.
Transfer of the highly advanced U.S. ocean systems
and mineral processing technology to an international
institution and less developed countries (and assuredly
in practice on to Eastern Bloc nations) is mandated.
The rights of the companies who would proceed with
exploration (and perhaps mining) of the resources

before entry into force of the Treaty are not assured.
It is doubtful that disputes could be fairly and effectively settled. A centrally planned, not market-
oriented economic system is established. [16]

Instead, the AMC suggested that the United States "should move
promptly to implement the reciprocating states provisions" of the
Deep Seabed Hard Minerals Act. [17]

In the beginning of December, Congressmen John B. Breaux
(D-La.) and 13 other members of Congress, including Edward J.
Derwinski (R-Ill.), Robert J. Lagomarsino (R-Calif.), and Jim
Santini (D-Nev.) wrote president-elect Ronald Reagan and suggested a review of the Draft Treaty. The group complained about
the provisions in respect to access, navigation, transfer of technology, revenue sharing, ISA powers, and Soviet and Third World
influence. [18]

The letter from the congressmen was followed up by a letter
from J. Allen Overton, Jr., president of the AMC, to the president-
elect on December 15, 1980. The AMC concurred in the recommendation to review the treaty. The letter also referred to the
national platform of the Republican Party in which it had been stated:

Multilateral negotiations have thus far insufficiently
focused attention on U.S. long-term security requirements. A pertinent example of this phenomenon is the
Law of the Sea Conference, where negotiations have
served to inhibit U.S. exploitation of the sea-bed for
its abundant mineral resources. [19]

In the platform it had further been stated:

A Republican Administration will conduct multilateral negotiations in a manner that reflects
America's abilities and long-term interest in access to raw material and energy resources. [20]

The letter to the president-elect stressed the strategic importance
of the minerals in question.

An earlier letter from Marne A. Dubs, chairman of the AMC
Committee on Undersea Mineral Resources, to George H. Aldrich,
the acting special representative to the Law of the Sea Conference,
had strongly criticized the Carter administration for failing to get
sufficient protection of preparatory investments into the Draft Convention. "Our more basic critiques, advice and suggestions have
been ignored," said Dubs, "and the Delegation has failed to negotiate

improvements . . . necessary to assure continued U.S. access to the strategic metals contained in ocean nodules."[21]

The National Ocean Industries Association also wrote the president-elect endorsing the idea of a treaty review: "We believe the draft treaty is heavily weighted against American interests."[22]

THE REAGAN REVIEW

The Reagan administration took office in January 1981. George H. Aldrich, who had been Richardson's deputy, remained as acting head of the U.S. UNCLOS team for the moment. Would the spring session of UNCLOS III become the last one as planned, or would the Reagan administration listen to the critiques of the Draft Convention?

It wasn't until March 2 that a senior interagency group met to discuss the law of the sea situation. The meeting was chaired by Deputy Secretary of State William P. Clark and, according to a newspaper account, "orchestrated" by James L. Malone, an incoming assistant secretary of state. Malone, who had been general counsel of the Arms Control and Disarmament Agency (ACDA) during 1973-76, is said to have relied heavily on Leigh S. Ratiner, a Washington attorney, who had been on the U.S. UNCLOS team during the Nixon and Ford administrations, and who had been a lobbyist for Kennecott Copper from January 1977 to 1979. Among those actively criticizing the Draft Law of the Sea Convention at the March 2 interagency meeting was also Deputy Secretary of Defense C. Fred Ikle, who had been head of ACDA when Malone was there.[23]

The March 2 interagency meeting resulted in the following statement issued by the Department of State that same day:

> After consultations with the other interested Departments and Agencies of the United States Government, the Secretary of State has instructed our representative to the UN Law of the Sea Conference to seek to ensure that the negotiations do not end at the present session of the Conference, pending a policy review by the United States Government. The interested Departments and Agencies have begun studies of the serious problems raised by the Draft Convention, and these will be the subject of a thorough review which will determine our position toward the negotiations.[24]

According to the New York Times, State Department officials explained the decision by a number of factors, "including intense pressure from private mining interests," and the plank in the Republican Party's platform that had critized the Law of the Sea Conference. [25]

In New York diplomats were arriving for what they believed would be the last negotiating session of UNCLOS when the U.S. decision was announced. "I am very upset," said Tommy Koh of Singapore, an influential participant in the international negotiations. "This is a major setback and I am extremely worried," said Koh. [26] "The world cannot stand still forever, waiting on Washington," was the comment from a NATO country ambassador, and many diplomats at the U.N. now feared that the intricate UNCLOS package might begin to unravel. [27]

On March 5 the Senate Foreign Relations Committee held hearings on the law of the sea, three days after the administration's decision to conduct a review and four days before the start of the tenth session of UNCLOS III. George Taft, who was still the State Department's director of the Office of the Law of the Sea Negotiations spoke about the remaining problems as already identified during the Carter administration: participation, the organization and functions of the Preparatory Commission, and preparatory investment protection. The Defense Department representative, Acting Under Secretary of Defense for Policy and International Security Affairs Franklin D. Kramer, announced that his department had "no final position" on the Draft Treaty. [28]

Representatives of resource related departments, however, were more critical. The Interior Department's Deputy Assistant Secretary of Energy and Minerals William P. Pendley talked about the "serious problems" of the Draft Convention in respect to "the availability of strategic and critical minerals" and the need for assured access to manganese nodules. According to the Interior's view, the Treaty did "not provide for assured access," nor did it "establish a secure investment climate." The acting administrator of the Commerce Department's National Oceanic and Atmospheric Administration (NOAA), James P. Walsh, concluded that his department did "not believe that the draft treaty text contains sufficient protection of the U.S. deep seabed mining companies." [29]

The administration's decision to conduct a review was not uniformly accepted in Washington. Senator Claiborne Pell (D-R.I.) was "deeply disappointed and troubled" by the decision. He hoped that President Reagan would be able to resist "the pleas of the mining industry and not permit that special interest to stand alone in the way of a fair and balanced treaty that would substantially advance American military and economic interests." [30]

Also, former special representative to UNCLOS, Elliot L. Richardson, warned the new administration that the United States had come to the conference "with a broader array of interests, perhaps, than any other single country." Most of these interests were well protected in the Draft Treaty and the proposed deep seabed mining regime was "workable."[31] It was necessary for the administration to "take a realistic view of the alternative":

> It is necessary at least to identify the fact that the seabed mining industry would not face plain sailing under U.S. domestic legislation even though the arrangements of that legislation are reciprocated by a handful of other advanced industrial countries.[32]

According to Richardson it was conceded by all international lawyers that there was "no way under which a single country or group of countries" could "acquire a legal right to exploit a particular area of the sea bottom." So unilateralism could have serious costs. Since the Draft Treaty was a package deal other countries might withdraw some of their concessions, for instance in respect to navigational rights.[33]

Needless to say, the mining industry supported the administration's decision to review the treaty. And their man on Capitol Hill, Congressman John B. Breaux, testified that the decision had sent a message "to the Third World and other members (sic) of the Soviet Bloc": "We will not meekly submit to the new international economic order; we will not mildly consent to the ruin of our system of values as a free enterprise society."[34]

On March 7 Deputy Secretary of State William P. Clark told the acting head of the U.S. delegation to UNCLOS, George H. Aldrich, that he was dismissed. So were several other members of the U.S. delegation, including George D. Taft, director of the Law of the Sea Office. Elliot L. Richardson told the New York Times that he was both "surprised and puzzled." He called the administration's move "a second Saturday night massacre," comparing it with October 20, 1973, when he had resigned as attorney general instead of carrying out President Nixon's order to discharge Archibald Cox, the special Watergate prosecutor. The 1973 order incidentally was conveyed by Alexander M. Haig, Jr., then White House chief of staff, later secretary of state.[35]

The administration appointed James L. Malone as the new special representative of the president for the Law of the Sea Conference. Leigh Ratiner was added to the delegation as an "expert."[36] What kind of opinions about the Draft Convention did James Malone have? Judging from his nomination hearings he had none. Pressed by Senator Paul E, Tsongas (D.-Mass.) he said: "I have no strong view as to the matter one way or another."[37]

On March 17 James L. Malone addressed the UNCLOS plenary in New York. He defended the U.S. right to conduct a review. The review would proceed as quickly as possible. He hoped it could be "completed in a few months."[38] Ambassador Tommy Koh of Singapore, who had been elected president of UNCLOS III on March 13, replacing H. Shirley Amerasinghe of Sri Lanka, who had died on December 4, 1980, said that all delegations had appealed to the United States "to organize its domestic affairs in such a way as . . . not to impede the Conference from being able to conclude its work in 1981."[39] The conference therefore considered calling a resumed session in Geneva in August. However, on April 14 the United States told the Conference that its review could not be completed by August.[40] But the conference did none the less decide to hold a resumed session in August, thus putting some pressure on the United States.

Very little was accomplished at the spring session. The other states were waiting for the U.S. review to be concluded. The Group of 77 explicitly refused to discuss one of the four major items on the agenda, preparatory investment protection. Some initial discussions took place in the Preparatory Commission. Delimitation problems were discussed, but no progress reported. Informal talks also continued about the question of participation. But no public report was given. The more interesting thing about the session was that a number of delegations expressed reservations about the "innocent passage" provision for warships through the territorial sea, favoring a change that would require prior authorization of the coastal state for such passage.[41] Some of them were probably trying to send a signal to the United States.

The first indications of the problems being reviewed by the Reagan administration came on April 29, 1981, when James Malone testified before the House Foreign Affairs Committee. His list of concerns sounded very much like those we have heard the mining industry produce:

burdensome international regulation of seabed development,
discriminatory advantages granted to the Enterprise,
transfer of technology provisions compelling the sale of proprietary
    technology,
production limits,
lack of guaranteed U.S. seat on the ISA Council,
a review conference that might adopt changes 20 years after the
    start of production by a two-thirds majority without U.S. consent,
revenue-sharing obligations,
possible benefits to liberation movements, including the PLO, and
lack of preparatory investment protection provisions.[42]

The conclusion followed: "it is the best judgment of this administration that this draft convention would not obtain the advice and consent of the U.S. Senate."[43]

However, some congressmen were not so easy to convince. When they asked questions Malone usually could not answer. It was all a question of what would be the result of the review process. Congressman Joel Pritchard (R-Wash.) and the committee chairman, Clement J. Zablocki (D-Wis.) were clearly frustrated. Pritchard at one point told Malone: "I must say that your answers here today really do not wash." And at another point Zablocki concluded: "I see it is futile to pursue the issue."[44]

Malone could give no indication of which might be the outcome of the review, only that it would determine "the net national interest of the United States" including also the national security interest.[45] Representative Pritchard found the U.S. timetable "very arrogant."[46] What would happen to multilateral negotiations if every state changing administration would conduct a nine-month review?

Some information was given about the organization of the review. It would be conducted at the deputy assistant secretary level and chaired by Theodore G. Kronmiller, the deputy assistant secretary for oceans and fisheries.[47] Kronmiller had been an aide to Congressman Breaux. He had drafted the letter that Breaux and 13 of his colleagues had sent to the president-elect in December.[48] Didn't this mean that the industry now had their man placed strategically in the State Department? Kronmiller is also the author of a three-volume work on the lawfulness of deep seabed mining.[49]

The members of Congress were very interested in congressional input. Would Congress be brought into the process at all, queried Representative Benjamin A. Gilman (R-N.Y.). The answers given by Malone and Kronmiller, who accompanied him, caused Gilman to remark: "It almost seems as though you are negotiating a treaty within our own administration."[50]

On May 14, 1981, Elliot Richardson appeared before the House Foreign Affairs Committee. He addressed "the remarkable persistence of distortions of the draft convention by critics apparently less interested in getting a good treaty than in scuttling any treaty whether satisfactory or not." Contrary to the critics, he maintained that the treaty would give the United States assured access to seabed minerals, an assured seat on the ISA council, and adequate compensation for transfer of technology. U.S. companies would not be required to sell national security-related technology. Liberation movements could only share in economic benefits if the United States concurred.[51]

Richardson strongly argued that the treaty would "bring substantial benefits to the United States." He predicted that "there
will be no investment in deep seabed mining without a treaty."
Reciprocal legislation in a number of states would not be enough.
No secure title to a specific area could be gained that way. Legal
harassment and litigation was the likely outcome. Would a company risk the investment of a billion dollars if the International
Court of Justice was likely to rule that there is no high seas right
to engage in deep seabed mining? Richardson had only supported
U.S. legislation "because we needed the negotiating leverage
created by the perception on the part of the Conference that we
were indeed prepared to go forward under that legislation."[52]

According to Richardson the mining companies had put pressure on the conference and the U.S. delegation to get a better
treaty. But, "their criticisms of the treaty have been picked up
by people whose basic objections to the treaty are essentially
ideological. . . . The shift of ideological content of the national
leadership" from the Carter to the Reagan administration "was
certainly more marked in degree" than the shifts in any recent
election that he could think of.[53] When he had been under secretary of state in 1970, "the paramount and overriding U.S. interest
in the negotiation of a comprehensive treaty was the politico-
military interest in freedom of navigation and overflight; second
came oil and gas; third fisheries; and seabed mining was a distant
fourth."[54] Now the whole thing had been "turned upside down."
Statist goals, clearly, are a matter of perceptions.

As predicted by Malone, the U.S. review had not been completed by the time of the resumed tenth session in August in Geneva.
Other states were increasingly frustrated. Said the Soviet deputy
foreign minister on August 3: "It is easy to imagine where international conferences would be if every new government considered
itself entitled to conduct similar endless 'reviews' of the previously
reached agreements and to make all other participants in international forums wait till such 'reviews' are completed."[55] Similarly,
the chairman of the Group of 77, Inam Ul-Haque of Pakistan, said
on August 10: "The United States government cannot reject the
work of over 150 nations including its own predecessor governments
for almost a decade, for in doing so it would be destroying the principle of good faith negotiations."[56]

These and other statements were made after James Malone
informally had revealed some of the U.S. concerns about Part XI
of the Draft Convention dealing with deep seabed mining. He saw
that part as "a stumbling-block to treaty ratification" in the United
States.[57] However, the United States was still not able to make
concrete proposals.

Most of the other states were determined to show some progress. In respect to the three Ps, progress was reported on two. A seven-article annex to the convention dealing with the participation of international organizations to which member states have transferred competence over some of the matters governed by the convention, such as the European Community, was proposed by President Koh. Progress was also reported on the arrangements for a Preparatory Commission, but important issues in this respect remained unresolved. Preparatory Investment Protection was not considered at the session.[58] The fourth remaining major issue, delimitation, was solved. On the closing day of the session President Koh reported "widespread and substantial support" for a new compromise formula: "The delimitation of the exclusive economic zone [continental shelf] between states with opposite or adjacent coasts shall be affected by agreement on the basis of international law, as referred to in Article 38 of the Statute of the International Court of Justice, in order to achieve an equitable solution."[59]

The formula might not give much direction in the future. But at least two groups of states, those favoring "equitable principles" and those favoring "equidistance" had realized that they couldn't get further. The resumed tenth session also selected Jamaica as the seat of the ISA and the Federal Republic of Germany as the seat of the proposed International Tribunal for the Law of the Sea.[60]

Finally it should be mentioned that the conference decided to upgrade the Draft Convention from an "informal text" to an official document. And a "final decision-making session for the adoption of the convention" was scheduled for New York, March 8–April 30, 1982.[61] President Koh told the press afterward that "with or without the United States—preferably with the United States"—delegations intended to bring the conference to a successful conclusion.[62]

In the meantime Washington was conducting its review. It was not until December that press reports emerged suggesting that the United States would return to the conference and seek improvements. The interdepartmental review had resulted in an "options paper" that suggested renegotiation of four important areas: production limitation, transfer of technology, decision making, and the review conference. A presidential announcement was expected by the end of the month.[63]

It was not until January 29, 1982, however, that President Reagan could announce that the U.S. review had been completed. Most provisions of the Draft Convention had been found acceptable, but some major elements of the deep seabed mining regime were not. However, the United States would return to the negotiations and work to achieve an acceptable treaty. Such a treaty should achieve six U.S. objectives:

—The treaty must not deter development of any deep seabed mineral resources to meet national and world demand.

—The treaty must assure national access to those resources by current and future qualified entities to enhance U.S. security of supply, avoid monopolization of the resources by the operating arm of the international Authority, and promote the economic development of the resources.

—The treaty must provide a decision-making role in the deep seabed regime that fairly reflects and effectively protects the political and economic interests and financial contributions of participating states.

—The treaty must not allow for amendments to come into force without approval of the participating states.

—The treaty must not set other undesirable precedents for international organizations.

—The treaty must be likely to receive the advice and consent of the Senate. In this regard, the convention should not contain provisions for the mandatory transfer of private technology, and participation by and funding for national liberation movements.[64]

According to one observer the review process had been a battle between essentially two views. According to the first view the Draft Treaty was flawed and incompatible with President Reagan's policy. Returning to international negotiations would entail great risks. This basically antitreaty group was led by Theodore Kronmiller and "supported by staff on the domestic side of the White House, the Interior Department and some civilians in the defense establishment as well as some members of Congress."[65] According to another observer the antitreaty group included presidential counselor Edwin Meese, Secretary of the Navy John Lehman, and Undersecretary of Defense for Policy Fred Ikle. The latter two "executed a 180° turn" in the Defense Department's position. Navigational rights were downplayed. Priority was instead given to "strategically essential" seabed minerals.[66]

Opposing the antitreaty group were more pragmatic participants in the review process, including Leigh Ratiner. They recognized problems with the Draft Treaty but believed it worthwhile to return to the negotiations and seek improvements. The president could then later decide whether the resulting changes were sufficient to gain U.S. signature.[67]

THE ELEVENTH SESSION OF UNCLOS III

President Reagan's announcement on January 29 signified that the treaty proponents had won the first round. But there was still

an important round ahead—the eleventh session. Detailed instruc-
tions to the U.S. delegation were only issued on March 8 as the
session started, and, according to Ratiner, they "reflected an interpretation of the President's objectives which was considerably
more constrained than the objectives themselves."[68]

During intersessional meetings, February 24–March 2, the
U.S. representatives had communicated the Reagan objectives in
the form of a comprehensive paper without suggesting specific
language. The Group of 77, however, wanted specific language.
The U.S. negotiators therefore prepared a set of amendments,
known as the "Green Book," which was presented to the Conference
on March 11.[69]

The Green Book, however, went too far. Most other states
saw it as a frontal assault on the parallel system. It could therefore not be accepted as a basis for negotiation. The result was a
stalemate. On the initiative of Canada and Denmark, a group of
smaller industrialized countries, eventually including Australia,
Austria, Canada, Denmark, Finland, Iceland, Ireland, the Netherlands, New Zealand, Norway, Sweden, and Switzerland, known as
Friends of the Conference (FOC), set out to prepare some compromise proposals. Included in these were a more production
oriented Article 150, a proposal that the review conference should
follow the consensus principle of UNCLOS III, a guaranteed U.S.
seat on the ISA Council "as the largest consumer," a more flexible
procedure for approval of applications, and weakened rules concerning transfer of technology.[70]

The U.S. delegation concluded that some of the FOC proposals
were adequate bases for addressing U.S. concerns, for example,
the proposals concerning contract approval and transfer of technology. But the FOC proposal concerning the review conference
was insufficient, and some U.S. concerns, such as production
limitation and decision making, weren't addressed by the FOC.[71]

In the following period both the Group of 77 and the United
States showed some rigidity. The developing countries felt that
they had given enough concessions to the United States already.
A further complication was hinted by a Jamaican delegate, who ob-
served that "the problem with the Americans was they were never
in a position to reveal their bottom line."[72] Other delegations
were aware of internal U.S. disagreements. There was therefore
a great amount of uncertainty as to whether Malone and Ratiner,
the chief and deputy U.S. representatives, could deliver.[73]

On April 3 Malone and Ratiner had a meeting with Secretary
of State Alexander Haig in Washington. It was agreed that the
United States should no longer insist on complete elimination of
the production limitation. Some greater U.S. flexibility on the

question of voting power of the U.S. and its allies in the ISA Council would also be indicated. [74]

However, Haig was losing influence in Washington. With many of the treaty proponents in New York, the antitreaty coalition had an easy game in Washington. They were joined by Robert Keating, a Defense Department adviser who was a member of the U.S. delegation. While negotiations took place he met with executives of several Fortune 500 companies in Dallas, Houston, and Washington in an effort to build up opposition to the Draft Treaty. And on April 15 he wrote to members of the business community that "the net result of [the Haig concession] will be to further enshrine the principle of the New International Economic Order." [75]

Keating was also instrumental in setting up a meeting between White House Counselor Meese and representatives of the mining industry on April 19. Those present included David Stang representing the Lockheed/Standard Oil of Indiana Consortium, Jeffrey Amsbaugh from the U.S. Steel/Sun Co. Consortium, and Richard Darman, a presidential assistant known to be critical of the Draft Treaty. The only treaty proponent at the meeting is said to have been Marne Dubs of the Kennecott Consortium. At this meeting Meese is said to have reassured the miners that the United States would not compromise. As a matter of fact, Meese is said to have wanted the U.S. negotiators to walk out of the U.N. then and there, but he was argued out of that position. [76] Ratiner describes the situation this way:

> The day-to-day negotiating process was monitored
> both within the delegation and back in Washington so
> closely by individuals who had supported the option
> of withdrawal from the Conference, that any nego-
> tiating move made by the American delegation was
> interpreted as a giant step down the slippery slope to
> compromise of principle and disaster. [77]

According to Ratiner the "countereffort launched" by the antitreaty coalition included "personal attacks" and attacks on the negotiation process that were often "marked by distortion and falsehood." The result was that U.S. negotiators were "held in check and did not make serious compromise proposals" on a number of issues where improvements might have been negotiated. [78]

A majority of the states at UNCLOS III were determined to proceed and solve the officially outstanding issues, the three Ps. A resolution on Preparatory Investment Protection was worked out. It established the concept of pioneer investors, defined as investors having spent $30 million on pioneer activities prior to

January 1, 1983. It was explicitly determined that this included
the four international consortia, Kennecott Consortium, Ocean
Mining Associates, Ocean Management Incorporated, and Ocean
Minerals Company (see Table 7) as well as four national companies
from France, Japan, the Soviet Union, and India.

Developing countries were given extra time, until December 1,
1985, to meet the financial requirements. The central idea of the
PIP resolution was that these pioneer investors would have a priority right to a specific mine site. The ISA Enterprise was guaranteed two production authorizations in the first round of allocation
for pioneer investors.[79] Another resolution was worked out concerning the establishment of a Preparatory Commission that would
administer PIP, prepare for the establishment of the ISA, and develop rates and regulations for deep seabed mining. The PrepCom
could start working 50 to 90 days after the convention had received
50 signatures.[80]

A third major step forward was a participation package that
gave international organizations that have taken over powers from
member states in respect to some ocean matters a right to accede
to the treaty under certain circumstances. National liberation
movements would be entitled to sign the Final Act in their capacity
as observers. Such signature would give them the right to participate in the deliberations of the PrepCom and later the ISA as observers.[81]

Despite inflexibility on the part of some negotiators, the deep
seabed section of the Draft Treaty, Part XI, did not remain unchanged. UNCLOS President Tommy Koh established himself as
arbiter. Eventually he suggested some changes that were incorporated in the Draft Treaty. As will be seen, some ideas were
borrowed from the FOC proposals. The United States was guaranteed a seat on the ISA Council as the largest consumer. The objectives of the ISA were made more production oriented, and the
votes needed for treaty amendments at the review conference were
raised from two-thirds to three-fourths.[82] But, states the U.S.
delegation report: "When Conference President Koh's last report
appeared on April 29, it became clear that the changes to the seabed mining provisions of the text failed to meet any of the U.S.
objectives. Consequently, the U.S. demanded that a recorded vote
be taken on the adoption of the Convention."[83]

REAGAN'S 'NO'

More than a decade's effort to arrive at a law of the sea
agreement by consensus ended on April 30, 1982. The conference

TABLE 7

International Deep Seabed Mining Consortia

Consortium	Participants	Country	Share (percent)	Spending until 1982	1982 Budget
Kennecott Consortium	SOHIO	U.S.	40	$50 million	$1 million
	Rio Tinto-Zinc	U.K.	12		
	Consolidated Gold Fields	U.K.	12		
	British Petroleum	U.K.	12		
	Mitsubishi	Japan	12		
Ocean Mining	U.S. Steel	U.S.	25	$100 million	$10 million
	Union Minière	Belgium	25		
	Sun	U.S.	25		
	Ente Nazionale Idrocarburi (ENI)	Italy	25		
Ocean Management Inc.	INCO	Canada	25	$60 million	$2 million
	AMR	West Germany	25		
	SEOCO	U.S.	25		
	DOMCO	Japan	25		
Ocean Minerals Co.	Standard Oil (Indiana)	U.S.	30.7	$120 million	$5 million
	Lockheed	U.S.	30.7		
	Royal Dutch Petroleum	Netherlands	30.7		
	Royal Bos Kalis Westminster	Netherlands	7.9		

Sources: Tom Alexander, "The Reaganites Misadventure at Sea, Fortune, August 23, 1982, p. 134; and David Tonge, "Why the 'Miners' Are Wary," Financial Times, April 20, 1982.

adopted the Draft Convention together with four resolutions, making up the package, by a vote of 130 in favor, 4 against, and with 17 abstentions. The United States and three other countries voted against: Israel, because of possible PLO signature of the Final Act; and Turkey and Venezuela because of problems with delimitation provisions. Abstaining were six European Economic Community (EEC) countries: Belgium, West Germany, Italy, Luxembourg, the Netherlands, and the United Kingdom, as well as the Soviet Union and its allies, except Rumania. Also abstaining were Spain and Thailand. Third World countries overwhelmingly voted in favor; as did a number of smaller industrialized countries, including the five Nordic countries. Finally, and not least, three potential seabed mining industrialized countries were included among those voting in favor, Japan, France, and Canada.[84]

According to Malone, speaking to the UNCLOS plenary on April 30, the United States had voted against the treaty "for reasons of deep conviction and principle."[85] After this it came as no great surprise that President Reagan announced on July 9, 1982, that the United States would not sign the convention as adopted by UNCLOS III.[86] The United States had decided to go it alone. Unilateralism had finally won; so had free market ideology—at least for the moment.

The decision not to sign the treaty was taken at a meeting of the National Security Council (NSC) on June 29. According to Washington Post columnist Lou Cannon the president's comment on that occasion was: "We are policed and patrolled on land and there is so much regulation that I kind of thought that when you go out on the high seas you can do what you want."[87] The leader of the so-called "Free World" had spoken. And the U.S. mining industry strongly supported him.[88] The losers might be more inclusive U.S. interests—not to speak of world community interests.

The June 29 NSC meeting, incidentally, was presided by Edwin Meese rather than William Clark, the titular head of the NSC. Walter Stoessel, Jr., the acting secretary of state reportedly offered no "official" State Department position. Only Secretary of Transportation Drew Lewis supported further negotiations. Secretary of Commerce Malcolm Baldrige, who had been expected to support further negotiations, failed to come through, admitting that he had not read his briefing book.[89] Or was it just concurrence-seeking behavior, the kind of "groupthink" phenomenon that psychologist Irving L. Janis argues can explain many U.S. foreign policy decisions and fiascoes?[90]

NOTES

1. For a perceptive study of the international seabed nego-
tiations, see Jesper Grolin, "The Deep Seabed: A North-South
Perspective," in Finn Laursen, ed., Toward a New International
Marine Order (The Hague: Martinus Nijhoff, 1982), pp. 119-49.

2. Lee Kimball, "UNCLOS Gains Momentum," Marine
Policy 2 (October 1978):334-37, at 335.

3. U.S. Congress, House, Foreign Affairs Committee,
Briefing on the Eighth Session of the Third United Nations Confer-
ence on the Law of the Sea, Hearing, 96th Cong., 1st Sess.,
March 7, 1979, p. 2.

4. U.S. Congress, House, Foreign Affairs Committee,
The Status of the Third United Nations Conference on the Law of the
Sea, Hearing, 96th Cong., 1st Sess., May 16, 1979, pp. 3-4.

5. U.S. Congress, House, Foreign Affairs Committee,
The Status of the Third United Nations Conference on the Law of
the Sea, Spring 1980, Hearing, 96th Cong., 2nd Sess., April 17,
1980, p. 2.

6. U.S. Congress, House, Foreign Affairs Committee,
The 1980 Geneva Session and Status of the Negotiations on the Law
of Sea, Hearing, 96th Cong., 2nd Sess., October 1, 1980, p. 2.

7. Ibid.

8. Ibid., passim. See also Elliot L. Richardson, "Concluding the Law Conference: Critical Remaining Steps," Columbia
Journal of World Business 15 (Winter 1980):42-44.

9. House, Foreign Affairs Committee, The 1980 Geneva
Session, p. 3.

10. See also Lee Kimball and Adolf R. H. Schneider, "At
the Threshold of a Sea Convention," Environmental Policy and Law
6 (1980):117-24, at 119. For the detailed provisions, see United
Nations, Third Conference in the Law of the Sea, "Draft Convention on the Law of the Sea," U.N. Doc. A/CONF. 62/L. 78,
28 Aug. 1981.

11. Elliot L. Richardson, "Seabed Mining and Law of the
Sea," Department of State Bulletin 80 (December 1980), pp. 60-54,
at 61.

12. Ibid., pp. 61-62.

13. Ibid., p. 62.

14. Ibid., pp. 62-63.

15. Ibid., p. 63.

16. Entered, U.S. Congress, Senate, Foreign Relations
Committee, Law of the Sea Negotiations, Hearing, 97th Cong., 1st
Sess., March 5, 1981, pp. 81-82, quotation at 82.

17. Ibid.

18. Ibid., pp. 144-45 (December 10, 1980 is given as the date in this publication. A copy provided by the AMC to the author gives the date of December 3, 1980).

19. Entered, ibid., pp. 158-59, quotation at 158.

20. Ibid.

21. Letter from Marne A. Dubs to Hon. George H. Aldrich, December 5, 1980. (Copy provided by the AMC.)

22. Entered, Senate, Foreign Relations Committee, Law of the Sea Negotiations, March 5, 1981, p. 155.

23. Nicholas Burnett, "The Ex-Kennecott Lobbyist and the Scuttled Sea Law," Washington Post, March 22, 1981, pp. D1 and D4.

24. Quoted from Bernard H. Oxman, "The Third United Nations Conference on the Law of the Sea. The Tenth Session (1981)," American Journal of International Law 76 (January 1982): 1-23, at 2.

25. Bernard Gwertzman, "U.S. Bars Treaty for Now on Use of Sea Resources," New York Times, March 4, 1981, pp. A1 and A-11. See also Don Oberdorfer, "Sea Law Treaty Blocked at White House," Washington Post, March 4, 1981, pp. A1 and A4.

26. Quoted from Bernard D. Nossiter, "Reagan's Delay in Sea Pact a Source of Dismay at U.N.," New York Times, March 5, 1981, p. A4.

27. Louis Halasz, "U.S. Shift on Sea Pact Upsets Many at U.N.," Washington Star, March 5, 1981, p. A11.

28. U.S. Congress, Senate, Foreign Relations Committee, Law of the Sea Negotiations, Hearing, 97th Cong., 1st Sess., March 5, 1981, pp. 1-4, 7-8.

29. Ibid., pp. 4-7, 8-10.

30. Ibid., pp. 13, 15.

31. Ibid., pp. 23-24.

32. Ibid., p. 25.

33. Ibid., passim. See also "Richardson Warns Against Revamping Law of Sea Treaty," Washington Post, March 6, 1981, p. A32.

34. Ibid., p. 37.

35. Bernard Gwertzman, "President Replaces Top U.S. Diplomats at Law of Sea Talks," New York Times, March 9, 1981, p. 1.

36. Ibid.

37. U.S. Congress, Senate, Foreign Relations Committee, Nomination of James L. Malone, Hearings, 97th Cong., 1st Sess., March 14 and April 2, 1981, p. 22.

38. Statement by Ambassador Malone, Plenary, March 17, 1981 (copy provided by U.S. State Department).

39. U.N. Press Release SEA/445, 16 April 1981, p. 4.

40. Lee Kimball, "U.S. Delegation Told Not to Seek End of Negotiations at Tenth Session," Soundings 6:1 (April-May 1981):1, 4.

41. U.N. Press Release SEA/445, p. 10. See also Lee Kimball, "Update—the Tenth Session," Marine Policy 5 (July 1981): 287-90.

42. U.S. Congress, House, Foreign Affairs Committee, U.S. Policy and the Third United Nations Conference on the Law of the Sea, Hearings, 97th Cong., 1st Sess., April 29 and May 14, 1980, pp. 3-5.

43. Ibid., p. 5.

44. Ibid., passim, quotations at pp. 16 and 19.

45. Ibid., p. 8.

46. Ibid., p. 17.

47. Ibid., pp. 8-9.

48. Burnett, "The Ex-Kennecott Lobbyist," p. D4.

49. Theodore G. Kronmiller, The Lawfulness of Deep Seabed Mining, 3 vols. (New York: Oceana Publications, 1980 and 1981). Vol. 3 with G. Wayne Smith.

50. U.S. Policy and the Third United Nations Conference, p. 24.

51. Ibid., pp. 28-29.

52. Ibid., pp. 30, 35-36, 48.

53. Ibid., pp. 36, 38.

54. Ibid., p. 39.

55. Quoted in Oxman, "The Third United Nations Conference on the Law of the Sea: The Tenth Session (1981)," p. 5.

56. Quoted, ibid.

57. U.N. Press Release SEA/151 (Geneva: 28 August 1981), p. 6.

58. Cecily Murphy, "Was Any Progress Made in Geneva?" Soundings 6:3 (September 1981):1-3; and Lee Kimball, "The Eleventh Hour," Marine Policy 6 (January 1982):69-71.

59. U.N. Press Release SEA/151, p. 15.

60. Ibid., p. 2.

61. Ibid., p. 5.

62. U.N. Press Release SEA/152 (Geneva: 28 August 1981), p. 2. See also Iain Guest, "Nations at Sea Law Talks Ready to Complete Treaty Without U.S.," International Herald Tribune, 29-30 August 1981, p. 1.

63. Bernard D. Nossiter, "Reagan Urged to Seek 4 Changes in Draft Treaty on Law of the Sea," International Herald Tribune, December 11, 1981, p. 3.

64. "Third United Nations Conference on the Law of the Sea: Statement by the President, January 29, 1982," Weekly Compilation of Presidential Documents 18 (February 1, 1982):94-95. See also James L. Malone, "U.S. Participation in Law of the Sea Conference," Department of State Bulletin 82 (May 1982), pp. 61-63; and Eliot Marshall, "U.S. Readies for Confrontation on Sea Law," Science 215 (March 19, 1982):1480-81.

65. Leigh S. Ratiner, "The Law of the Sea: A Crossroads for American Foreign Policy," Foreign Affairs 60 (Summer 1982): 1006-21, at 1008. See also Theodore G. Kronmiller, "Law of the Sea: An Administration Review of Mineral Supply Issues," Mining Congress Journal, March 1982, pp. 41-43.

66. Jennifer Seymour Whitaker, "Outside the Mainstream," Atlantic, October 1982, pp. 18-26, at 19.

67. Ratiner, "The Law of the Sea," p. 1009.

68. Ibid., p. 1009.

69. Report of the United States Delegation to the Eleventh Session of the United Nations Conference on the Law of the Sea, March 8-April 30, 1982 (Washington, D.C.: State Department, June 1982), p. 2. (Hereafter cited as U.S. Delegation Report, 1982.)

70. Denmark, Foreign Ministry, Beretning. FN's 3. havretskonference. Mødesamlingen, New York, 8. marts-30. april 1982 (Copenhagen, July 1982), 2, 7, 19. (Hereafter cited as Danish delegation report, 1982.)

71. US Delegation Report, 1982, p. 3.

72. Quoted, Whitaker, "Outside the Mainstream," p. 21.

73. Interview material.

74. U.S. Delegation Report, 1982, p. 4; and Daniel D. Nossiter, "Underwater Treaty: The Fascinating Story of How the Law of the Sea Was Sunk," Barron's, July 26, 1982, pp. 10-11, 19, at 11.

75. Quoted from Nossiter, "Underwater Treaty," p. 11.

76. Ibid., pp. 10-11.

77. Ratiner, "The Law of the Sea," p. 1013.

78. Ibid., p. 1013.

79. U.S. Delegation Report, 1982, pp. 8-10.

80. Ibid., p. 11; Danish Delegation Report, 1982, p. 16.

81. U.S. Delegation Report, 1982, pp. 13-14.

82. Ibid., pp. 5-6.

83. Ibid., p. 6.

84. U.N. Press Release SEA/494 (New York, 30 April 1982), p. 10. See also "Sea Law—A Rendezvous with History," UN Chronicle 19 (June 1982):3-22, at 13.

85. U.S. Delegation Report, 1982, p. 97. See also Bernard D. Nossiter, "Sea Treaty Approved Despite U.S. 'No' Vote," International Herald Tribune, May 3, 1982, p. 1.

86. "U.S. Votes Against Law of the Sea Treaty: President's Statement, July 9, 1982," Department of State Bulletin 82 (August 1982), p. 71.

87. Quoted in "A Reagan Viewpoint," Soundings 7 (July 1982): 6.

88. "Statement on the Law of the Sea of the American Mining Congress to the Committee on Foreign Affairs, House of Representatives, August 12, 1982. (Provided by the AMC.)

89. "President Reagan Decides against Signing the Law of the Sea Treaty," Strategic Materials Management 2 (July 15, 1982):1-2, at 2.

90. Irving L. Janis, Victims of Groupthink: A Psychological Study of Foreign-Policy Decisions and Fiascoes (Boston: Houghton Mifflin, 1972).

8

EXPLANATORY ASSESSMENTS

STATIST GOALS

It is time to return to our initial analytical models and hypotheses and discuss their relevance for our understanding of U.S. ocean policy from the Nixon proposals in 1970 to Reagan's "no" to multilateralism in 1982. Our job would be so much easier were we only to draw conclusions about the 1970s because of the continuity of the Nixon, Ford, and Carter administrations. So let us do that first before looking at the problems of interpretation that have been created by Reagan's unilateralism.

We recall the gist of our hypotheses in respect to statist goals: A primary importance of security goals, but also great importance attached to access to resources. There can be no doubt that security interests played a primary role in the considerations of the central U.S. decision makers during the 1970s. The proposals made by the United States in the U.N. Seabed Committee and at UNCLOS III fit the hypotheses quite well. We recall that the first major U.S. proposal was a Draft Convention submitted to the Seabed Committee in Geneva on August 3, 1970, that proposed an International Seabed Area seaward of the 200-meter isobath. The proposal was designed to help arrest the process of "creeping jurisdiction."

Evidence in support of the argument that security interests were of primary importance was also found in congressional hearings. Various central decision makers, including Under Secretary of State Elliot L. Richardson in 1970, argued against broad U.S. claims to ocean resources because such claims would raise serious national security questions.

A similar fear of creeping jurisdiction determined U.S. straits policy. At an early stage in the U.N. Seabed Committee negotiations, the United States made it clear that it considered freedom of transit of international straits to be a nonnegotiable right. The

U.S. straits proposal in 1971 was designed to secure this freedom. John R. Stevenson explicitly mentioned the security aspect when the proposal was introduced in 1971.

The early U.S. proposals thus clearly concentrated on maintaining freedom of navigation. They stipulated that, if territorial seas were allowed to go beyond the 3 nautical miles so far accepted by the United States, 12 nautical miles should be a maximum; and that could only be accepted if a special regime was introduced for international straits narrower than 24 nautical miles. Jurisdiction over continental shelf resources was to be limited to the area within the 200-meter isobath. The outer continental margin beyond the 200-meter isobath, including the continental slope and rise, should be an intermediate "Trusteeship Zone," basically international, but with the coastal state exercising some limited functions on behalf of the international community in respect to authorization of oil and gas exploration and exploitation. The basic purpose of the states' limited coastal jurisdiction was to secure the high seas status of the area for navigation.

The importance the United States attached to keeping the oceans free for the navy was also seen in the way it approached the question of seabed arms control. The Seabed Treaty signed in 1971 was a success from a navy point of view. It only outlawed weapons of mass destruction on the seabed. All important naval operations remained legal.

The question that follows is whether all this has changed with the Reagan administration. According to Richardson it has. We recall his May 14, 1981 testimony in which he defined the 1970 priorities in this order: (1) the politico-military interest in freedom of navigation and overflight, (2) oil and gas, (3) fisheries, and (4) deep seabed mining. He then went on to say "the whole thing has been turned upside down."[1]

This is also the view found in an article by Foreign Affairs associate editor Jennifer Seymour Whitaker, according to whom the new civilian appointees at the Defense Department, led by John Lehman and Fred Iklé, had "executed a 180° turn in the department's position."[2]

However, the changes that took place with the inauguration of Reagan did not mean that security goals lost their importance. The change was first of all a change in strategy. Whereas earlier administrations had believed it to be important to secure those goals in a widely accepted multilateral treaty, the new administration believed that they could be realized through unilateral measures and bilateral agreements with key states. To that should be added the increased emphasis on the strategic value of nickel, cobalt, and manganese to the United States.

When Secretary of the Navy John Lehman delivered the Sixth Annual Doherty Lecture in Oceans Policy at the University of Virginia on May 26, 1982, he spoke about two major national tasks, national security and the economy, in that order. One interpretation of the November 1980 "mandate" of the electorate that appealed to him was a "wish to reject the pessimistic and Spenglerian vision of a declining American future": "'The shining city on the hill' which President Reagan campaigned to achieve, symbolized a deep and uniquely American optimism that has now been returned to American politics."[3]

It was from this perspective that the secretary of the navy mentioned "the major and ambitious naval recovery program" upon which the United States had embarked "to achieve a 600-ship Navy and clear maritime superiority within the decade." It was from this perspective that he saw navies becoming "ever more prominent as instruments of national power and physical symbols of sovereignty." It was from this perspective that he talked about "the nearly two dozen strategic minerals on which America is now virtually wholly dependent on overseas sources," but which could nearly all be "provided from the seabottom."[4]

> Because of this enlightened and visionary awareness
> of the promise within the deep oceans, the United
> States . . . had the courage and wisdom to vote
> against the acceptance of the current draft of the
> Law of the Sea Treaty. . . . The effect that this
> Treaty Draft embodies was, I believe, ill-fated from
> the start. It was based on a fundamentally false
> ideological premise that the seas are somehow owned
> by all mankind, and that therefore a creation of the
> United Nations should assume the property rights and
> administer them.[5]

Clearly, a new kind of political ideology had come to power in Washington. Vietnams and Irans had to be forgotten. Superpower USA was now going for maritime superiority. With such superiority straits, states, and archipelagic states better be quiet. And all talk about a New International Economic Order better stop. The United States already had navigational rights according to customary law, it was argued in Washington. And deep seabed mining was a high seas freedom.

The basic goals of security and access to resources had really not changed that much. It was the strategic issue of multilateralism versus unilateralism that was now viewed differently. Access to resources had been important for central decision makers during the 1970s, too. But they were willing to pay a price for such access if U.S. security interests could be guaranteed in a treaty. Not so the Reagan administration, or the faction of it that won the game.

Stated narrowly it can be argued that all U.S. administrations—from Nixon to Reagan—have had security and access to resources as their main goals in ocean policy. As such the statist perspective must be said to have predictive power. And yet, it does not really explain the change in policy from the Carter to the Reagan administration. It does not help us understand strategic shifts. It assumes stability of interests and continuity in policy; "astounding continuity," according to Hans Morgenthau. But our case study did not demonstrate such astounding continuity, at least not in respect to strategy, which is also part of policy.

All U.S. proposals through the 1970s can be said to have aimed at protecting its access to ocean resources—although, as is consistent with the statist perspective, these proposals were often criticized by the U.S. industries that were directly concerned. With respect to continental margin resources and coastal fishing, the U.S. moved toward greater congruence with the policies advocated by the affected industries relatively early. It was only with respect to deep seabed resources that the U.S. can be said to have moved away from the policy preferred by domestic firms in the mid-1970s, in connection with Secretary of State Henry Kissinger's acceptance of the parallel system. As it has been argued, that particular change took place in an effort to strike an international bargain. It can therefore possibly be explained from an international interdependence perspective.

But what about the Reagan shift? In the last analysis it can be seen as domestic politics. As such it was the last major change forced upon central decision makers to satisfy the affected industry. Clearly, central decision makers are not as insulated from society as the statist model suggests. Who the central decision makers are, in the last analysis, depends on presidential elections. And new presidents do occasionally bring new perceptions and ideologies into the White House, the State Department, and the Defense Department. Statism is too apolitical. Contrary to Morgenthau's assertion, "motives, preferences, and intellectual and moral qualities" of presidents do matter. Statism then is too apsychological as well. It insulates central decision makers too much, and it downgrades the importance of mind-sets too much. It does matter who occupies the White House.

INTERNATIONAL INTERDEPENDENCE

The Reagan decision to go unilateral tout court also raises serious problems for the predictive capacity of the international interdependence perspective. Again, had our analysis been limited to the Nixon, Ford, and Carter administrations, our assessment would have been easier and more positive.

The very fact that, despite adversity, the United States stayed in the international negotiations through the 1970s was due to international interdependence. It may be argued that it was a paradox of that interdependence that it was mainly perceived to exist in respect to security and navigation, while there was a widespread feeling that the United States could respond to resource-related sensitivities through unilateral measures. This perception had an impact on offshore oil and fisheries policies as the United States moved to accept broad coastal state jurisdiction over these resources in the 1970s. But we recall that U.S. decision makers did resist the enclosure movement for quite some time. This was done because coastal state jurisdiction was used as a bargaining chip in the international negotiations and despite the fact that the United States would be a winner if the concept of the 200-mile economic zone were accepted.

Since domestic politics undermined the use of continental shelf oil and coastal area fish as international bargaining chips, the major area left for linkage politics was deep seabed mining. This was an excellent linkage instrument for the United States, which, contrary to most states, had the technological lead and the financial capacity to start this new activity. The United States was a credible linker; the linkee group, mainly the developing countries (Group of 77), would be worse off if the United States carried out its threat to go unilateral. Therefore the United States could expect a quid pro quo in the form of navigational freedom in return for contributing to the creation of an operational ISA. The U.S. acceptance of the idea of a parallel regime for deep seabed mining was announced by Secretary of State Henry Kissinger in the mid-1970s as a way to reach a compromise between the industrialized countries (which preferred simple registration of claims or licensing of mining activities), and the Group of 77 (which demanded an ISA with an active "enterprise" that would engage in mining, either alone or through joint ventures with private companies). The basic linkage was clearly on Secretary Kissinger's mind when he spoke to the American Bar Association in Montreal on August 11, 1975. It was on this occasion that he indicated the conditional U.S. acceptance of the parallel system. The reason for his willingness was stated this way:

> The breakdown of the current negotiation, a failure
> to reach a legal consensus, will lead to unrestrained
> military and commercial rivalry and mounting polit-
> ical turmoil.
>
> Ultimately, unless basic rules regulate exploi-
> tation, rivalry will lead to tests of power. A race
> to carve out exclusive domains of exploration on the
> deep seabed, even without claims of sovereignty, will
> menace freedom of navigation, and invite a competi-
> tion like that of the colonial powers in Africa and
> Asia in the last century. [6]

On the other hand, the establishment of an international regime
for the deep seabed could "turn interdependence from a slogan into
reality."[7]

That Secretary of State Kissinger attached importance to the
conclusion of an international agreement can also be gathered from
the fact that he attended the fourth and fifth sessions of UNCLOS III
in 1976. On both occasions he suggested further U.S. concessions.
At the fourth session, in the spring, he stated that the United States
was prepared to accept a temporary limitation on production of
seabed minerals, tying such limitation to the growth of demand for
nickel in the world market. Further, the U.S. would agree to the
ISA's participation in international commodity agreements and to
the use of some seabed mining revenues for adjustment assistance
to land-based producers of nickel, copper, cobalt, and manganese.[8]
Finally, at the fifth session, Kissinger said that the United States
was prepared to help financing the Enterprise so that it could get
started "either concurrently with the mining of state or private
enterprises or within an agreed timespan that was practically concurrent."[9]

Although the domestic mining industry criticized Secretary
Kissinger's concessions, the Carter administration continued the
efforts to reach an international agreement based upon the parallel
system. It was widely believed that the world was close to reaching such an agreement when UNCLOS III issued a Draft Convention
after the ninth session in Geneva in August 1980. Despite the difficulties of the negotiations and the temptation to go unilateral, the
United States continued trying to hammer out acceptable details on
the deep seabed mining sections of the negotiating text. That the
United States had security reasons for such a policy has been admitted on a number of occasions by President Carter's chief
UNCLOS negotiator, Elliot Richardson. In an article that dealt
with U.S. naval missions, the increasing naval capacities of other
states, and the dangers of creeping jurisdiction, he said about the

participants in the international negotiations that they had "understood from the outset that the accommodation of navigational and resource interests must be at the core of any eventual 'package deal.'"[10]

After the publication of the Draft Convention in 1980, Richardson told a meeting of the American Mining Congress in San Francisco that the result was "an unprecedented achievement for multilateral negotiations." Although the United States had now enacted the Deep Seabed Hard Mineral Resources Act, which would allow U.S. companies to start commercial deep seabed mining in 1988 even in the absence of a treaty, Ambassador Richardson suggested to representatives of U.S. mining companies that the uncertainties and threats of reprisal that were associated with the unilateral legislative approach could only be removed "through the establishment of a universally recognized international regime for the exploitation of deep seabed minerals."[11]

Richardson also went over the detailed provisions of the Draft Convention, arguing that there was assured access for U.S. companies, "a fair chance to earn a return on investment commensurate with the risk undertaken," and "solid protection against the arbitrary or unpredictable use or abuse of the Authority's power."[12] The statement was of course designed to sell the Draft Convention to the U.S. mining industry. While the emphasis on access also fits the statist perspective, the adopted linkage strategy is best explained by international interdependence.

However, the Kissinger-Richardson analysis was brushed aside by Kronmiller, Lehman, Meese, and other Reagan conservatives. Their approach to U.S. sensitivities was not one of international regime formation and linkage strategies, but one of unilateralism. They clearly perceived of U.S. sensitivity in respect to minerals. The remedy: get U.S. seabed mining started unilaterally. No quid pro quo was considered necessary to assure U.S. navigational and military interests. According to the Reagan conservatives, superpower USA can ignore international agenda setting. Officials who may have "learned" too much in an international setting can be dismissed. Linkages can be unlinked.

That the Reagan conservatives feared learning and actor socialization in international negotiations was suggested by Ratiner, who found it "fair to say" that the antitreaty group in the administration found it impossible "for any American to participate actively in the negotiation of [the law of the sea] treaty without being seduced by it."[13] This was seen as an argument against returning to the negotiating table. And, as we have seen, Aldrich, Taft, and other law of the sea officials left over from the Carter administration were dismissed on the eve of the eleventh session.

According to Kronmiller, international consensus negotiations take too long, and majority votes are unfair. Speaking at a luncheon of the American Oceanic Organization in late May, 1981, he stated: "There was no consensus and precisely what the western nations feared occurred. We were rolled." And he continued: "It is not for one-third of [the] world's countries that are landlocked and an additional number that have very little in the way of coastal interest to determine for those countries that are most widely affected and do use the oceans what universal law will be."[14] Kronmiller concluded: "If we descend into a regime where the majority nations make international law, life will not only be challenging but intolerable."[15]

Kronmiller obviously did not trust other states, with the possible exception of some Western states. The possibility of mutual gain through international regime formation was ruled out a priori. The positions of the Reagan conservatives is that of dogmatic nationalism. Their victory in Washington may mean the return of gunboat diplomacy in the future, if the coastal and straits states that consider the Law of the Sea Treaty to be a deal decide not to heed their part of the deal. Harassment may also be the result if U.S. companies go ahead and start seabed mining unilaterally. A majority of the world's states have clearly indicated that they consider unilateral seabed mining illegal. But the Reagan conservatives obviously feel that these concerns can be brushed aside.

According to Congressman Gerry Studds (D-Mass.), the Reagan position is one of "arrogance and ethnocentrism." And the Reagan decision not to sign the Law of the Sea Treaty was made in terms of a simplistic view of the world.[16]

Although the Reagan decision seems to have negated the central assertions of international interdependence a caveat is in order. The future may negate the Reagan analysis. The other industrialized states may decide to join the ISA instead of accepting the U.S. invitation to join a reciprocating states arrangement, an alternative mini-treaty. In that case there may be no U.S. flag seabed mining at all. Said Ratiner of that scenario: "We will stand as the emperor without clothes—for the entire world will see that it can do amazing and stupendous things without American money, leadership or technology."[17] Who knows, a future U.S. administration may then decide to accept the Kissinger-Richardson analysis and join the world again. Such a future change of events would be a vindication of international interdependence.

BUREAUCRATIC POLITICS

As bureaucratic politics hypotheses we offered the following two: (1) The State and Defense Departments will work toward an international agreement, and (2) resource-related agencies will support their "client" industries. Was that the case, and if so, what is the significance for our understanding of the making of U.S. ocean policy? Again it will be useful first to discuss the 1970s before looking at what happened with the arrival of President Reagan.

In connection with our explication of the logic of bureaucratic politics, it was suggested that bureaucratic pulling and hauling may lead to incoherence or stalemate. To know the outcome of political games within the administration it will often be necessary to study wider societal forces since such forces may lend weight to the arguments of particular agencies. Such wider forces may be decisive when bureaucrats appeal to the president for decisions. This point emerges clearly if we look at the role of the Interior Department with respect to offshore oil-leasing rights. The Nixon administration's original effort to limit coastal state authority to the area landward of the 200-meter isobath was strongly criticized by the oil industry. Through the National Petroleum Council (NPC)—established in 1946 as the oil companies' advisory body to the Interior Department—the industry issued a report in March 1969 in which it argued that the 1958 Continental Shelf Convention already gave the coastal state jurisdiction over the entire continental margin. The Interior Department worked for this position within the administration, but was unsuccessful in 1970. President Nixon proposed exactly what the Interior Department and its "client," the oil industry, did not want, a Trusteeship Zone between the 200-meter isobath and the outer edge of the continental margin.

After the presentation of the U.S. Draft Convention in Geneva in 1970, the Interior Department again invited the NPC to submit its opinions, in the form of "an article-by-article analysis" of the U.S. draft. The criticism that followed was harsh. The new NPC report objected strongly to "the relinquishment by the coastal state of its existing mineral resource rights in the outer continental margin," and maintained that an international authority holding a "residuum of powers" would create instability and uncertainty. [18]

The second NPC report and the work of the Interior Department did not change U.S. policy in 1971. The decisive event in that respect was the emergence of a widespread perception of an energy crisis in 1973. Even before OPEC's oil embargo, President Nixon, on April 18, 1973, had directed the secretary of the interior to triple the amount of offshore oil leasing. [19] A few days later, the Interior Department issued a call for bids for offshore oil and gas leasing off Louisiana that included areas beyond the 200-meter isobath. Leases beyond the 200-meter isobath were specified to "be subject to the international regime to be agreed upon." [20] But despite the reference to a future international regime, it was clear that U.S. policy was changing. Partly, this was due to lack of international support for the Trusteeship Zone idea. But the new perceptions of the national interest that followed the energy crisis were of critical importance.

A further indication of changes in U.S. policy was a draft document presented by the United States in July 1973 to the U.N. Seabed Committee, proposing a "coastal sea-bed economic area." The idea of a Trusteeship Zone had been dropped, and the idea of the economic zone was creeping into U.S. policy.

The 1973 changes in U.S. continental margin policy were crowned by a notice in the Federal Register that leases beyond the 200-meter isobath would no longer require provisions subjecting them to future international agreements.[21] Secretary of the Interior Rogers C. B. Morton referred to a feeling in Washington that the 1970 policy was not accepted by the majority of the nations"; but he also suggested that "our own national interests" had perhaps changed.[22] The latter part of the statement had to be a reference to the energy crisis, which had increased the weight of the Interior Department in determining ocean policy. Thus, the decisive event was exogenous to the bureaucratic system per se. The bureaucratic politics aspects of the policy change were rather epiphenomenal.

The role of the Department of Defense (DOD) also fits this pattern. The central importance of security goals in U.S. policy in the 1970s is not so much explained by DOD politicking as by the fact that the United States is a superpower; by its size, economy, and resources; and by the perceptions of its people and politicians. These are factors that are exogenous to the bureaucracy, but they explain the DOD's clout in Washington politics.

In other agencies, we will find that the bureaucratic politics perspective often explains the position taken by those agencies. But in a conflict between, say, the State and Commerce Departments, much will depend on the issues, the constituents, and congressional involvement. Further, it does happen that sectors of the industry do not receive strong bureaucratic support. When coastal fishermen thought that the support they got from the Commerce Department was not adequate, they contacted their representatives in the Congress.

What about the Reagan review then? The Reagan administration is very interesting from a bureaucratic politics perspective, not because of the bureaucratic pulling and hauling during the review process—there clearly was such a phenomenon—but because some of the bureaucrats did not take the positions predicted by the model. Where you stand does not always depend on where you sit! The State and Defense Departments had clearly worked for an international agreement through the 1970s, in correspondence with predictions based on the missions of those departments. But the Reagan

administration appointed officials for those two departments that
contributed decisively to a reversal of policy. Kronmiller, Iklé,
and others changed the input of State and Defense in a manner that
was unpredictable from a bureaucratic politics perspective. It took
a Reagan politics perspective to understand what happened. It had
to do with the changing mood of the country. It had to do with the
man himself, his conservative ideology, and his lack of leadership
in respect to ocean politics. In the last analysis his domestic advisor Edwin Meese may have had a decisive influence. Traditional
foreign policy input seems to have been weak. The NSC meeting in
June 29, 1982 that decided that the U.S. should not sign the Law of
the Sea Convention took place during the Haig-Shultz interregnum.

The resource-related departments have largely given the kind
of input in the interagency policy-making process that one would
predict from the bureaucratic politics model, from the late 1960s
to the early 1980s. The Interior Department has been a very active
player on the side of industry. This has also been the case under
the Reagan administration, where Secretary of the Interior James
Watt was one of those objecting to the Law of the Sea Treaty because it was found to represent too great a concession to the Group
of 77.[23] The Commerce Department has been less powerful, partly
because of internal conflicts between its Maritime Administration
and NOAA. This may be one reason why it played a rather timid
role in connection with the Fishery Conservation and Management
Act (FCMA) of 1976.

It is probably fair to say that there have been anti- and protreaty officials in most departments. And it should not be forgotten
that many proindustry officials were also protreaty, because they
felt that a widely accepted treaty would be the best way, or maybe
the only way, to provide security of tenure for U.S. seabed mining.
That the antitreaty coalition eventually won the game under Reagan
was not so much due to a specific constellation of bureaucratic
forces as the fact that the White House leaned that way.

We must therefore conclude that the impact of bureaucratic
politics has been limited. Exogenous phenomena such as the energy
crisis, presidential elections, and the changing mood of country
must be taken into account to explain the enclosure of continental
margin resources, the FCMA, and Reagan's final "no" to multilateralism.

DOMESTIC POLITICS

Of our four models, domestic politics emerges as the most
powerful and accurate. We recall that this model focused upon

domestic groups and Congress and the likelihood of unilateral actions to gain access to resources. In examining the empirical aspects of U.S. ocean policy, we find that the enactment of the FCMA of 1976 fits the domestic politics model very well. It was a major event of U.S. ocean policy. Early in the 1970s, coastal fishermen concluded that the executive branch was not providing adequate support for their views. They therefore went to their senators and congressmen, who eventually acted by passing the 200-mile fisheries bill. President Ford signed it against the advice of the Departments of State, Defense, and Justice, as well as that of the National Security Council.

The FCMA went against the premise of international interdependence. In fact, it was the State Department and NSC opposition to the bill that fitted the interdependence perspective. John Norton Moore, chairman of the NSC Interagency Task Force on the Law of the Sea, stated five reasons against enactment of the bill:

it would be counter to U.S. policy of resisting unilateral claims to ocean space, and could thus interfere with other U.S. interests;
it could be seriously harmful to important foreign relations interests;
it would not be compatible with international law, in particular the 1958 Convention on the High Seas;
it would pose serious risks for U.S. fishing interests, in particular the U.S. distant-water fishing interests;
it could seriously undercut efforts to conclude the Law of the Sea Treaty.[24]

Some of the central U.S. decision makers were clearly concerned about sensitivities and vulnerabilities. How would Japan and the Soviet Union react? Both countries were customarily fishing within 200 miles of the U.S. coastline. Moreover, if the United States could unilaterally abrogate one of the freedoms of the sea, such as fishing, could not other countries unilaterally abrogate other freedoms of the sea, such as freedom of navigation? If so, U.S. interests might be seriously hurt. There was also a bargaining aspect: if the United States unilaterally introduced a 200-mile fishing zone, then such a zone would no longer be a bargaining chip in the international negotiations. Thus, a part of the U.S. linkage strategy was at stake.

By passing the bill, Congress brushed aside all these concerns about sensitivities and linkages. Members of Congress from the New England and Pacific Northwest states had listened to their constituents and provided leadership in a coalition-building effort that secured the passage of the 200-mile bill in January 1976. Only pressures from constituents can explain what happened. To remain legitimate representatives of their constituents, congressmen from coastal states had to work for the 200-mile fishing zone. The pressures were enormous. At one point, Senator Bob Packwood (R-Oregon) stated that he had received over 400 letters during the two preceding weeks demanding immediate and effective action to help coastal fishermen. [25]

But why did President Ford sign the bill? The answer is that he was seeking reelection. The final Senate vote on the bill came on January 28, 1976. At that time, the president was concerned about the upcoming New Hampshire primary, where he faced a tough and important battle with Governor Ronald Reagan. Eventually he signed the bill on April 13, in the middle of the fourth session of UNCLOS III. The FCMA extended U.S. jurisdiction over 2.2 million square miles of ocean that had hitherto been considered high seas and open to fishermen of all countries.

The dictates of domestic politics thus turned out to be more important than the dictates of international interdependence. Moreover, the president's decision to sign the 200-mile bill against the advice of his chief foreign and security policy advisors suggests problems for the statist perspective: "central decision makers" are not always a unitary body. The president is a political figure sui generis. He is not as insulated from societal pressures as the statist perspective suggests. Even a relatively small group, such as maybe 100,000 coastal fishermen, can be important as marginal voters in a tight political race. The wide sympathy that the coastal fishermen received from the press and the general public, and the support from conservation and environmental groups, were important factors. Senator Warren Magnuson (D-Wash.) and Congressman Gerry Studds (D-Mass.), provided strong leadership, which the president had to follow in order to avoid high domestic political costs.

The case of deep seabed mining is somewhat different; and yet some similarities eventually emerged in connection with the final Reagan decisions.

Although the first deep seabed mining bill was introduced before the first 200-mile fishing bill, it was only in June 1980 that Congress passed and President Carter signed the Deep Seabed Hard Mineral Resources Act. Despite pressures from the mining industry, the Nixon and Ford administrations had successfully opposed unilateral steps with respect to deep seabed mining. These pressures did contribute to the Carter administration's decision to support the legislation, but in this case there was a further reason: deep seabed mining was an excellent linkage instrument from a U.S. point of view, and through support for the legislation Washington was able to put pressure on the international negotiations. It was a way of telling the Group of 77 that, if it did not enter real bargaining on the details of the parallel system in such a way that U.S. companies would get guaranteed access to a reasonable number of mine sites, the United States could start deep seabed mining unilaterally.

When the Carter administration decided to support the legislation, Ambassador Richardson gave three reasons. First, the administration had concluded that legislation would "be needed with or without a successful law of the sea treaty." Second, it believed that "the orderly development of deep seabed mining should not only be continued but also . . . encouraged." And finally, it believed that legislation would not "negatively affect the prospects for reaching agreement at the Law of the Sea Conference." On the latter point, Ambassador Richardson added an indirect threat to the Group of 77: "Administration opposition to deep seabed mining legislation could be misunderstood as a total reliance on the Law of the Sea Conference for achievement of our seabed objectives."[26]

The Carter-Richardson strategy was aimed in two directions. Domestically it tried to pacify the mining industry; internationally the purpose was to put pressure on the Group of 77 and improve the negotiating text. The process was ably spearheaded by Ambassador Richardson. In June 1980 the Deep Seabed Hard Mineral Resources Act, which postponed unilateral deep seabed mining until 1988, was passed. And in August 1980, a Draft Convention acceptable to the Carter administration emerged from the ninth session of UNCLOS III in Geneva. It looked as if the Richardson strategy was succeeding.

Many observers now believed that the world was on the way to adopt a legal regime for 71 percent of the surface of the globe. Although it was a difficult, tedious, and frustrating multilateral effort of international legislation, it could be viewed as a remarkable example of rational politics. It had been a process of true give-and-take—although, as is normally the case in politics, some had taken more than others. With respect to coastal resources, the winners were the United States, the Soviet Union, Canada, Australia, and other states with long coastlines and broad continental margins.[27] The losers, of course, were the landlocked and geographically disadvantaged states, although they were supposed to have some access to the living resources of the economic zones of the neighboring countries. They might further expect some revenues from the exploitation of minerals beyond the 200-mile limit. But, since the most important oil and fish resources are within the 200-mile limit, geography had indeed been an important distributive factor. In respect to navigational rights, the maritime powers were the winners; so the United States fared well on this account, too. The price was the parallel deep seabed mining regime, with certain production limits and rules about transfer of technology. For a moment it looked as if this price was considered a fair one by nearly everybody except the mining industry. That moment lasted until the sudden announcement, on March 2, 1981, that the Reagan administration was not ready to complete the negotiations during the tenth session of UNCLOS III, scheduled to start in New York on March 9. According to the new administration, serious problems had been found in the Draft Convention; future U.S. policy would be determined through a review process.

We now know the outcome of that review. The United States decided to return to the bargaining table and seek improvements in the Draft Convention at the eleventh session in the spring of 1982. We also know that the United States eventually decided that the improvements obtained at the eleventh session were insufficient to gain U.S. adherence to the treaty. Was it domestic politics?

Yes, at least it had a strong element of domestic politics. The Republican platform adopted at the Detroit convention in 1980 had violently criticized UNCLOS III, stating that "too much concern has been lavished on nations unable to carry out seabed mining, with insufficient attention paid to gaining early American access to it." Senator Jesse Helms (R-N.C.) had this clause inserted at the request of the mining companies.[28] So there was a campaign promise. Industry also had easy access to Congress, various officials in key departments, and the White House. The domestic politics of Keating, Stang, Amsbaugh, Breaux, Watt, Iklé, Lehman, and Meese were able to undermine UNCLOS politics. World order groups did not have the clout of industry in Reagan's Washington.

A hypothetical question follows: What would have happened if President Carter had been reelected in November 1980? We cannot know for sure, but judging from Ambassador Richardson's statements both before and after November 1980 it seems fair to say that there is a high probability that a Carter administration could have negotiated and adhered to a consensus agreement. If so, we have to add that the Reagan decision was not only a question of domestic politics. It was also a question of ideology or psychological factors. As James Barber has argued so well in The Presidential Character, it does matter who occupies the White House.[29] But who occupies the White House is determined by the U.S. people. And that's domestic politics, too.

So, if we should summarize our conclusion in a few words it will have to be this: U.S. ocean policy has largely been determined by domestic politics. Put differently, the domestic politics model has more explanatory power than any other model of foreign policy, at least for this case, but we believe for many other cases too. Our explanatory conclusions are summarized in Table 8.

TABLE 8

Explanatory Conclusions of U.S. Ocean Policy

Model	Hypothesis	Explanatory Power
Statism	Primacy of security	Confirmed for 1970s
	Importance of access to resources	Confirmed
		Model does not explain changes in policy or conflict between the president and foreign policy advisors. Nor does it explain ideological shifts in connection with presidential elections
International interdependence	Use of linkage strategies	Confirmed for 1970s
	Likelihood of international agreement	Disconfirmed
Bureaucratic politics	Incoherence, infighting, stalemate	Epiphenomenal
	Bureaucratic missions determined bureaucratic positions	Not always the case
Domestic politics	Unilateral actions	Explains passage of the FCMA and other enclosure decisions. Explains Reagan's decision not to sign Law of the Sea Treaty

Source: Compiled by the author.

The statist perspective was useful for understanding the primacy of security interests through the 1970s. The general predictions about statist policies with respect to access to resources were useful, too; but because of the complex nature of these issues, it was more difficult to make specific predictions. A major weakness of this perspective was its inability to explain changes in policy; it presumed a rather well-defined static national interest. The model was not able to foresee conflict between the president and his foreign policy and security advisors. Nor was it able to predict ideological shifts in connection with presidential elections.

The model of international interdependence explains why the United States decided to take part in the international law of the sea negotiations: certain vulnerabilities were perceived, and linkage strategies were adopted. However, the enactment of the FCMA in 1976—which meant de-linkage of the fisheries aspect from the international negotiations—can only be explained by domestic politics. The legislation was demanded by constituents who built an effective coalition in an election year.

With respect to deep seabed mining, domestic politics and international interdependence were pulling in different directions. Eventually the domestic pulls were stronger than the international ones. So Reagan's "no" to multilateralism must be seen as a disconfirmation of international interdependence, at least for the moment.

Although there were a lot of bureaucratic politics, it was not found very important for any of the major outcomes.

Domestic politics thus emerges as the most important of our models. It was, however, a special kind of domestic politics. It may to some extent have been a kind of pluralism, but it was clearly skewed. Business groups had special impact on decisions. Countervailing powers remained weak or were practically nonexistent. The voice of consumers was, to say the least, very timid. The lack of general public concern about the international repercussions of law of the sea policies gave industry groups a disproportionate influence. If not at the outset, the national interest eventually became equated with business interests. A government-business symbiosis emerged. Policy making took on some of the characteristics of a corporatist system.[30]

NOTES

1. U.S. Congress, House, Foreign Affairs Committee, U.S. Policy and the Third United Nations Conference on the Law of the Sea, Hearings, 97th Cong., 1st Sess., April 29 and May 14, 1981, p. 39.

172 / SUPERPOWER AT SEA

2. Jennifer Seymour Whitaker, "Outside the Mainstream," Atlantic, October 1982, pp. 18-26, at 19.

3. John Lehman, "Going for the High Ground in the Deep Seas," Marine Technology Society Journal 16:2 (1982):3-6, at 3.

4. Ibid., pp. 4-5.

5. Ibid., pp. 5-6.

6. "International Law, World Order and Human Progress," in Henry A. Kissinger, American Foreign Policy, 3d ed. (New York: W. W. Norton, 1977), pp. 217-36, at 222 and 225.

7. Ibid., pp. 226-27.

8. Henry A. Kissinger, "The Law of the Sea: A Test of International Cooperation," Department of State Bulletin 74 (April 26, 1976), pp. 533-42.

9. "Secretary Kissinger Discusses U.S. Position of Law of the Sea Conference," Department of State Bulletin 75 (September 27, 1976), pp. 395-403, at 398.

10. Elliot L. Richardson, "Power, Mobility and the Law of the Sea," Foreign Affairs 58 (Spring 1980):902-12, at 911.

11. Elliot L. Richardson, "Seabed Mining and the Law of the Sea," Department of State Bulletin 80 (December 1980), pp. 60-64, at 61.

12. Ibid., pp. 61-63.

13. Leigh S. Ratiner, "The Law of the Sea: A Crossroad for American Foreign Policy," Foreign Affairs 60 (Summer 1982): 1006-21.

14. "Administration Speaker Doubtful on Law of the Sea Treaty," Sea Technology, June 1982, p. 55.

15. Ibid.

16. Ocean Science News 24 (July 20, 1982):1.

17. Ratiner, "The Law of the Sea," p. 1020.

18. National Petroleum Council, Petroleum Resources under the Ocean Floor: A Supplemental Report (Washington, D.C., March 1971).

19. U.S. Congress, House, Judiciary Committee, Outer Continental Shelf Oil and Gas, Hearings, 93rd Cong., 2nd Sess. (1974), p. 76.

20. U.S. Department of the Interior, "Outer Continental Shelf Off Louisiana," Federal Register 38 (April 20, 1973), p. 9839.

21. "Outer Continental Shelf Leasing Beyond 200 Meters," Federal Register 38 (November 5, 1973), p. 30457.

22. House, Judiciary Committee, Outer Continental Shelf Oil and Gas, p. 227.

23. See Elizabeth Drew, "A Reporter at Large: Secretary Watt," The New Yorker, May 4, 1981, pp. 104-38, at 120.

24. U.S. Congress, Senate, Foreign Relations Committee, Emergency Marine Fisheries Protection Act of 1974, Hearings, 93d Cong., 2d Sess. (1974), pp. 49-51.

25. U.S. Congress, Senate, Commerce Committee, Emergency Marine Fisheries Protection Act of 1975, part I, Hearing, 94th Cong., 1st Sess. (1975), pp. 29-32.

26. U.S. Congress, House, International Relations Committee, Deep Seabed Hard Mineral Resources Act, Hearings and Mark-up, 95th Cong., 2d Sess. (1978), p. 28.

27. See Lewis M. Alexander and Robert D. Hodgson, "The Impact of the 200-Mile Economic Zone on the Law of the Sea," San Diego Law Review 12 (1975):569-99.

28. Ursula Wassermann, "UNCLOS: 1981 Session," Journal of World Trade Law 16 (January-February 1982):81-82.

29. James David Barber, The Presidential Character: Predicting Performance in the White House (Englewood Cliffs, N.J.: Prentice Hall, 1972).

30. For an argument along similar lines, see Maria E. Conalis, "The Evolution of U.S. Ocean Policy: The Power Elite and Government Interaction," M.A. thesis, American University, Washington, D.C., 1982.

9

CONCLUDING REMARKS

All four perspectives or models that have been applied in this volume are based on a premise of rationality. The statist perspective assumes that central decision makers will pursue national interests in a rational manner—that is, they will try to maximize the values and interests they perceive to be important from the national point of view. The three other models suggest that central decision makers are constrained in their value maximization by both international and domestic factors. Although there have been tendencies in the literature on bureaucratic politics—and to a lesser extent in the literature on international interdependence—to downgrade or to dispense with the premise of rationality, the assumption here has been that rationality is essential for making predictions, and that attaining a predictive capacity is and should be one of the goals of social science.

Thus it can be considered rational to use linkage strategies internationally. Obviously, the interests of other countries will have to be taken into consideration if an international bargain is to be arrived at. Moreover, the procedural aspects—such as the consensus approach often applied in international negotiations—may influence the outcome. At the same time, it is quite rational for central decision makers to consider the domestic reaction. After all, any treaty will have to be ratified by the Senate. And the Senate does—at least to a certain extent—listen to the mood of the country. Nor should it be considered irrational if a president calculates the impact of his decisions on his chances for reelection.

The assumption is rationality of individuals. It is through a political process of decision making that individual rationalities add up to outcomes. That political process primarily consists of bargaining: actors seek to influence events through efforts at coalition building. The models suggest basically that ocean politics is a very complex matter involving both international and domestic aspects. In this case, the term "intermestic" applies.[1]

The central decision makers were caught up in an "intermestic" bargaining situation; they had to listen to both international and domestic demands, and try gradually to adjust the conflicts between them. Changes in policy during the 1970s can therefore to a large degree be seen as resulting from feedback from these two bargaining forums.

Since domestic bargaining (and legislation) is often simpler than international bargaining (and treaty making), timing tends to become an important variable. International decision making is usually very slow—for both cultural and procedural reasons. That is why there is always a high probability that domestic politics will undercut the politics of international linkages. This problem was raised by Senator Mike Gravel (D-Alaska) in the debate on the 200-mile fishing zone; he castigated his colleagues for not seeing that UNCLOS III had made tremendous progress during its first two sessions. He felt that members of Congress did not understand UNCLOS III "because we are operating from our perception and our experience. We legislate from a basis of sovereignty. In the international community you don't legislate from a basis of sovereignty. You legislate from a basis of consensus."[2]

Had UNCLOS negotiations advanced faster or were states ready to accept majority decisions, the situation might look different today.

If we look at the international negotiations as a game between two actors, the United States (Actor A) and the Group of 77 (Actor B), it is possible to discuss some of the events from 1980 to 1982 as a game in terms of a two-by-two matrix. If we look at the situation in the summer of 1980 when the informal Draft Treaty was issued, it can be argued that the Carter administration had a dominant strategy of a treaty approach, despite its use of the threat of unilateralism.[3] The Draft Treaty is given the value 3 and the improved treaty that might result from further negotiations the value 4. Unilateralism is given the lower value of 2 for the United States. The G-77 had a dominant strategy of sticking to the Draft Treaty and not reopening negotiations that could only lead to further concessions. But the G-77 preferred a Draft Treaty with U.S. participation (value 4) to one without U.S. participation (value 2). In both cases reopened negotiations would lead to poorer results (values 3 and 1 respectively). The resulting situation was an equilibrium outcome A_1B_1 (see Figure 1). That outcome, however, was slightly better for the G-77 than the United States (value 4 against value 3). The G-77 could be satisfied. But the outcome left the United States slightly aggrieved. However, the costs of unilateralism were perceived by Richardson and other central decision makers to be so high (lower value 2) that it was not seriously contemplated. For this reason the situation was such that no further concessions could be expected from the G-77 as long as its negotiators analyzed the situation in a similar way.

FIGURE 1

The Bargaining Situation, Summer 1980

Actor B: G-77

	B_1^* Slightly Amended Treaty	B_2 Further Amended Treaty
A_1 Treaty Approach	A_1B_1 2,4	A_1B_2 4,3
A_2 Unilateralism	A_2B_1** 3,2	A_2B_2 3,1

Actor A: U.S.A.

* Actor's dominant strategy
**Equilibrium outcome

Source: Compiled by the author.

This was the situation inherited by the Reagan administration. That administration, however, attached different values to the two options of treaty approach and unilateralism. So the ideological shift that took place with the Reagan inauguration in January 1981 changed the structure of the bargaining situation. However, the exact structure of that situation remained uncertain while the review process was conducted. But the mere fact that the Reagan administration questioned the Draft Treaty made the G-77 reconsider the value of U.S. participation and created a situation where it was more likely to allow a reopening of some issues. The exact structure of U.S. values probably also remained uncertain for the G-77 after negotiations started again. Not only is communication often incomplete in such situations, but there was also uncertainty as to which faction represented the Reagan administration. And U.S. negotiators probably did not know themselves how far they could go. The outcome of the eleventh session can probably be illustrated by Figure 2.

FIGURE 2

Bargaining Situation, Eleventh Session of UNCLOS III, 1982

Actor B: G-77

	B_1^* Slightly Amended Treaty	B_2 Further Amended Treaty
A_1 Treaty Approach Actor A: U.S.A.	A_1B_1 2, 4	A_1B_2 4, 3
A_2 Unilateralism	A_2B_1 ** 3, 2	A_2B_2 3, 1

* Actor's dominant strategy
**Equilibrium outcome

Source: Compiled by the author.

The United States tried to get rather radical changes at the eleventh session, but could probably have accepted what we have termed a further amended treaty, something like improved FOC proposals (value 4). However, the Reagan conservatives did not attach the same costs to unilateralism as the Carter administration had done, thus the value of 3. But a treaty that was only slightly improved was considered more costly than unilateralism (value 2). The United States thus had a contingent strategy. Treaty or unilateralism depended on how far G-77 would go in giving concessions to the U.S. demands.

The G-77, however, had a dominant strategy. Given the direction of the changes, a slightly amended treaty was more valuable than a much more amended treaty. But they might have accepted a further amended treaty had they been sure that the United States would have stayed on the treaty line. Efforts from the G-77 to get such an assurance from the United States were not successful. Because the antitreaty lobby in Washington was undermining the position of U.S. negotiators in New York they could not give such assurances. The G-77 therefore had to stick to their dominant strategy, and the United States voted against the only slightly amended treaty. The outcome, A_2B_1, is suboptimal compared to A_1B_2. The matrix suggests that the result could have been better if there had been more trust, communication, and flexibility. It especially suggests the importance of giving delegations to international conferences clear negotiating mandates and of executive branch leadership to deliver afterward. For these various reasons suboptimal outcomes are not uncommon in international politics.[4]

That the outcome was suboptimal may be denied by the Reagan conservatives. I shall therefore try to substantiate the argument further. It will be argued that it is suboptimal because it creates a situation of legal uncertainty that may hamper both navigation and investments in the exploitation of ocean resources.

Some of these issues of legal uncertainty were dealt with by the president of the American Society of International Law, Covey T. Oliver, in his address to the 1982 annual meeting of the American Bar Association. He seriously questioned that one can pick and choose from a treaty arrived at as a "package deal." The Reagan administration's view that the treaty's provisions dealing with navigation and overflight can be considered customary international law is therefore problematic. "It is novel . . . to entertain a contention that a treaty in force that derogates from older customary law or carves out new international authority gives rights to non-signers," said Covey Oliver.[5] Nationally it is not the administration, but the federal courts that say "what international law is." And internationally, "situations that are widely perceived . . . as grossly inequitable, become unstable." International bodies, including the International Court of Justice, are increasingly supporting concepts of distributive justice.[6] "States do not yield territory—or claims to territory—lightly, and only when conquered, for less than a quid pro quo," said Oliver. The United States, therefore, could only claim rights for a price. "The minimum price would be reciprocity—legally assured reciprocity."[7] And he finished along these lines:

> The globe is not easy for commanders, civilian masters, and air pilots as to where they may legally go. UNCLOS III gives them a bridge book if the flag state is a party thereto. But I pity American navigators if we do not sign. Uncertainty will be compounded.[8]

In this connection it may be worth remembering that many states tried to reopen the question of passage of warships through territorial seas at the last sessions of UNCLOS III.

The U.S. pick-and-choose theory was also criticized by Alfonso Areas-Schreiber of Peru, speaking on behalf of the Group of 77 at the short resumed eleventh session of UNCLOS III in New

York, September 1982. No states could invoke isolated provisions if they were not parties, he said.[9] Similarly, conference president Tommy Koh stated at the signing session at Montego Bay, Jamaica in December 1982 that it had emerged from the statements there that the provisions of the convention were considered closely inter-related: "it is not permissible to claim rights under the Convention without being willing to shoulder the corresponding obligations."[10] Koh specifically mentioned transit passage through straits, the re-gime of archipelagic sea lanes passage, and the concept of the con-tinental shelf to include the continental slope and the continental rise as new legal concepts, which could not be invoked by nonparties.

The Reagan "no" also creates serious problems in respect to deep seabed mining. We recall that Elliot Richardson told the House Foreign Affairs Committee in May 1981 that "there will be no invest-ment in deep seabed mining without a treaty." The administration's alternative, some mini-treaty with reciprocating states, was said not to give the miners "a sufficiently secure title to mine sites. In-vestment would be too risky."[11] Similarly, a staff paper that cir-culated in the Department of Commerce after the Reagan decision concluded: "If the U.S. remains outside the convention, then ocean mining by domestic operators is extremely unlikely—absent finan-cial incentives to overcome the legal uncertainties of operating out-side of a widely accepted legal regime."[12]

Financial incentives could possibly be provided through U.S. legislation, through risk insurance, loan guarantees, or subsidies. But would an administration professing free market ideology take such steps? The mining consortia might also do the mining under the flag of one of the states adhering to the treaty, which would fore-close a U.S. flag mining industry. The staff paper therefore con-cluded that "although the interests of the ocean mining industry were cited as a major reason for U.S. opposition to the draft convention, it appears that the U.S. ocean mining industry is now in the worst situation possible."[13]

Also a recent report by the General Accounting Office (GAO) raised the question whether the mini-treaty alternative is viable. Banking officials told the GAO that they did not consider a recipro-cating states agreement "as providing adequate protection if a non-reciprocating state should encroach upon an established mine site."[14]

Another question of course is whether other potential mining states will join such an arrangement. Of the eleven states accorded the special status of pioneer investors, five signed the Convention at Montego Bay, namely, Canada, France, India, the Netherlands, and the Soviet Union. The United Kingdom said it would seek im-provements in the deep seabed mining provisions. Italy suggested that the Preparatory Committee should help solve some of the difficulties. Belgium and the Federal Republic of Germany were still studying the text, and Japan stated that the convention "merits its support and signature" but was under review by its new government.[15] Japan indeed is expected to adhere to the treaty. That leaves a few West European states that seem to want to see the rules and regulations to be adopted by the Preparatory Commission before they decide. But it is worth mentioning that the Commission of the European Communities has decided to support European adherence to the convention. Europe depends much more than the United States on free navigation for trade and good relations with Third World countries for supplies of a number of commodities.

The Reagan administration commissioned Donald Rumsfeld, a former member of the Ford administration, to try to talk U.S. allies out of signing the treaty in the fall of 1982.[16] His trip to West European capitals is reported not to have been very successful.

At the resumed eleventh session in September 1982, Arias-Schreiber stated clearly on behalf of the Group of 77 that any unilateral action or mini-treaty outside the U.N. Convention "would have no international validity and would lead to the adoption of appropriate measures to defend the interests of all States in the utilization of this area as the common heritage of mankind."[17] Similarly, Tommy Koh summed up the statements at Montego Bay: "Speakers from every regional and interest group expressed the view that the doctrine of the freedom of the high seas can provide no legal basis for the grant by any State of exclusive title to a specific mine site in the international Area."[18] And his warning to the United States was straightforward: "Any attempt by any state to mine the resources of the deep seabed outside the Convention will earn the universal condemnation of the international community and will incur grave political and legal consequences."[19]

No doubt, a great majority of states are determined to go ahead and implement the U.N. Convention. The Preparatory Commission will begin its work in March 1983. In reality it can address most of President Reagan's stated concerns, maybe all of them except the Review Conference.[20] But the United States has decided not to be present. One can hope, as Tommy Koh did, that the PrepCom will carry out its work "in an efficient, objective, and businesslike manner." Then, maybe the resulting seabed mining system "will induce those who are standing on the sidelines to come in and support the Convention."[21] Then maybe a future administration in Washington will give up confrontation and return to law and diplomacy.

NOTES

1. The term was proposed by Bayless Manning in "The Congress, the Executive and Intermestic Affairs: Three Proposals," Foreign Affairs 55 (January 1977):306-24. See also Douglas J. Bennett, Jr., "Congress in Foreign Policy: Who Needs it?" Foreign Affairs 57 (Fall 1978):40-50.

2. U.S. Congress, Senate, Foreign Relations Committee, Two Hundred-Mile Fishing Zone, Hearing, 94th Cong., 1st Sess. (1975), p. 105.

3. See Arthur A. Stein, "The Politics of Linkage," World Politics 33 (October 1980):62-81.

4. See also Arthur A. Stein, "Coordination and Collaboration: Regimes in an Anarchic World," International Organization 36 (Spring 1982):299-324.

5. Covey T. Oliver, "The Rule of Law at Sea—Uncustomary Law," Presentation at 1982 annual meeting, American Bar Association (mimeo), p. 4.

6. Ibid., pp. 7-8.

7. Ibid., p. 10.

8. Ibid., p. 11.

9. U.N. Press Release SEA/496 (New York), 22 September 1982, p. 3.

10. U.N. Press Release SEA/MB/14 (Montego Bay), 10 December 1982, p. 2.

11. U.S. Congress, House, Foreign Affairs Committee, U.S. Policy and the Third United Nations Conference on the Law of the Sea, Hearings, 97th Cong., 1st Sess., April 29 and May 14, 1981, pp. 35, 48-49.

12. Quoted, "Some in the Administration Are Reconsidering What the U.S. Has Done at the LOS Conference," Strategic Materials Management, July 1, 1982, p. 6.

13. Ibid.

14. U.S. General Accounting Office, Impediments to U.S. Involvement in Deep Ocean Mining Can Be Overcome, Report to the Congress, EMD-82-31, February 3, 1982, p. 32.

15. U.N. Press Release SEA/514 (New York), 10 December 1982, pp. 3-4.

16. Charles Maechling, Jr., "On Top of the Pipeline Fracas, A Coming Clash on Sea Law," International Herald Tribune, October 26, 1982.

17. U.N. Press Release SEA/496, p. 3.

18. U.N. Press Release SEA/MB/14, p. 3.

19. Ibid.

20. Lee Kimball, "What Happens Next for the U.S. in Ocean Law?" Presentation to the Marine Technology Society Annual Meeting, September 21, 1982 (mimeo).

21. U.N. Press Release SEA/MB/14, pp. 3-4.

SELECTED BIBLIOGRAPHY

Aldrich, George H. "Law of the Sea." Department of State Bulletin 81 (February 1981):56-59.

Alexander, Lewis M. "The Extended Economic Zone and U.S. Ocean Interests." Columbia Journal of World Business 10 (Spring 1975):34-41.

Alexander, Tom. "The Reaganites Misadventure at Sea." Fortune, August 23, 1982, pp. 129-44.

Allen, Edward W. "Law, Fish and Policy." International Lawyer 5 (October 1971):621-36.

Amacher, Ryan L., and Richard James Sweeney, eds. The Law of the Sea: U.S. Interests and Alternatives. Washington, D.C.: American Enterprise Institute, 1976.

Arrow, Dennis W. "The Proposed Regime for the Unilateral Exploitation of Deep Seabed Mineral Resources by the United States." Harvard International Law Journal 21 (Summer 1980):337-417.

Auburn, F. M. "The Deep Seabed Hard Mineral Resources Bill." San Diego Law Review 9 (May 1972):491-513.

Bandow, Doug. "UNCLOS III: A Flawed Treaty." San Diego Law Review 19 (April 1982):475-92.

Barkenbus, Jack N. Deep Seabed Resources: Politics and Technology. Riverside, N.J.: The Free Press, 1979.

Barry, James A. "The Seabed Arms Control Issue, 1967-1971: A Superpower Symbiosis?" Naval War College Review 25 (September-October 1972):87-101.

Breaux, John. "The Diminishing Prospects for an Acceptable Law of the Sea Treaty." Virginia Journal of International Law 19 (Winter 1979):257-97.

Brown, Seyom, and Larry L. Fabian. "Diplomats at Sea." Foreign Affairs 52 (January 1974):301-21.

Burke, William T. "Law, Science, and the Ocean." Natural Resources Lawyer 3 (May 1970):195-226.

Buzan, Barry. Seabed Politics. New York: Praeger, 1976.

Carlisle, Geoffrey E. "Three-Mile Limit: Obsolete Concept?"
U.S. Naval Institute Proceedings 93 (1967):24-33.

Caron, David D. "Deep Seabed Mining—A Comparative Study of
U.S. and West German Legislation." Marine Policy 5 (January
1981):4-16.

Charney, Jonathan I. "United States Interests in a Convention on
the Law of the Sea: The Case for Continued Efforts." Vanderbilt
Journal of Transnational Law 11 (Winter 1978):39-75.

Christy, Francis T., Jr. "Northwest Atlantic Fisheries Arrangements: A Test of the Species Approach." Ocean Development
and International Law Journal 1 (Spring 1973):65-91.

Clarkson, Kenneth W. "International Law, U.S. Seabeds Policy
and Ocean Resource Development." Journal of Law and Economics 17 (April 1974):117-42.

Clingan, Thomas A., Jr. "The U.S. and Unilateral Action: Changing Patterns of Fisheries Conservation and Management."
German Yearbook of International Law 22 (1979):178-99.

Danzig, Aaron L. "Draft Treaty Proposals by the United States,
the United Kingdom and France on the Exploitation of the Seabed:
An Analysis." Ocean Management 1 (March 1973):55-82.

Darman, Richard G. "The Law of the Sea: Rethinking U.S. Interests." Foreign Affairs 56 (January 1978):373-95.

Doumani, George A. Ocean Wealth: Policy and Potential. Rochelle
Park, N.J.: Hayden, 1973.

Eckert, Ross D. The Enclosure of Ocean Resources: Economics
and the Law of the Sea. Stanford: Hoover Institution Press,
1979.

Ely, Northcutt. "United States Seabed Minerals Policy." Natural
Resources Lawyer 4 (July 1971):597-621.

_____. "Deep Seabed Minerals: Congress Steams to the Rescue." International Lawyer 10 (Summer 1976):537-43.

Finlay, Luke W. "The Position of the American Bar Association on the Law of the Sea." Case Western Reserve Journal of International Law 8 (Winter 1976):84-109.

_____. "United States Policy with Respect to High Seas Fisheries and Deep Seabed Minerals—A Study in Contrasts." Natural Resources Lawyer 9 (1976):629-43.

Frank, Richard A. "Jumping Ship." Foreign Policy no. 43 (Summer 1981):121-38.

Friedheim, Robert L., ed. Managing Ocean Resources: A Primer. Boulder: Westview Press, 1979.

Friedman, Alan G. U.S. Law of the Sea Policy—A Bureaucratic Politics Analysis." Marine Policy 2 (October 1978):304-20.

Friedmann, Wolfgang. The Future of the Oceans. New York: Braziller, 1971.

Garwin, Richard L. "Anti-Submarine Warfare and National Security." Scientific American 227 (July 1972):14-25.

Goldwin, Robert A. "Locke and the Law of the Sea." Commentary, June 1981, pp. 46-50.

Haight, G. W. "Law of the Sea Conference—Why Paralysis?" Journal of Maritime Law and Commerce 8 (April 1977):281-93.

Henkin, Louis. "Politics and the Changing Law of the Sea." Political Science Quarterly 89 (March 1974):46-67.

Hill, Clarence A., Jr. "U.S. Law of the Sea Position and Its Effect on the Operating Navy." Ocean Development and International Law Journal 3 (1976):341-59.

Hollick, Ann L. "The Origins of the 200-Mile Offshore Zones." American Journal of International Law 71 (July 1977):494-500.

_____. U.S. Foreign Policy and the Law of the Sea. Princeton: Princeton University Press, 1981.

Hollick, Ann L., and Robert E. Osgood. New Era of Ocean Politics. Baltimore: Johns Hopkins University Press, 1974.

Hoole, Francis W.; Robert L. Friedheim; and Timothy M. Hennessey, eds. Making Ocean Policy: The Politics of Government Organization and Management. Boulder: Westview Press, 1981.

Humphreys, Donald L. "An International Regime for the Exploration for and Exploitation of the Resources of the Deep Seabed—The United States Hard Minerals Industry Position." Natural Resources Lawyer 5 (Fall 1972):731-51.

Jackson, Jon Gregory. "Deepsea Ventures: Exclusive Mining Rights to the Deep Seabed as a Freedom of the Sea." Baylor Law Review 28 (1976):170-86.

Jacobs, Michael J. "United States Participation in International Fisheries Agreements." Journal of Maritime Law and Commerce 6 (July 1975):471-529.

Jacobson, Jon L. "Bridging the Gap to International Fisheries Agreement: A Guide for Unilateral Action." San Diego Law Review 9 (May 1972):454-90.

Janis, Mark W. Sea Power and the Law of the Sea. Lexington: Lexington Books, 1976.

Jennings, R. Y. "The United States Draft Treaty on the International Sea-Bed Area—Basic Principles." International and Comparative Law Quarterly 20 (July 1971):433-52.

Johnson, Barbara, and Frank Langdon. "Two Hundred Mile Zones: The Politics of North Pacific Fisheries." Pacific Affairs 49 (Spring 1976):5-27.

Juda, Lawrence. Ocean Space Rights: Developing U.S. Policy. New York: Praeger, 1975.

Kildow, Judith T., ed. Deepsea Mining. Cambridge, Mass.: MIT Press, 1980.

Kissinger, Henry A. "The Law of the Sea: A Test of International Cooperation." Department of State Bulletin 74 (April 26, 1976): 533-42.

Knight, H. Gary. "The Draft United Nations Convention on the International Seabed Area: Background, Description and Some Preliminary Thoughts." San Diego Law Review 8 (May 1971): 459-550.

_____. "The 1971 United States Proposals on the Breadth of the Territorial Sea and Passage through International Straits." Oregon Law Review 51 (Summer 1972):759-87.

_____. "The Deep Seabed Hard Mineral Resources Act: A Negative View." San Diego Law Review 10 (May 1973):446-66.

_____. "United States Oceans Policy: Perspective 1974." Notre Dame Lawyer 49 (December 1973):241-75.

_____. Managing the Sea's Living Resources: Legal and Political Aspects of High Seas Fisheries. Lexington: Lexington Books, 1977.

_____. "The Law of the Sea and Naval Missions." U.S. Naval Institute Proceedings 103 (June 1977):32-39.

Kolb, Kenneth H. "Congress and the Ocean Policy Process." Ocean Development and International Law 3 (1976):261-86.

Krueger, Robert B. "An Evaluation of United States Oceans Policy." McGill Law Journal 17 (1971):603-98.

LaQue, F. L. "Different Approaches to International Regulation of Exploitation of Deep-Ocean Ferromanganese Nodules." San Diego Law Review 15 (April 1978):477-92.

Larson, David L. "The United States Position on the Deep Seabed." Suffolk Transnational Law Journal 3 (1979):1-33.

_____. "Security, Disarmament and the Law of the Sea." Marine Policy 3 (January 1979):40-58.

Laylin, John G. "The Legal Regime of the Deep Seabed Pending Multinational Agreement." Virginia Journal of International Law 13 (Spring 1973):319-30.

Logue, John J., ed. The Fate of the Oceans. Villanova: Villanova University Press, 1972.

McCloskey, Paul N., Jr. "Domestic Legislation and the Law of the Sea Conference." Syracuse Journal of International Law and Commerce 6 (1978-79):225-32.

Magnuson, Warren G. "U.S. Oceans Policy: The Congressional View." Columbia Journal of World Business 10 (Spring 1975): 20-28.

_____. "The Fishery Conservation and Management Act of 1976: First Step Toward Improved Management of Marine Fisheries." Washington Law Review 52 (1977):427-50.

Mangone, Gerard J. Marine Policy for America: The United States at Sea. Lexington: Lexington Books, 1977.

Mero, John L. "A Legal Regime for Deep Sea Mining." San Diego Law Review 7 (1970):488-503.

Meron, Theodor. "The Fishermen's Protective Act: A Case Study in Contemporary Legal Strategy of the United States." American Journal of International Law 69 (April 1975):290-309.

Metcalf, Lee. "The U.S. Congress and the Law of the Sea." Marine Technology Society Journal 11 (May 1977):43-53.

Moore, John Norton. "Salvaging UNCLOS III from the Rocks of the Deep Seabed." Virginia Journal of International Law 17 (Fall 1976):1-7.

_____. "Foreign Policy and Fidelity to Law: The Anatomy of a Treaty Violation." American Journal of International Law 70 (October 1976):802-08.

_____. "In Search of Common Nodules at UNCLOS III." Virginia Journal of International Law 18 (Fall 1977):1-29.

_____. "Law and Foreign Policy of the Oceans." California Western International Law Journal 9 (1979):522-39.

_____. "Charting a New Course in the Law of the Sea Negotiations." Denver Journal of International Law and Policy 10 (1981):207-19.

Morris, Michael A. "Have U.S. Security Interests Really Been Sacrificed? A Reply to Admiral Hill." Ocean Development and International Law 4 (1977):381-97.

Murphy, John M. "Deep Ocean Mining: Beginning a New Era." Case Western Reserve Journal of International Law 8 (Winter 1976):46–68.

_____. "The Politics of Manganese Nodules: International Considerations and Domestic Legislation." San Diego Law Review 16 (April 1979):531–54.

Nolta, Frank. "Passage through International Straits: Free or Innocent? The Interests at Stake." San Diego Law Review 11 (May 1974):815–33.

Nye, J. S. "Ocean Rule Making from a World Politics Perspective." Ocean Development and International Law 3 (1975):29–52.

Oda, Shigeru. The Law of the Sea in Our Time. Vol. I: New Developments (1966–1975). Leyden: Sijthoff, 1977.

_____. The Law of the Sea in Our Time. Vol. II: The United Nations Seabed Committee (1968–1973). Leyden: Sijthoff, 1977.

Ohly, D. Christopher. "International Seabed Resources: The U.S. Position." Virginia Journal of International Law 15 (Summer 1975):903–25.

Osgood, Robert E. "U.S. Security Interests in Ocean Law." Ocean Development and International Law 2 (Spring 1974):1–36.

Osgood, Robert E.; Ann L. Hollick; Charles S. Pearson; and James C. Orr. Toward a National Ocean Policy: 1976 and Beyond. Washington, D.C.: U.S. Government Printing Office, 1976.

Ott, Dana B. "An Analysis of Deep Seabed Mining Legislation." Natural Resources Lawyer 10 (1977):591–604.

Oxman, Bernard H. "The Third United Nations Conference on the Law of the Sea: The 1976 New York Sessions." American Journal of International Law 71 (April 1977):247–69.

_____. "The Third United Nations Conference on the Law of the Sea: The 1977 New York Session." American Journal of International Law 72 (January 1978):57–83.

_____. "The Third United Nations Conference on the Law of the Sea: The Seventh Session (1978)." American Journal of International Law 73 (January 1979):1–41.

_____. "The Third United Nations Conference on the Law of the Sea: The Eighth Session (1979)." American Journal of International Law 74 (January 1980):1-47.

_____. "The Third United Nations Conference on the Law of the Sea: The Ninth Session (1980)." American Journal of International Law 75 (April 1981):211-56.

_____. "The Third United Nations Conference on the Law of the Sea: The Tenth Session (1981)." American Journal of International Law 76 (January 1982):1-23.

Palmer, William. "The United States Draft United Nations Convention on the International Sea-Bed Area and the Accommodation of Ocean Uses." Syracuse Journal of International Law 1 (October 1972):110-15.

Pirtle, Charles E. "Transit Rights and U.S. Security Interests in International Straits: The 'Straits Debate' Revisited." Ocean Development and International Law 5 (1978):477-97.

Ratiner, Leigh S. "United States Oceans Policy: An Analysis." Journal of Maritime Law and Commerce 2 (January 1971):225-66.

_____. "National Security Interests in Ocean Space." Natural Resources Lawyer 4 (July 1971):582-96.

_____. "The Law of the Sea: A Crossroads for American Foreign Policy." Foreign Affairs 60 (Summer 1982):1006-21.

Ratiner, Leigh S., and Rebecca L. Wright. "The Billion Dollar Decision: Is Deep Sea Mining a Prudent Investment?" Lawyer of the Americas 10 (1978):712-73.

Reisman, W. Michael. "The Regime of Straits and National Security: An Appraisal of International Lawmaking." American Journal of International Law 74 (January 1980):48-76.

Richardson, Elliot L. "Power, Mobility and the Law of the Sea." Foreign Affairs 58 (Spring 1980):902-19.

_____. "Law of the Sea: Navigation and Other Traditional National Security Considerations." San Diego Law Review 19 (April 1982):553-76.

Stevens, Ted. "The Future of Our Continental Shelf and the Sea-beds." Natural Resources Lawyer 4 (July 1971):646-53.

Stevenson, John R. "The United States Proposal for Legal Regulation of Seabed Mineral Exploitation beyond National Jurisdiction." Natural Resources Lawyer 4 (July 1971):570-81.

_____. "Who Is to Control the Oceans: U.S. Policy and the 1973 Law of the Sea Conference." International Lawyer 6 (July 1972): 465-77.

Stevenson, John R., and Bernard H. Oxman. "The Preparations for the Law of the Sea Conference." American Journal of International Law 68 (January 1974):1-32.

_____. "The Third United Nations Conference on the Law of the Sea: The 1974 Caracas Session." American Journal of International Law 69 (January 1975):1-30.

_____. "The Third United Nations Conference on the Law of the Sea: The 1975 Geneva Session." American Journal of International Law 69 (1975):763-97.

Stone, Oliver L. "United States Legislation Relating to the Continental Shelf." International and Comparative Law Quarterly 17 (January 1968):103-17.

_____. "The United States Draft Convention on the International Sea-Bed Area." Tulane Law Review 45 (April 1971):527-45.

Swing, John Temple. "Who Will Own the Oceans?" Foreign Affairs 54 (1976):527-46.

Tassi, Arthur J. "Fishery Conservation and Management Act of 1976: An Accommodation of State, Federal, and International Interests." Case Western Reserve Journal of International Law 10 (Summer 1978):703-38.

Turner, Stansfield. "Missions of the U.S. Navy." Naval War College Review 26 (March-April 1974):2-17.

Walsh, Don. "Some Thoughts on National Ocean Policy: The Critical Issue." San Diego Law Review 13 (March 1976):594-627.

_____, ed. The Law of the Sea: Issues in Ocean Resource Management. New York: Praeger, 1977.

Wirsing, Robert G., ed. International Relations and the Future of Ocean Space. Columbia: University of South Carolina Press, 1974.

Zacklin, Ralph, ed. The Changing Law of the Sea: Western Hemisphere Perspectives. Leiden: Sijthoff, 1974.

Books Written under the Auspices of
The Center of International Studies,
Princeton University

Gabriel A. Almond, The Appeals of Communism (Princeton University Press, 1954).

William W. Kaufmann, ed., Military Policy and National Security (Princeton University Press, 1956).

Klaus Knorr, The War Potential of Nations (Princeton University Press, 1956).

Lucian W. Pye, Guerrilla Communism in Malaya (Princeton University Press, 1956).

Charles De Visscher, Theory and Reality in Public International Law, trans. by P. E. Corbett (Princeton University Press, 1957; rev. ed., 1968).

Bernard C. Cohen, The Political Process and Foreign Policy: The Making of the Japanese Peace Settlement (Princeton University Press, 1957).

Myron Weiner, Party Politics in India: The Development of a Multi-Party System (Princeton University Press, 1957).

Percy E. Corbett, Law in Diplomacy (Princeton University Press, 1959).

Rolf Sannwald and Jacques Stohler, Economic Integration: Theoretical Assumptions and Consequences of European Unification, trans. by Herman Karreman (Princeton University Press, 1959).

Klaus Knorr, ed., NATO and American Security (Princeton University Press, 1959).

Gabriel A. Almond and James S. Coleman, eds., The Politics of the Developing Areas (Princeton University Press, 1960).

Herman Kahn, On Thermonuclear War (Princeton University Press, 1960).

Sidney Verba, Small Groups and Political Behavior: A Study of Leadership (Princeton University Press, 1961).

Robert J. C. Butow, Tojo and the Coming of the War (Princeton University Press, 1961).

Glenn H. Snyder, Deterrence and Defense: Toward a Theory of National Security (Princeton University Press, 1961).

Klaus Knorr and Sidney Verba, eds., The International System: Theoretical Essays (Princeton University Press, 1961).

Peter Paret and John W. Shy, Guerrillas in the 1960's (Praeger, 1962).

George Modelski, A Theory of Foreign Policy (Praeger, 1962).

Klaus Knorr and Thornton Read, eds., Limited Strategic War (Praeger, 1963).

Frederick S. Dunn, Peace-Making and the Settlement with Japan (Princeton University Press, 1963).

Arthur L. Burns and Nina Heathcote, Peace-Keeping by United Nations Forces (Praeger, 1963).

Richard A. Falk, Law, Morality, and War in the Contemporary World (Praeger, 1963).

James N. Rosenau, National Leadership and Foreign Policy: A Case Study in the Mobilization of Public Support (Princeton University Press, 1963).

Gabriel A. Almond and Sidney Verba, The Civic Culture: Political Attitudes and Democracy in Five Nations (Princeton University Press, 1963).

Bernard C. Cohen, The Press and Foreign Policy (Princeton University Press, 1963).

Richard L. Sklar, Nigerian Political Parties: Power in an Emergent African Nation (Princeton University Press, 1963).

Peter Paret, French Revolutionary Warfare from Indochina to Algeria: The Analysis of a Political and Military Doctrine (Praeger, 1964).

Harry Eckstein, ed., Internal War: Problems and Approaches (Free Press, 1964).

Cyril E. Black and Thomas P. Thornton, eds., Communism and Revolution: The Strategic Uses of Political Violence (Princeton University Press, 1964).

Miriam Camps, Britain and the European Community 1955-1963 (Princeton University Press, 1964).

Thomas P. Thornton, ed., The Third World in Soviet Perspective: Studies by Soviet Writers on the Developing Areas (Princeton University Press, 1964).

James N. Rosenau, ed., International Aspects of Civil Strife (Princeton University Press, 1964).

Sidney I. Ploss, Conflict and Decision-Making in Soviet Russia: A Case Study of Agricultural Policy, 1953-1963 (Princeton University Press, 1965).

Richard A. Falk and Richard J. Barnet, eds., Security in Disarmament (Princeton University Press, 1965).

Karl von Vorys, Political Development in Pakistan (Princeton University Press, 1965).

Harold and Margaret Sprout, The Ecological Perspective on Human Affairs, with Special Reference to International Politics (Princeton University Press, 1965).

Klaus Knorr, On the Uses of Military Power in the Nuclear Age (Princeton University Press, 1966).

Harry Eckstein, Division and Cohesion in Democracy: A Study of Norway (Princeton University Press, 1966).

Cyril E. Black, The Dynamics of Modernization: A Study in Comparative History (Harper & Row, 1966).

Peter Kunstadter, ed., Southeast Asian Tribes, Minorities, and Nations (Princeton University Press, 1967).

E. Victor Wolfenstein, The Revolutionary Personality: Lenin, Trotsky, Gandhi (Princeton University Press, 1967).

Leon Gordenker, The UN Secretary-General and the Maintenance of Peace (Columbia University Press, 1967).

Oran R. Young, The Intermediaries: Third Parties in International Crises (Princeton University Press, 1967).

James N. Rosenau, ed., Domestic Sources of Foreign Policy (Free Press, 1967).

Richard F. Hamilton, Affluence and the French Worker in the Fourth Republic (Princeton University Press, 1967).

Linda B. Miller, World Order and Local Disorder: The United Nations and Internal Conflicts (Princeton University Press, 1967).

Henry Bienen, Tanzania: Party Transformation and Economic Development (Princeton University Press, 1967).

Wolfram F. Hanrieder, West German Foreign Policy, 1949-1963: International Pressures and Domestic Response (Stanford University Press, 1967).

Richard H. Ullman, Britain and the Russian Civil War: November 1919-February 1920 (Princeton University Press, 1968).

Robert Gilpin, France in the Age of the Scientific State (Princeton University Press, 1968).

William B. Bader, The United States and the Spread of Nuclear Weapons (Pegasus, 1968).

Richard A. Falk, Legal Order in a Violent World (Princeton University Press, 1968).

Cyril E. Black, Richard A. Falk, Klaus Knorr, and Oran R. Young, Neutralization and World Politics (Princeton University Press, 1968).

Oran R. Young, The Politics of Force: Bargaining During International Crises (Princeton University Press, 1969).

Klaus Knorr and James N. Rosenau, eds., Contending Approaches to International Politics (Princeton University Press, 1969).

James N. Rosenau, ed., Linkage Politics: Essays on the Convergence of National and International Systems (Free Press, 1969).

John T. McAlister, Jr., Viet Nam: The Origins of Revolution (Knopf, 1969).

Jean Edward Smith, Germany Beyond the Wall: People, Politics and Prosperity (Little, Brown, 1969).

James Barros, Betrayal from Within: Joseph Avenol, Secretary-General of the League of Nations, 1933-1940 (Yale University Press, 1969).

Charles Hermann, Crises in Foreign Policy: A Simulation Analysis (Bobbs-Merrill, 1969).

Robert C. Tucker, The Marxian Revolutionary Idea: Essays on Marxist Thought and Its Impact on Radical Movements (W. W. Norton, 1969).

Harvey Waterman, Political Change in Contemporary France: The Politics of an Industrial Democracy (Charles E. Merrill, 1969).

Cyril E. Black and Richard A. Falk, eds., The Future of the International Legal Order. Vol. I: Trends and Patterns (Princeton University Press, 1969).

Ted Robert Gurr, Why Men Rebel (Princeton University Press, 1969).

C. Sylvester Whitaker, The Politics of Tradition: Continuity and Change in Northern Nigeria 1946-1966 (Princeton University Press, 1970).

Richard A. Falk, The Status of Law in International Society (Princeton University Press, 1970).

John T. McAlister, Jr., and Paul Mus, The Vietnamese and Their Revolution (Harper & Row, 1970).

Klaus Knorr, Military Power and Potential (D. C. Heath, 1970).

Cyril E. Black and Richard A. Falk, eds. The Future of the International Legal Order. Vol. II: Wealth and Resources (Princeton University Press, 1970).

Leon Gordenker, ed., The United Nations in International Politics (Princeton University Press, 1971).

Cyril E. Black and Richard A. Falk, eds., The Future of the International Legal Order. Vol. III: Conflict Management (Princeton University Press, 1971).

Francine R. Frankel, India's Green Revolution: Political Costs of Economic Growth (Princeton University Press, 1971).

Harold and Margaret Sprout, Toward a Politics of the Planet Earth (Van Nostrand Reinhold, 1971).

Cyril E. Black and Richard A. Falk, eds., The Future of the International Legal Order. Vol. IV: The Structure of the International Environment (Princeton University Press, 1972).

Gerald Garvey, Energy, Ecology, Economy (W. W. Norton, 1972).

Richard Ullman, The Anglo-Soviet Accord (Princeton University Press, 1973).

Klaus Knorr, Power and Wealth: The Political Economy of International Power (Basic Books, 1973).

Anton Bebler, Military Role in Africa: Dahomey, Ghana, Sierra Leone, and Mali (Praeger, 1973).

Robert C. Tucker, Stalin as Revolutionary 1879-1929: A Study in History and Personality (W. W. Norton, 1973).

Edward L. Morse, Foreign Policy and Interdependence in Gaullist France (Princeton University Press, 1973).

Henry Bienen, Kenya: The Politics of Participation and Control (Princeton University Press, 1974).

Gregory J. Massell, The Surrogate Proletariat: Moslem Women and Revolutionary Strategies in Soviet Central Asia, 1919-1929 (Princeton University Press, 1974).

James N. Rosenau, Citizenship Between Elections: An Inquiry into the Mobilizable American (Free Press, 1974).

Ervin Laszlo, A Strategy for the Future: The Systems Approach to World Order (Braziller, 1974).

John R. Vincent, Nonintervention and International Order (Princeton University Press, 1974).

Jan H. Kalicki, The Pattern of Sino-American Crises: Political-Military Interactions in the 1950s (Cambridge University Press, 1975).

Klaus Knorr, The Power of Nations: The Political Economy of International Relations (Basic Books, 1975).

James P. Sewell, UNESCO and World Politics: Engaging in International Relations (Princeton University Press, 1975).

Richard A. Falk, A Global Approach to National Policy (Harvard University Press, 1975).

Harry Eckstein and Ted Robert Gurr, Patterns of Authority: A Structural Basis for Political Inquiry (John Wiley & Sons, 1975).

Cyril E. Black, Marius B. Jansen, Herbert S. Levine, Marion J. Levy, Jr., Henry Rosovsky, Gilbert Rozman, Henry D. Smith, II, and S. Frederick Starr, The Modernization of Japan and Russia (Free Press, 1975).

Leon Gordenker, International Aid and National Decisions: Development Programs in Malawi, Tanzania, and Zambia (Princeton University Press, 1976).

Carl Von Clausewitz, On War, edited and translated by Michael Howard and Peter Paret (Princeton University Press, 1976).

Gerald Garvey and Lou Ann Garvey, eds., International Resource Flows (D. C. Heath, 1977).

Walter F. Murphy and Joseph Tanenhaus, Comparative Constitutional Law Cases and Commentaries (St. Martin's Press, 1977).

Gerald Garvey, Nuclear Power and Social Planning: The City of the Second Sun (D. C. Heath, 1977).

Richard E. Bissell, Apartheid and International Organizations (Westview Press, 1977).

David P. Forsythe, Humanitarian Politics: The International Committee of the Red Cross (Johns Hopkins University Press, 1977).

Paul E. Sigmund, The Overthrow of Allende and the Politics of Chile, 1964-1976 (University of Pittsburgh Press, 1977).

Henry S. Bienen, Armies and Parties in Africa (Holmes and Meier, 1978).

Harold and Margaret Sprout, The Context of Environmental Politics (The University Press of Kentucky, 1978).

Samuel S. Kim, China, the United Nations, and World Order (Princeton University Press, 1979).

S. Basheer Ahmed, Nuclear Fuel and Energy Policy (D. C. Heath, 1979).

Robert C. Johansen, The National Interest and the Human Interest: An Analysis of U.S. Foreign Policy (Princeton University Press, 1980).

Richard A. Falk and Samuel S. Kim, eds., The War System: An Interdisciplinary Approach (Westview Press, 1980).

James H. Billington, Fire in the Minds of Men: Origins of the Revolutionary Faith (Basic Books, 1980).

Bennett Ramberg, Destruction of Nuclear Energy Facilities in War: The Problem and the Implications (D. C. Heath, 1980).

Gregory T. Kruglak, The Politics of United States Decision-Making in United Nations Specialized Agencies: The Case of the International Labor Organization (University Press of America, 1980).

W. P. Davison and Leon Gordenker, eds., Resolving Nationality Conflicts: The Role of Public Opinion Research (Praeger, 1980).

James C. Hsiung and Samuel S. Kim, eds., China in the Global Community (Praeger, 1980).

Douglas Kinnard, The Secretary of Defense (The University Press of Kentucky, 1980).

Richard Falk, Human Rights and State Sovereignty (Holmes and Meier Publishers, 1981).

James H. Mittelman, Underdevelopment and the Transition to Socialism: Mozambique and Tanzania (Academic Press, 1981).

Gilbert Rozman, ed., The Modernization of China (The Free Press, 1981).

Robert C. Tucker, Politics as Leadership. The Paul Anthony Brick Lectures. Eleventh Series (University of Missouri Press, 1981.

Robert Gilpin, War and Change in World Politics (Cambridge University Press, 1981).

Nicholas G. Onuf, ed., Law-Making in the Global Community (Carolina Academic Press, 1982).

Ali E. Hillal Dessouki, ed., Islamic Resurgence in the Arab World (Praeger, 1982).

INDEX

Aboureszk, James, 117
Aldrich, George H., 135-36, 138
Allison, Graham, 20
American Bar Association (ABA), 53-54
American Mining Congress (AMC): alternative to international treaty, 94, 104; and criticism of Draft Treaty, 134-35; and Draft Convention of 1970, 93-95; at San Francisco in 1980, 133
American Petroleum Institute (API), 52
Anti-Submarine Warfare program (ASW), 35
Areas-Schreiber, Alfonso, 179, 181

Baldrige, Malcolm, 148
Barber, James, 169
"Basic Conditions of Exploration and Exploitation," 100-104, 111
Bedell, Berkley, 118, 121
Biemiller, Andrew J., 116
Breaux, John B., 113, 138; and H.R. 3350, 113-17
Brower, Charles N., 61, 105
bureaucratic politics: assessment of, 162-65; and bargaining games, 20; hypotheses of, 21-22, 162-63; missions in, 21-22
Byrd, Robert, 117

Cannon, Lou, 148
Carlisle, Geoffrey E., 32-33
Carter administration: and Deep Seabed Hard Mineral Resources Act, 11, 121; and deep seabed mining policy, 10; and hypothesis of reelection, 11, 169; and mining legislation, 114; ocean policy of, and change with Reagan administration, 158; and unilateralism, 10-11

Center for Naval Analysis, 31-32
Chile, 3
Clark, William P., 136, 138
Cohen, Stephen, 22
Cohen, William S., 72-73
Commission on Marine Science Engineering and Resources, 50
Conference on the Committee of Disarmament (CCD), 37
Convention on Fishing and Conservation of the Living Resources of the High Seas of 1958, 74-75, 81
Convention on the Continental Shelf, 3, 48, 67, 163
Convention on the Territorial Sea and the Contiguous Zone of 1958, 33
Cook, Charles F., Jr., 58
Corfu Channel Case in 1949, 33
creeping jurisdiction: fear of, 31-34, 36; and fishing policy, 72; and mining industry, 94; Navy's concern about, 34-36; Nixon proposal of 1970, 6; and Truman Proclamations of 1945, 2-3; and U.S. straits policy, 155

Dean, Arthur H., 32
Deep Seabed Hard Mineral Resources Act (S. 2801): Carter's signing of, 11, 167; introduction of, 104; passage of, 117-21; provisions of, 135; reintroduction of, as S.713, 108; reintroduction of, S. 1134, 105-10; sponsors of, 104
deep seabed mining industry: and creeping jurisdiction, 94; and Draft Convention, 134-36, 138, 180; and parallel or dual access system, 9, 99-104, 160;

policy of, 10; and Reagan veto of
Draft Convention, 180
deep seabed mining industry, politics of: congressional action
(1971-76), 104-5, 107-9; and
Deep Seabed Hard Mineral Resources Act of 1980, 117; and
developing countries, 95-96, 98-
99; and Informal Composite Negotiating Text of 1977, 110-13; and
Nixon proposal of 1970, 91-95;
and parallel system, 99-104; and
unilateral action, 113-17
Deep Sea Mineral Resources, Committee on, 55
Department of Defense, 32, 164
Department of the Interior, 47
domestic politics: assessment of,
165-69; and deep seabed mining,
171; hypotheses, 24-25; and resource interests, 23; view of,
22-23
Downing, Thomas: and H.R. 9,
105, 107; and H.R. 1270, 108;
and H.R. 13904, 104
Draft Convention on the Law of the
Sea of 1982: countries abstaining
from, 4; countries favoring, 4;
countries opposing, 4; deep seabed section of, 146; and freedom
of navigation, 42; international
progress of, 131-34; and mining
industry, 134-36, 138; provisions
of, 134
Draft Convention on the Law of the
Sea of 1982, Reagan review of:
on April 29, 1981, 139; assessment of, 164-65; completion of,
141-43; March 2, 1981 interagency meeting, 136-37; objectives of, 142-43; veto of, 1,
146, 148
dual access system, 9 (see also
parallel system)
Dubs, Marne A.: and criticism of
Carter administration, 135-36;
and H.R. 9, 105; and mining

legislation, 118; and OPEC
analogy, 107; and sea law legislation, 114; and sea law negotiations, 113
Dykstia, Jacob, 69

economic zone, exclusive, 57, 59,
63 (see also trusteeship zone);
and United States' conditions
for acceptance of, 60
Ecuador, 3
Eighteen-Nation Disarmament
Committee (ENDC), 36-37
Ely, Northcutt, 54-55, 95, 109,
118
Emergency Marine Fisheries Pro-
tection Act of 1975 (S. 961):
amendment to, 79; passage of,
78-82; sponsors of, 77-78; tes-
timonies against, 79-82
Energy Crisis, The, 62
Englund, Merrill, 58-59
Engo, Paul, 110
Evensen, Jens, 110

Finlay, Luke W., 52-53
First Committee of the General
Assembly (see Seabed Com-
mittee)
Fisher, Adrian, 37
Fishery Conservation and Management Act of 1976 (FCMA):
Ford's signing of, 83-85, 166-
67; and national enclosure, 8;
passing of, 82-83; and unilateralism in fisheries area, 8
fishing industry: and creeping
jurisdiction, 72; and foreign
fishing, 82; in North Atlantic,
70; in North Pacific, 69; problems of, 7; rights of, 67;
shrimp, 69; and tuna in California, 19, 69-70
fishing industry, politics of: and
coastal fishermen, 72-73; congressional action (1973-75),
73-77; Fishery Conservation

and Management Act, 77-82; and species approach, 7, 68, 71
Flipse, John E., 105, 109
Ford, Gerald, 77, 80, 83
Foreign Affairs, 156
Foreign Relations Committee: and H.R. 2759, 119-20; and law of the sea, 137; and S. 493, 118; and S. 713 (Deep Seabed Hard Mineral Resources Act), 109-10; and S. 961 (Emergency Marine Fisheries Protection Act of 1975), 79-80; and S. 1988 (Magnuson bill), 75-76; and S. 2053, 116
Frank, Richard A., 107
freedom of the seas, 1
French, Stuart P., 41
Friends of the Conference (FOC), 144

General Accounting Office (GAO) report, 180
General Assembly (see United Nations General Assembly)
Geneva Conventions of 1958 (see United Nations Conference on the Law of the Sea of 1958)
Gravel, Mike, 80
Great Britain, 2
"Green Book," 144
Griffin, Robert, 116
Grotius, Hugo, 1-2
Group of 77 (G-77): and eleventh session of UNCLOS III, 144; political goals of, 103-4; problems with, 100; proposals of, 101; and reconsideration of value of United States' participation, 177; and Revised Single Negotiating Text (RSNT), 102-4; strategy of, 178-79; United States' concession to, 102
groupthink, 148

Haig, Alexander, 144-45
Halperin, Morton, 21
Hearn, Wilfred A., 32
Hedberg, Hollis D., 48

High Seas Fisheries Conservation bill (H.R. 4760), 72
House International Relations Committee, 81
House of Representatives (see Foreign Relations Committee; House International Relations Committee)
H.R. 9, 105, 107
H.R. 200 (Fishery Conservation and Management Act), 81-83
H.R. 1270, 108
H.R. 2759, 117-21
H.R. 3350 (Murphy-Breaux bill), 113-17
H.R. 4760 (High Seas Fisheries Conservation bill), 72
H.R. 8665, 73, 75, 77
H.R. 13904, 104

Informal Composite Negotiating Text of 1977 (ICNT), 110-13; second revision of, 132
innocent passage, right of, 2, 33
Intergovernmental Maritime Consultative Organization (IMCO), 41
international agreement (see unilateralism)
International Civil Aviation Organization (ICA), 41
International Commission for the Northwest Atlantic Fisheries (ICNAF), 70-71
International Court of Justice, 33, 49
international interdependence: assessment of, 159-62; and deep seabed mining, 171; hypotheses of, 19-20; and international law of the sea negotiations, 171; literature on, 18; scholars, 20
International Law Association (ILA), American Branch, 55
International Law Commission (ILC), 33, 48-49

International Seabed Authority (ISA), 9, 11, 38, 95, 98-99
International Seabed Resource Authority (ISRA), proposed, 91-92

Janis, Irving L., 148
Johansen, Robert, 24

Keating, Robert, 145
Kennedy, Ted, 117
Kenya, 59
Keohane, Robert O., 18
Kinder, Donald, 26
Kissinger, Henry: and law of the sea bargain, 101-2; and Magnuson bill, 76; and parallel or dual access system, 9, 160-61; at UNCLOS III, fifth session of, 10; and unilateralism, dangers of, 10
Koh, Tommy, 139, 142, 180-81
Kohl, Wilfrid, 22
Kramer, Franklin D., 137
Krasner, Stephen, 15-16
Kronmiller, Theodore G., 140, 143, 161-62

law of the sea: classical, 1; and international agreement, 1, 3; international treaty approach to, 12; negotiations, 11, 41-42; in 1967, 3; regime of 1958 conventions, 33-34
Leggett, Robert L., 119
Lehman, John, 156-57
Levering, Samuel R., 74, 107, 118
Lewis, Drew, 148
Lima Declaration, 57
Lowi, Theodore, 23

McKernan, Donald L., 71, 73
Magnuson, Warren G., 73; and S. 961 (see Emergency Fisheries Protection Act of 1975)
Magnuson bill (S. 1988), 73-77
Malone, James L.: and Reagan review of Draft Convention, 136; as representative to UNCLOS, 138-41, 148

Maltese proposal, United Nations General Assembly, 50
manganese nodules, 3, 9
Mare Clausum of 1635, 2
Mare Liberum of 1609, 1
Marine Science, Engineering and Resources, Commission on, 50
Matsunaga, Spark M., and S. 493, 117-21
Maw, Carlyle E., 8, 78
Meese, Edwin, 143, 148, 165
Merchant Marine Fisheries Committee, 81, 113, 119
Metcalf, Lee: and S. 713, 108-10; and S. 1134, 105, 108; and S. 2053, 113-17; and S. 2801 (Deep Seabed Hard Mineral Resources Act), 104; and Subcommittee on the Outer Continental Shelf, 55; as supporter of oil industry, 55
Metcalf bill (see Deep Seabed Hard Mineral Resources Act)
Minerals, Materials and Fuels of the Senate Interior and Insular Affairs Committee, Subcommittee on, 52, 54
mining industry, deep seabed (see deep seabed mining industry)
Montevideo Declaration, 57
Moore, John Norton: and coastal seabed economic area, 62; and Fishery Conservation and Management Act, 166; and Magnuson bills, opposition to, 75-76, 81; statement to House Committee on International Relations on September 24, 1975, 8; and trusteeship, 61
Morgenthau, Hans, 15-17, 158
Morton, Rogers C. B., 62, 164
Murphy, John M., 113; and H. R. 2759, 117-21
Murphy-Breaux bill (H. R. 3350, 113-17
Muskie, Edmund, 77-78

national enclosure, 8, 24, 67

national interests, 15-16
National Ocean Industries Association, 136
National Petroleum Council (NPC): establishment of, 47, 163; 1969 report of, 50, 163; 1971 report of, 51, 163; study by, 48-51
National Security Council (NSC), 148; Interagency Task Force on the Law of the Sea, 8
Netherlands, 2
Nixon administration: and limitation of national claims to continental shelf, 55; and ocean policy of United States, 6, 56; and offshore oil leasings, 62, 163
Nixon proposal of 1970, 1; aim of, 6; and creeping jurisdiction, 6; and fishing policy, 7; and National Petroleum Council, 51; and national security, 38-39
North Sea Continental Shelf Case of 1969, 49
Nye, Joseph S., 18

Oceanography, Subcommittee on, 113
ocean regime: international, 4; new, 1; traditional, 1-2
oil industry: and law of the sea, 47; and national jurisdiction, 67; and National Petroleum Council study, 47-51
oil industry, politics of: allies of, 53-56; and continental margin, 62-63; and enclosure, 60-63; and energy crisis, 60, 62; and international developments, 56-59
Oliver, Covey T., 179
Organization of African Unity, 98-99
Organization of American States (OAS), 49
Organization of Petroleum Exporting Countries (OPEC), 11, 163
Our Nation and the Sea, 50
Outer Continental Shelf, Subcommittee on the, 55-56

Outer Continental Shelf Lands Act (OCSLA) of 1953, 32, 48, 52, 55
Overton, J. Allen, Jr., 135

Packwood, Bob, 77, 167
Palestine Liberation Organization (PLO), 132
parallel system: and International Seabed Authority, 9; and mining industry, 99-104, 160; and sea law negotiations, 131
Pardo, Arvid, 3-4
Pastore, John O., 78
patrimonial sea, 58
Pell, Claiborne, 81, 137
Pendley, William P., 137
Peru, 3
Petroleum Resources Under the Ocean Floor, 48
Petroleum Resources Under the Ocean Floor, Committee on, 48
Pinto, Christopher, 100-104
pluralism, 23
politics (see bureaucratic politics; domestic politics)
Pollock, Howard W., 69
Preparatory Commission (PrepCom), 132, 142, 181
Preparatory Investment Protection (PIP), 132, 142, 145
Presidential Character, The, 169
Public Law 94-265 (see Fishery Conservation and Management Act of 1976)

Quandt, William, 22

Ratiner, Leigh, 39, 136, 138, 143, 162
rationality, premise of, 15-16, 175
Reagan administration: conservatives in, 161-62; and Draft Convention on the Law of the Sea, 1, 136-39, 143, 146, 148; and ocean policy of United States, 11, 165; policy of, and

change from Carter administration, 158; and unilateralism,
11, 156, 158, 177
Reagan Shift, 158
Regional Fishery Management Councils, 79
Revised Single Negotiating Text
(RSNT), 102-4, 109, 110
Richardson, Elliot L.: and Carter's
mining policy, 10; and Deep Seabed Hard Mineral Resources Act,
168; and defense of United States'
ocean policy, 160; and Draft Convention, 137-38, 140-41, 161;
and House Merchant Marine and
Fisheries Committee, statement
to, 10; and mining policy, 114,
180; and Nixon proposal of 1970,
38-39; opposition to S. 493, 117-
18, 120; priorities of policy, 156;
and UNCLOS III, ninth session of,
132-33
Rumsfeld, Donald, 181
Rush, Kenneth, 75

S. 493, 117-21
S. 713, 108-10 (see also Deep
Seabed Hard Mineral Resources
Act)
S. 961 (see Emergency Marine Fish-
eries Protection Act of 1975)
S. 1134, 105-10 (see also Deep Sea-
bed Hard Mineral Resources Act)
S. 1988 (see Magnuson bill)
S. 2053, 113-17
S. 2801 (see Deep Seabed Hard
Mineral Resources Act)
Santo Domingo Declaration of 1972,
58, 99
Schattschneider, E. E., 23
seabed arms control, 36-38
Seabed Committee of United Nations
General Assembly: and Draft Con-
vention of 1970, 38, 91; and draft
on fisheries, revised, 70-71; es-
tablishment of, 36; 1970 resolution
of, 4; and seabed arms control,

36-37, 156; and species ap-
proach, 7; and transit of inter-
national straits, 39; and UNCLOS
III, 4; United States' proposals
in, 31, 155
Seabed Treaty of 1971, 38, 156
seas (see also law of the sea;
UNCLOS III); freedom of, 1;
territorial, 1, 33
Seldon, John, 2
Senate Armed Service Committee:
and Deep Seabed Hard Mineral
Resources Act (S. 713), 109;
and Emergency Marine Fisheries
Protection Act of 1975 (S. 961),
79, 81; and Magnuson bill
(S. 1988), 76-77
Senate Commerce Committee: and
Deep Seabed Hard Mineral Re-
sources Act (S. 713), 109; and
Emergency Marine Fisheries
Protection Act of 1975 (S. 961),
78-79; and Magnuson bill
(S. 1988), 74
Senate Energy and Natural Re-
sources and Commerce Com-
mittee, 114
Senate Interior and Insular Affairs
Committee: and H. R. 2759,
119; and S. 713, 108-9; and
Subcommittee on Minerals,
Materials and Fuel, 52-54; and
Subcommittee on the Outer Continental Shelf, 55-56
Soviet Union, 36
Spain, 40
species approach: and anadromous
species, 68; and coastal stocks,
68; and draft article on fisheries in 1971, 68; and migratory
species, 68; outline of, 7-8;
and politics of fishing industry,
67-72; problem of, 70
Stang, David P., 59, 61
statist approach: assessment of,
155-58; goals of, 15-17; hypotheses of, 17, 31, 155; and
national interest, static, 18

Stevens, Ted, 78
Stevenson, Adlai E., III, 82
Stevenson, John R., 6-7, 38, 40; and continental margin policy, 61-62; and species approach, 71; and U.S. straits proposal, 156
Strategic Arms Limitation Talks (SALT), 34
Stoessel, Walter, Jr., 148
Studds, Gerry E., 72-73, 162; and H. R. 200, 81-83 (see also Fishery Conservation and Management Act); and H. R. 8665, 73, 75, 77
Sullivan, William, 70
Taft, George, 137
Tanzania, 40, 96
Tanzanian proposal, 96, 98
Technical Subcommittee, 48
territorial seas, 1, 33
Third World countries, and mining industry, 95-96, 98-99
Truman Proclamations of 1945, 2-3, 32
trusteeship zone, 6-7, 61, 67, 156; lack of support of, 163-64; shift from, to economic zone, 164
Tsongas, Paul E., 138-39

Ul-Haque, Inam, 141
unilateralism: and coastal fishermen, 73; policy of, 8-12; and Reagan administration, 11, 156, 158, 177
United Nations Conference on the Law of the Sea (UNCLOS): of 1958, 3, 32-33; of 1960, 3, 32
UNCLOS III: and Draft Convention on the Law of the Sea, 4; in 1974, 6, 63, 108; in 1975, 99; in 1977, 131; negotiations of, 20, 176; and Seabed Committee, 4; United States' proposals at, 31; work of, 1
UNCLOS III, sessions of: fourth, 9, 83, 102, 160; fifth, 103, 110, 160; sixth, 113; seventh, 131-32; eighth, 132; ninth, 132-33; tenth, 132, 137, 142, 168; eleventh, 143-46, 169
United Nations General Assembly, 1, 50 (see also Seabed Committee of United Nations General Assembly)
United States: deep seabed mining policy of, 100-104; sensitivity, 18-19, 161; and 12-mile fishery limit, 67; and United Nations Seabed Committee, 31, 155
United States, ocean policy of: (see also Nixon proposal of 1970; Draft Convention on the Law of the Sea; species approach; trusteeship zone; unilateralism): aspects of, 27; changes in, 1; and coastal zones, 8, 61; and continental margin policy, 62-63, 164; and energy crisis, 60, 62; flexibility in, 60; interests involved in, 15-17, 23, 31; making of (see bureaucratic politics; domestic politics; international interdependence; statist approach); and military operations, 17, 31; multilateral route of, 19-20; Nixon administration, 6; pick-and-choose theory, 179; proposals of, through 1970s, 158; and revenue sharing, 9; and transfer of technology, 9; and 200-mile economic zone, 6-7, 159; in UNCLOS III, eleventh session of, 178
United States Straits Proposal of, 1971, 39-40, 155-56; and international developments, 40-42

Wallace, David, 78
Walsh, James P., 137
Weicker, Lowell O., 78-79
Weiss, Janet, 26
Whitaker, Jennifer Seymour, 156
White, Robert M., 72
Working Group of Committee I, 100

Yaounde Report, 59, 61

zonal approach (see species approach)

ABOUT THE AUTHOR

FINN LAURSEN is associate professor of political science at Odense University, Odense, Denmark. He was a research fellow at the European University Institute, Florence, Italy, 1977-80, and a visiting fellow at Princeton University, 1980-81.

Dr. Laursen has published widely in the area of international politics. His articles have appeared in Europe en formation, Internasjonal Politikk, and World Politics. He is the editor of Toward a New International Marine Order (The Hague: Martinus Nijhoff, 1982).

Dr. Laursen holds a diploma from the Institut Européen des Hautes Etudes Internationales, Nice, France, a graduate degree in political science from Aarhus University, Denmark, and a Ph.D. from the University of Pennsylvania, Philadelphia.